Microsoft Press

Step by Step

Microsoft WebPublishing

/Active**Education**

PUBLISHED BY
Microsoft Press
A Division of Microsoft Corporation
One Microsoft Way
Redmond, Washington 98052-6399

Library of Congress Cataloging-in-Publication Data
Web Publishing Step by Step / ActiveEducation.
      p. cm.
  ISBN 0-7356-1156-4
   1. Web sites--Design. 2. Web publishing. 3. Microsoft FrontPage.
4. Microsoft Photodraw.   I. ActiveEducation (Firm)   II. Microsoft
Press.
TK5105.888.W3735   1999
005.7'2--dc21   99-33266
                                                 CIP

Printed and bound in the United States of America.

1 2 3 4 5 6 7 8 9 WCWC   4 3 2 1 0

Distributed in Canada by Penguin Books Canada Limited.

A CIP catalogue record for this book is available from the British Library.

Microsoft Press books are available through booksellers and distributors worldwide. For further information about international editions, contact your local Microsoft Corporation office or contact Microsoft Press International directly at fax (425) 936-7329. Visit our Web site at mspress.microsoft.com.

For ActiveEducation, Inc.
Managing Editor: Ron Pronk
Project Editor: Kate Dawson
Writer: Scott Palmer
Production/Layout: Katherine Stark
Technical Editors: Amy Carpenter,
   Rebecca Van Esselstine, Patrick Vincent
Indexer: Jenifer F. Walker
Proofreader: Holly Freeman

For Microsoft Press
Acquisitions Editor: Susanne M. Forderer
Project Editor: Jenny Moss Benson
Technical Editor: Jim McCarter
Copy Editor: Kristen Weatherby

Contents

QuickLook Guide

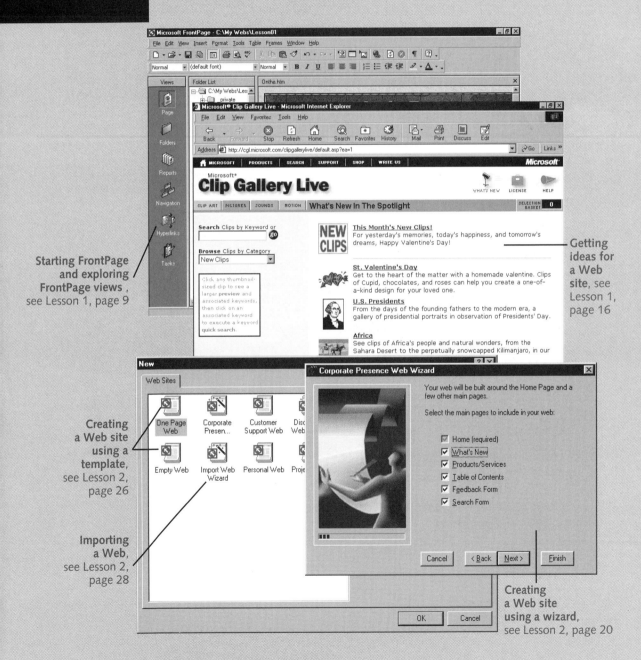

Starting FrontPage and exploring FrontPage views , see Lesson 1, page 9

Getting ideas for a Web site, see Lesson 1, page 16

Creating a Web site using a template, see Lesson 2, page 26

Importing a Web, see Lesson 2, page 28

Creating a Web site using a wizard, see Lesson 2, page 20

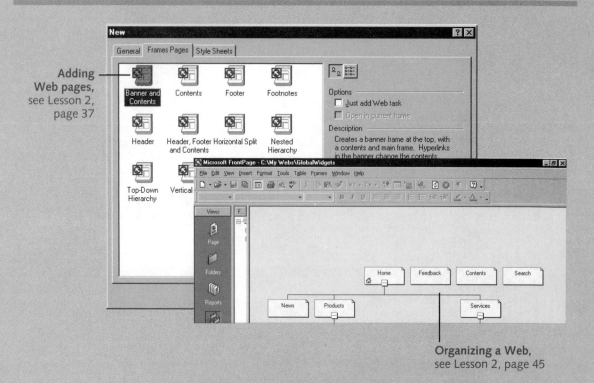

Adding Web pages, see Lesson 2, page 37

Organizing a Web, see Lesson 2, page 45

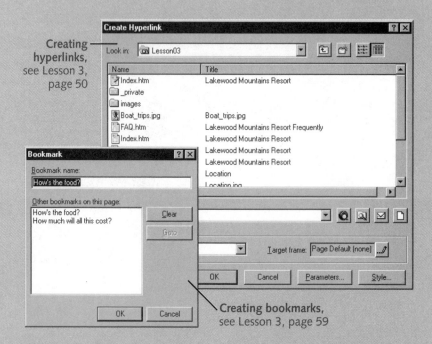

Creating hyperlinks, see Lesson 3, page 50

Creating bookmarks, see Lesson 3, page 59

Using components, see Lesson 4, page 78

Using themes, see Lesson 4, page 72

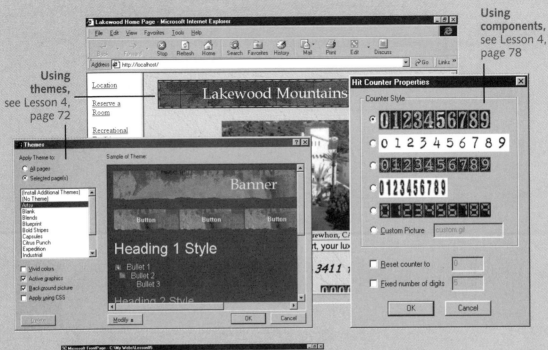

Creating lists, see Lesson 5, page 94

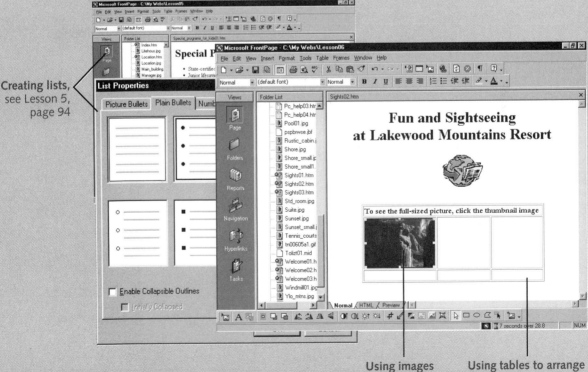

Using images on Web pages, see Lesson 6, page 110

Using tables to arrange Web page elements, see Lesson 5, page 99

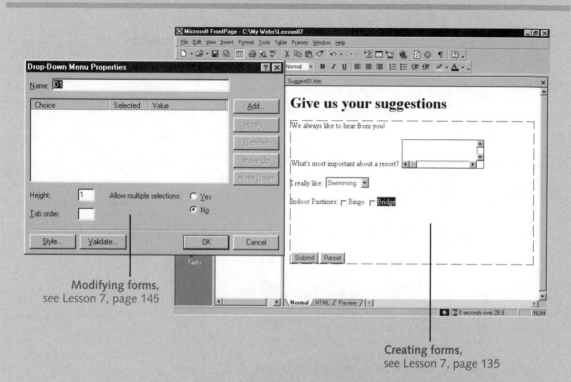

Modifying forms,
see Lesson 7, page 145

Creating forms,
see Lesson 7, page 135

**Using shared borders
and navigation bars,**
see Lesson 8, page 170

Creating frames pages,
see Lesson 8, page 160

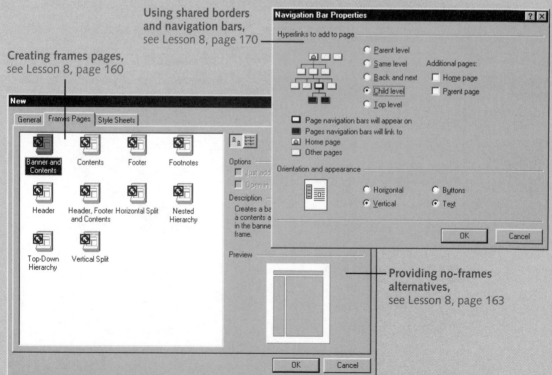

**Providing no-frames
alternatives,**
see Lesson 8, page 163

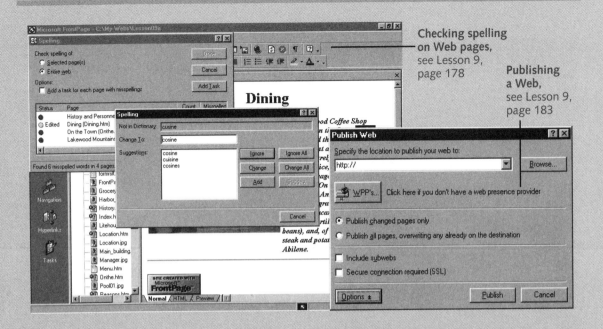

Checking spelling on Web pages, see Lesson 9, page 178

Publishing a Web, see Lesson 9, page 183

Getting reports on a Web, see Lesson 10, page 200

Enhancing a Web, see Lesson 10, page 208

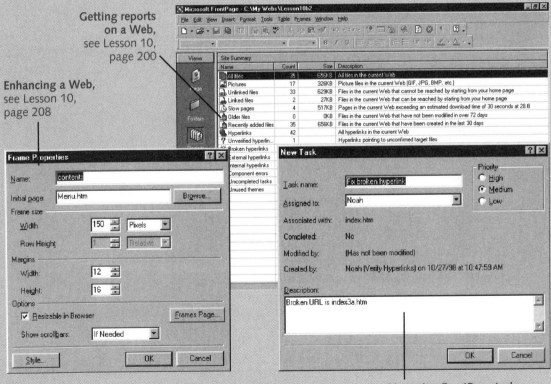

Managing FrontPage tasks, see Lesson 10, page 204

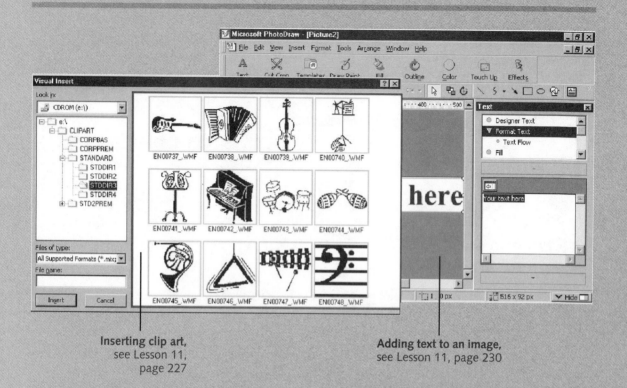

Inserting clip art,
see Lesson 11,
page 227

Adding text to an image,
see Lesson 11, page 230

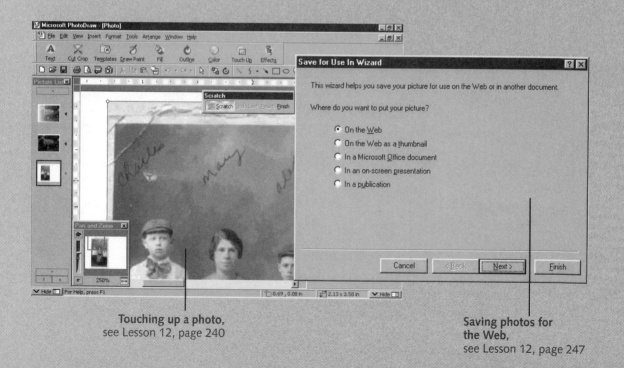

Touching up a photo,
see Lesson 12, page 240

**Saving photos for
the Web,**
see Lesson 12, page 247

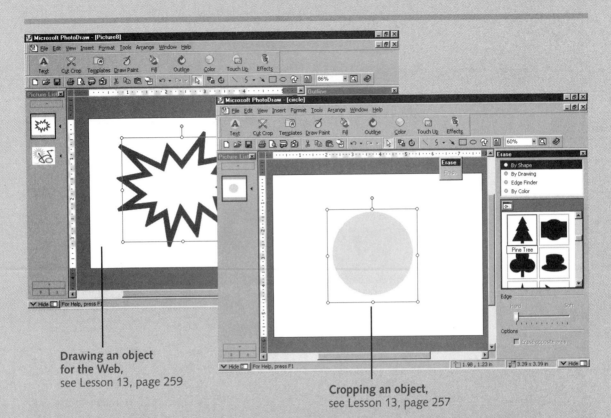

Drawing an object for the Web, see Lesson 13, page 259

Cropping an object, see Lesson 13, page 257

Add a designer edge to a photo, see Lesson 14 page 271

Creating a Web page button, see Lesson 14, page 268

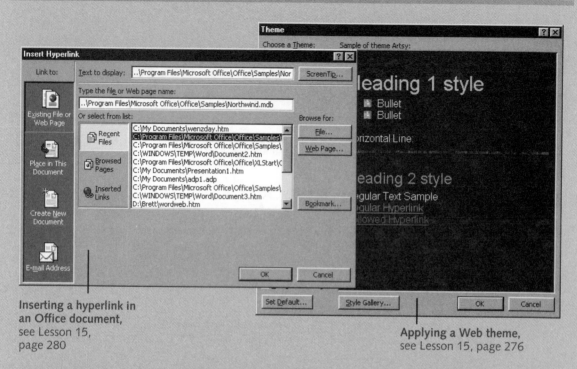

Inserting a hyperlink in an Office document,
see Lesson 15,
page 280

Applying a Web theme,
see Lesson 15, page 276

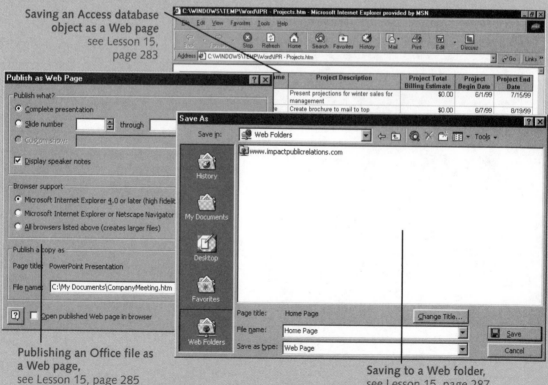

Saving an Access database object as a Web page
see Lesson 15,
page 283

Publishing an Office file as a Web page,
see Lesson 15, page 285

Saving to a Web folder,
see Lesson 15, page 287

Finding Your Best Starting Point

Microsoft Office 2000 Premium is a powerful family of integrated programs that you can use to publish on the Web. With *Web Publishing Step by Step*, you'll quickly and easily learn how to use FrontPage 2000 to build and manage Web and intranet sites, PhotoDraw 2000 to create, import, refine, and optimize Web photos and graphics, and other Office 2000 applications to publish information and communicate over intranets and the World Wide Web.

important

This book is designed for use with Microsoft Office 2000 Premium for the Windows and Windows NT operating systems. If your software is not compatible with this book, a Step by Step book matching your software is probably available. Please visit our World Wide Web site at *http://mspress.microsoft.com* or call 1-800-MSPRESS (1-800-677-7377) for more information.

Finding the Best Starting Point for You

This book is designed for beginning Web designers, as well as readers who have had experience with these types of programs and are switching or upgrading their current Web design tool to FrontPage 2000. Use the following tables to find your best starting point in this book.

If you are	Follow these steps
New	
To Microsoft FrontPage or Microsoft PhotoDraw	**1** Install the practice files as described in "Using the Web Publishing Step by Step Learning Kit CD-ROM."
	2 Learn basic skills for using Microsoft FrontPage 2000 by working through Lessons 1 through 3.
	3 Learn basic skills for using Microsoft PhotoDraw by working through Lesson 11.

If you are	Follow these steps
New	
To Web page design and creation	**1** Install the practice files as described in "Using the Web Publishing Step by Step Learning Kit CD-ROM."
	2 Work through Lessons 1 through 3 in sequence.
	3 Work through Lessons 4 through 10 as needed.
	4 Work through Lessons 11 through 14 to learn how to create images for Web pages.
	5 Work through Lesson 15 to learn how to publish Office documents to the Web.

If you are	Follow these steps
Switching	
From a different Web design tool	**1** Install the practice files as described in "Using the Web Publishing Step by Step Learning Kit CD-ROM."
	2 Skim through Lesson 1 to review basic Web design concepts.
	3 Work through Lessons 2 through 10 in sequence to learn the FrontPage approach to Web design.
	4 Work through Lessons 11 through 14 to learn how to use PhotoDraw to create elements for Web pages.

If you are	Follow these steps
Upgrading	
From FrontPage 98	**1** Install the practice files as described in "Using the Web Publishing Step by Step Learning Kit CD-ROM."
	2 Skim through Lessons 1 and 2 to review basic Web design concepts and learn about some of the new features in FrontPage.
	3 Work through Lesson 6 to learn how FrontPage 2000 allows you to place items in precise locations on a Web page by using CSS positioning.
	4 Work through the other lessons as needed to review FrontPage and learn about other new features.

If you are	Follow these steps
Referencing	
This book after working through the lessons	**1** Use the index to locate information about specific topics, and use the table of contents and the *Quick*Look Guide to locate information about general topics.
	2 Read the Quick Reference at the end of each lesson for a brief review of the major tasks in the lesson. The Quick Reference topics are listed in the same order as they are presented in the lesson.

New Features in Microsoft FrontPage 2000

The following table lists the major new features of FrontPage 2000 covered in this book and the lesson in which you can learn how to use each feature. You can also use the index to find specific information about a feature or about a task you want to perform. Appendix A, "Upgrading from FrontPage 98," details each new feature.

The New! 2000 icon appears in the margin throughout this book to indicate these new features of FrontPage 2000.

To learn how to	See
Manage a Web site with FrontPage.	Lesson 1
Create or edit a Web page with FrontPage's integrated Web page editor.	Lesson 2
Open recently used Webs in FrontPage.	Lesson 3
Use the FrontPage Themes dialog box to create an overall "look" for your Web.	Lesson 4
Change table properties.	Lesson 5
Use Cascading Style Sheets (CSS) to position items on Web pages.	Lesson 6
Test a form with FrontPage.	Lesson 7
Assign or create pages for Web site frames.	Lesson 8
Use background spelling checking.	Lesson 9
Animate text with dynamic HTML.	Lesson 10

Corrections, Comments, and Help

Every effort has been made to ensure the accuracy of this book and the contents of the Web Publishing Step by Step CD-ROM. Microsoft Press provides corrections and additional content for its books through the World Wide Web at *http://mspress.microsoft.com/support*

If you have comments, questions, or ideas regarding this book or the CD-ROM, please send them to us.

Send e-mail to:

mspinput@microsoft.com

Or send postal mail to:

Microsoft Press

Attn: Step by Step Editor

One Microsoft Way

Redmond, WA 98052-6399

Please note that support for Office 2000 Premium software products is not offered through the above addresses. For help using Office 2000, you can call Office 2000 Technical Support at (425) 635-7070 on weekdays between 6 A.M. and 6 P.M. Pacific Time.

Visit Our World Wide Web Site

We invite you to visit the Microsoft Press World Wide Web site. You can visit us at the following location:

http://mspress.microsoft.com

You'll find descriptions for all of our books, information about ordering titles, notices of special features and events, additional content for Microsoft Press books, and much more.

You can also find out the latest in software developments and news from Microsoft Corporation by visiting the following World Wide Web site:

http://www.microsoft.com/

We look forward to your visit on the Web!

Using the Web Publishing Step by Step CD-ROM

The CD-ROM inside this book contains *Web Publishing Step by Step Interactive* and the practice files that you'll use as you perform the exercises in the book. The interactive training is a complete self-contained course that features simulations, pre- and post- assessment, exercises, a glossary, and tips. The practice files are included on the CD so you won't waste time creating the samples used in the lessons in this book, and you can concentrate on learning how to use the applications in Microsoft Office 2000 to publish to the Web.

important

Before you break the seal on the practice CD-ROM package, be sure that this book matches your version of the software. This book is designed for use with Microsoft Office 2000 Premium for the Windows operating systems. If your program is not compatible with this book, a Step by Step book matching your software is probably available. Please visit our World Wide Web site at *http://mspress.microsoft.com* or call 1-800-MSPRESS (1-800-677-7377) for more information.

To use this CD-ROM, you need: PC with a Pentium 75MHz or higher processor; Microsoft Windows 95 or later or Windows NT Workstation 4.0 or later; Microsoft Internet Explorer 4.0 or later; 16 MB of RAM minimum; 21 MB of hard disk space; 2X or faster CD-ROM drive; SVGA display at 800 x 600 pixels with 256 or more colors; Microsoft Mouse or compatible pointing device; Windows-compatible sound board and headphones or speakers for audio syllabus.

Installing *Web Publishing Step by Step Interactive* and the Practice Files

Follow these steps to install *Web Publishing Step by Step Interactive*. The setup program will also install the practice files on your computer's hard disk so that you can use them with the exercises in this book.

1 Remove the CD-ROM from the package inside the back cover of this book and insert it in the CD-ROM drive of your computer.

Follow the setup instructions on the screen.

important

If the setup instructions do not appear automatically, click the Start menu, and then click Run. Then type **d:\setup**, where d is the letter of your CD-ROM drive.

There are two installation options for the interactive training product: typical and full. If you choose typical, you'll need to keep the CD in the computer. If you choose full, all of the training files will be copied to your machine and you can remove the CD after installation. Keep in mind that the full installation requires 160 MB of hard disk space.

2 After the files have been installed, remove the CD-ROM from your CD-ROM drive and replace it in the package inside the back cover of the book.

A folder called Web Publishing SBS Practice has been created on your hard disk, and the practice files have been placed in that folder. A shortcut to Web Publishing Step by Step Interactive and to the Microsoft Press Web site is placed on your desktop.

If your computer is set up to connect to the Internet, you can double-click the Microsoft Press Welcome shortcut to visit the Microsoft Press Web site. You can also connect to this Web site directly at *http://mspress.microsoft.com*

Using *Web Publishing Step by Step Interactive*

Web Publishing Step by Step Interactive is a multimedia training program. Simulations, animated conceptual topics, step-by-step practice, and self-assessment quizzes create an easy and flexible learning environment. Throughout the lessons in *Web Publishing Step by Step Interactive*, you'll have both audio guidance and text instructions to read. When you've finished the training, post-assessment exams let you test what you've learned.

Using the Practice Files

Each lesson in this book explains when and how to use any practice files for that lesson. When a practice file is needed for a lesson, the book will list instructions on how to open the file. The lessons are built around scenarios that simulate a real work environment, so you can easily apply the skills you learn to your own work. For the scenario in this book, imagine that you're a partner in Impact Public Relations, a small public relations firm. Your company recently installed Office 2000 Premium, and you are eager to use its software programs to publish to the Web.

important

For each lesson in Part 1, "Creating Web Sites with Microsoft FrontPage 2000," you must first work through the exercise "Import the Lesson Web," which creates the practice Web for that lesson.

For those of you who like to know all the details, here's a list of the practice files used in the lessons.

File name	Description
Lesson01 - folder	Folder used in Lesson 1
Welcome.htm	File used in Lesson 1
Lesson02 – folder	Folder used in Lesson 2
Recreati.htm	File used in Lesson 2
Boat_trips.jpg	Picture used in Lesson 2
Pool01.jpg	Picture used in Lesson 2
Tennis_courts.jpg	Picture used in Lesson 2
Location02.htm	File used in Lesson 2
Extras – folder	Folder used in Lesson 2
Lesson03 - folder	Folder used in Lesson 3
Index.htm	File used in Lesson 3
Location.htm	File used in Lesson 3
Index01.htm	File used in Lesson 3
Index02.htm	File used in Lesson 3

FAQ.htm   File used in Lesson 3
Main_building.jpg   Picture used in Lesson 3

File name	Description
Lesson04 - folder	Folder used in Lesson 4
Copyrigh.htm	File used in Lesson 4
Reasons.htm	File used in Lesson 4
Lesson05 – folder	Folder used in Lesson 5
Special_programs_for_kids01.htm	File used in Lesson 5
Directions_to_Lakewood.htm	File used in Lesson 5
On_the_town01.htm	File used in Lesson 5
Exptextb.jpg	Picture used in Lesson 5
Lesson06 – folder	Folder used in Lesson 6
Welcome01.htm	File used in Lesson 6
Sights01.htm	File used in Lesson 6
Sights02.htm	File used in Lesson 6
Bry_gap.jpg	Picture used in Lesson 6
FP Logo.gif	Image used in Lesson 6
Welcome02.htm	File used in Lesson 6
Welcome03.htm	File used in Lesson 6
Tolizt01.mid	Sound clip used in Lesson 6
Pc_help01.htm	File used in Lesson 6
Closewin.avi	Motion clip used in Lesson 6
Pc_help03.htm	File used in Lesson 6
Dragdrop.avi	Motion clip used in Lesson 6
Bry_gap_small.jpg	Picture used in Lesson 6
Shore_small.jpg	Picture used in Lesson 6
Frontdr01.htm	File used in Lesson 6
The Microsoft Sound.wav	Sound clip used in Lesson 6
Lesson07 – folder	Folder used in Lesson 7
Lesson08 – folder	Folder used in Lesson 8
Menu01.htm	File used in Lesson 8
Roomres.htm	File used in Lesson 8
Location1.htm	File used in Lesson 8
Frontdr.htm	File used in Lesson 8
Index03.htm	File used in Lesson 8
Location.htm	File used in Lesson 8
On the.htm	File used in Lesson 8

Lesson09 – folder   Folder used in Lesson 9
   History.htm   File used in Lesson 9
   Dining.htm   File used in Lesson 9

File name	Description
Lesson10 – folder	Folder used in Lesson 10
Dhtml01.htm	File used in Lesson 10
Darkphoto.jpg	Picture used in Lesson 12
Scratchphoto.mix	PhotoDraw file used in Lesson 12
Colorpicture.jpg	Picture used in Lessons 12 and 14
B&Wphoto.jpg	Picture used in Lesson 12
Rectangle.gif	Image used in Lesson 13
Circle.gif	Image used in Lesson 13
Swirl.gif	Image used in Lesson 13
AnnualReport.doc	File used in Lesson 15
SampleIPR.mdb	File used in Lesson 15
CompanyMeeting.ppt	File used in Lesson 15
WebPage.htm	File used in Lesson 15

Replying to Install Messages

You might see a message indicating that the feature you are trying to use is not installed. If you see this message, insert the appropriate Microsoft Office CD-ROM in your CD-ROM drive and click Yes to install the feature.

Uninstalling Web Publishing Step by Step Interactive

Use the following steps when you want to delete Web Publishing Step by Step Interactive.

❶   On the Windows taskbar, click the Start button and point to Programs. Point to Microsoft Press, and then point to Microsoft Press Interactive Training. Click Uninstall Microsoft Press Interactive Training.

The Microsoft Interactive Training Uninstall box appears.

② Follow the directions on your screen.

Uninstalling the Practice Files

Use the following steps when you want to delete the practice files added to your hard disk by the Step by Step setup program.

① On the Windows taskbar, click Start, point to Settings, and then click Control Panel.

② Double-click the Add/Remove Programs icon.

The Add/Remove Programs Properties dialog box appears.

③ On the Install/Uninstall tab, select Web Publishing SBS Practice from the list, and then click Add/Remove.

A confirmation message appears.

④ Click Yes or OK.

The practice files are uninstalled.

⑤ Click OK to close the Add/Remove Programs Properties dialog box.

⑥ Close the Control Panel window.

Need Help with Web Publishing Step by Step?

Every effort has been made to ensure the accuracy of this kit. If you do run into a problem, Microsoft Press provides corrections for its books and kits through the World Wide Web at:

http://mspress.microsoft.com/support/

We invite you to visit our main Web page at:

http://mspress.microsoft.com

You'll find descriptions for all of our books, information about ordering titles, notices of special features and events, additional content for Microsoft Press books, and much more.

Conventions and Features in This Book

You can save time when you use this book by understanding, before you start the lessons, how instructions, keys to press, and so on, are shown in the book. Please take a moment to read the following list, which also points out helpful features of the book that you might want to use.

Conventions

■ Hands-on exercises for you to follow are given in numbered lists of steps (1, 2, and so on). A round bullet (●) indicates an exercise that has only one step.

■ Text that you are to type appears in **bold.**

■ A plus sign (+) between two key names means that you must press those keys at the same time. For example, "Press Alt+Tab" means that you hold down the Alt key while you press Tab.

 ■ The New! 2000 icon in the margin is used to identify features that are new in Microsoft Office 2000.

Other Features of This Book

■ You can learn about techniques that build on what you learned in a lesson by trying the optional "One Step Further" exercise at the end of the lesson.

■ You can get a quick reminder of how to perform the tasks you learned by reading the Quick Reference at the end of each lesson.

PART 1

Creating Web Sites with Microsoft FrontPage 2000

1

Planning
a Web Site

**ESTIMATED
TIME
20 min.**

In this lesson you will learn how to:

✔ *Plan a Web site.*

✔ *Start FrontPage.*

✔ *View a Web site in different ways.*

✔ *Open and close a Web.*

Imagine that you are an account executive at Impact Public Relations, an innovative public relations firm that uses the Internet to spread the word about its clients. You've just been assigned to an important new account with Lakewood Mountains Resort, a posh California vacation spot. Your first job will be to create a Web site that spotlights the resort's most attractive features.

There's just one problem. You've been on the World Wide Web, but you don't understand how it works. And the idea of *creating* a Web site—especially for a crucial new account—is very intimidating. But you're in luck. A fellow account executive tells you about a Web tool called Microsoft FrontPage 2000, and volunteers to help you along as you learn to use it.

In this lesson, you will learn how the Web operates and how Web pages make up Webs, or Web sites. You will also learn how to plan your own Web site, complete with hyperlinks. Finally, you will learn how to start FrontPage, use FrontPage views, open and close a Web, and quit FrontPage.

Understanding the World Wide Web

The World Wide Web (or the *Web*) makes it easy to use the *Internet*, a worldwide network of computers created in the late 1960s. Originally, the Internet required you to learn many arcane commands—not only to use it, but also to get data from computers connected to it. If you wanted to get data from a computer that used the UNIX operating system, for example, you needed to know the commands for using UNIX; to get data from a VAX computer that used the VMS operating system, you needed to know the commands for VMS. The Internet worked, but it was difficult to use.

In 1992, however, Tim Berners-Lee and other researchers helped launch the Web, which allowed users to "browse" the Internet without knowing complex commands. In the years that followed, Web *browsers* such as Microsoft Internet Explorer made the Web even easier and more powerful.

> **important**
>
> In this book (and elsewhere), you'll see the word *Web* used in two different ways. Usually, *Web* refers to the World Wide Web. However, it can also refer to a *FrontPage-based Web*, a set of Web pages you create in FrontPage for your Web site. The context should make it clear what *Web* means in each particular case.

The key to creating the Web was *hypertext,* a method for linking blocks, or "pages," of data that was first conceived in the 1960s. It wasn't until the 1990s, however, that Berners-Lee and his coworkers applied the hypertext concept to the Internet with what they called *HTTP* (Hypertext Transfer Protocol). And with HTTP, the World Wide Web was born.

Today, there are millions of Web sites. You can access information on a wide range of topics, you can run a Web-based business, and you can even learn about the Web and its underlying technology.

Understanding Web Pages and HTML

If hypertext and HTTP were the keys to creating the World Wide Web, the key to creating Web pages is *HTML* (Hypertext Markup Language). *HTML* uses codes, called *tags*, to format and define text on a Web page. The Web browser that you use translates these codes into the Web page text and graphics you see on your screen.

HTML tags do more than tell Web browsers how to format text and place graphics. Hyperlinks, for example, tell the Web browser to locate a different

Web page on the Internet and display it on the user's screen. The code for a typical Web page and the page it creates are shown in the following illustrations.

Start of HTML document

Start of page header

End of page header

Start of table

Start of row in table

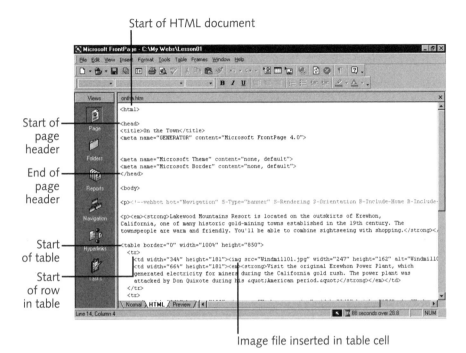

Image file inserted in table cell

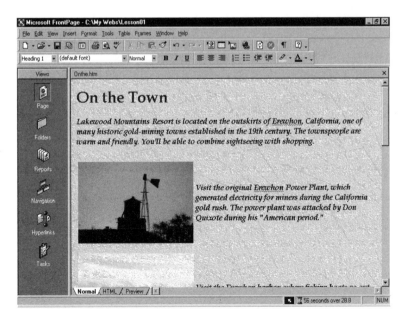

Many Web pages today use *scripts* created with languages such as Microsoft VBScript and JavaScript. These "mini-programs" are embedded in Web pages, where they handle formatting, images, and multimedia display routines much like any other programming language. A new and more advanced way to handle many scripting tasks is to use *Dynamic HTML* (DHTML). With DHTML, you can create simple animations and many other effects.

So, you're feeling overwhelmed by HTML and its many options? Now your coworker gives you the good news. To create Web sites with FrontPage, you don't have to learn anything about HTML, scripts, or DHTML unless you want to. With FrontPage, you simply type the text you want on your Web page, drop in any pictures or sounds you desire, and use FrontPage's features to do anything for which you would normally have to write a script or DHTML. You can still write HTML, scripts, or DHTML if you want, but it's not required.

tip

This book teaches you how to create Web sites for the World Wide Web. You can use the same techniques to create Web sites for an *intranet*—a network that works like the World Wide Web but has security features that restrict parts of it so that only users within your company or organization can access its pages.

Understanding Web Pages and Web Sites

You'll learn more about wizards and templates in Lesson 2, "Creating a Web Site."

A Web *site* is a collection of related Web pages and other files linked together. Web sites usually have a specific purpose, whether it be personal or business-related. FrontPage comes with *wizards*, which walk you step by step through the process of creating a Web site, and *templates*, which are built-in Web pages containing all the formatting required to build and customize your own Web pages. Wizards and templates can help you create several different kinds of Web sites.

A hyperlink is text or an image on a Web page that, when clicked, immediately sends you to another Web page or site.

On each Web site, one page is designated as the *home page*. This is the page that users see first when they visit the Web site. From the home page, users can click *hyperlinks* to jump to other pages on the Web site or to pages on different Web sites. Those hyperlinks might be Web sites on the same computer as the first Web site, or they might be stored on a computer halfway around the world. A typical Web site organization is shown in the following illustration.

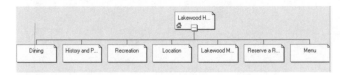

The home page is at the top, with linked pages on the row below it. Usually, each page under the home page—called a "child page" of the home page—contains hyperlinks to the other pages on the Web site, as well as hyperlinks back to the home page. Often, child pages will have hyperlinks to still other pages that are below them in the organization, and so forth.

You can use FrontPage to create and manage Web sites on the Internet or on an intranet.

A Web site resides on a *Web server,* which is a computer dedicated to making Web pages available to people who want to visit the site. (However, with FrontPage, you can create your Web site right in your computer's file system and publish the Web site to a server when you are ready.) Normally, a Web server is connected to the Internet, which makes its Web pages available for viewing on the World Wide Web. Many companies and organizations are setting up Web servers on intranets. These private Web servers are ideal for hosting Web sites that contain project files and other internal data that need to be shared by staff members. Some pages of the intranet Web site are made available to the world, while other pages remain accessible only to users within the organization.

Finding a Web Server

Before you set up the Web site for your client, Lakewood Mountains Resort, you need to find a place to put it: a Web server.

Most Internet service providers (ISPs) offer Web hosting as part of the package when you buy an Internet account. Web hosting simply means that the ISP provides space on a Web server computer for your Web files. Online services such as America Online also offer Web hosting. For simple Webs, an ISP's Web hosting services are often adequate. For larger and more sophisticated Webs, though, an account with a *dedicated* Web host can be a good investment. A dedicated Web host can offer more disk space for your Web files and, often, faster equipment.

Whether you choose an Internet service provider or a dedicated Web host, there's an important question you should always ask: "Do you have the FrontPage Server Extensions?" FrontPage has a slew of extra features to help you create exciting Web sites and put them on the Web with minimal effort. But some ISPs and Web hosts do not have the FrontPage Server Extensions. Some ISPs have them for business Internet accounts but not for the less-expensive personal accounts.

So, where can you find a FrontPage-supporting Web host? On the Web, of course. Navigate to Microsoft's Web Presence Provider site at *microsoft.saltmine.com/frontpage/wpp/list/* to view lists of ISPs and Web hosts that have the FrontPage Server Extensions.

Planning Your Web Site

Let's assume you've found a Web host that has the FrontPage Server Extensions. Now you need to decide what should go into the Web site you present to your client. You must first decide on the purpose of the Web site. In the case of Lakewood Mountains Resort, there are two main purposes.

- To provide information about the resort for prospective customers.
- To enable customers to request room reservations over the Web.

Of course, Web sites can have many additional purposes. One Web site might provide technical support for a computer product. Another might have a catalog and allow customers to place secure orders over the Web. The purpose of a Web site determines its design and the pages it should include.

Like all Web sites, the resort's Web site will start with a home page. From there, it needs at least one page about each of the resort's major selling points. So that customers can request reservations over the Web, the site will also need a form on which customers can enter their name, address, and reservation data.

You call the resort manager to learn about the resort's major selling points. You end up with a list of topics, each of which will get its own Web page.

- The resort's secluded location.
- The resort's recreational facilities.
- The resort's fine food.
- The picturesque town just a few minutes away.
- The resort's colorful history and helpful staff.

Based on this information, you come up with a diagram of the Web site.

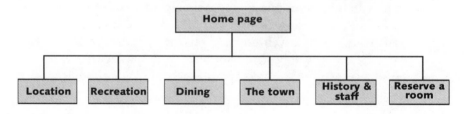

Now is the time to ask how the pages will be linked together. The obvious answer is "by hyperlinks," but FrontPage helps you use hyperlinks in a variety of ways. You can put all your hyperlinks on the home page, or, if you're interested in a more high-tech alternative, you can use a *navigation bar*, one of FrontPage's special features. You can also create an *image map*—a picture with "hot spots," or hyperlinks within an image, that users can click to go to the desired pages.

Your coworker suggests a simple yet elegant solution: a menu *frame*. A frame is a pane in a Web site that works independently of the main pane. A frame is displayed continuously even as the user selects other hyperlinks that are displayed in the main pane. As the user moves around the Web site, pages are displayed in the right frame, while a menu of hyperlinks stays constant in the left frame. After considering these options, you decide to use frames in the Web site.

Managing a Web Site with FrontPage

The Views bar now provides an easy way to switch between views of Web structure and pages, and it includes an all new Reports view.

FrontPage makes it easy not only to create Web pages and Web sites, but also to manage them. The FrontPage window is divided into three main sections, each of which gives you a different kind of control over your Web site.

Views bar   Folder List   Page view

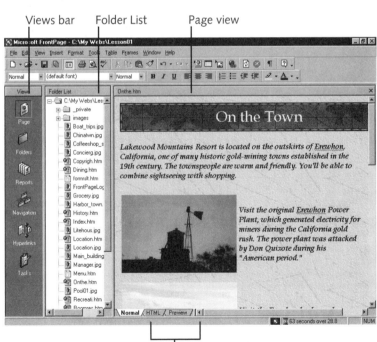

Tabs let you view and edit the currently selected file in different ways.

In FrontPage, you can view a Web in several different ways. Th⌐
plays icons that let you view and edit different aspects of yo⌐

Icon	Name	Description
	Folders	Displays a list of folders and files in ⌐ current Web.
	Reports	Displays a list of reports on different aspects of the current Web, such as the number of linked files, broken links, and the number of "slow" pages that would take more than 30 seconds to download to a computer over a 28.8-KB connection. (Thirty seconds is the default value, but it can be changed by the user.)
	Navigation	Displays a tree diagram of the current Web and makes the Folder List display a list of folders and files in the current Web.
	Tasks	Displays a list of tasks to be done on the current Web. When you use some of the wizards to create a Web, FrontPage compiles a task list. You can also add tasks on your own.
	Page	Displays a Web page for viewing or editing.
	Hyperlinks	Displays a diagram of hyperlinks to and from the current page.

You'll learn more about tasks in Lesson 10, "Managing and Enhancing a Web."

The Folder List displays all folders and files in the current Web, while the currently selected page is displayed in Page view. At the bottom of the screen, a status bar displays information about the current page or operation. When a page is displayed in Page view, for example, the status bar shows an estimated download time for the page over a 28.8-KB modem connection.

Import the Lesson 1 practice Web

Before you can work with any of the exercise files, you must install the files from the Web Publishing Step by Step CD-ROM. For installation instructions, see "Installing Web Publishing Step by Step Interactive and the Practice Files" on page xxii.

In this exercise, you create a new Web based on the files in the Lesson01 folder in the Web Publishing SBS Practice folder. You will use this Web for all the exercises in Lesson 1.

1 On the Windows taskbar, click the Start button, point to Programs, and then click Microsoft FrontPage.

FrontPage starts.

If a dialog box appears asking if you'd like to make FrontPage your default HTML editor, click Yes.

② On the File menu, point to New, and then click Web.

FrontPage displays the New dialog box.

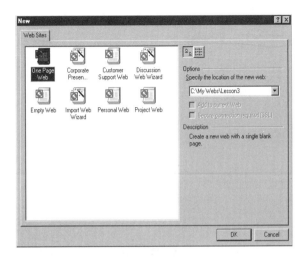

If your hard disk drive is not drive C, substitute the appropriate drive letter in step 3.

③ Click the Import Web Wizard icon. In the Specify The Location Of The New Web text box, delete the default text and type **C:\My Webs\Lesson01**, and then click OK.

FrontPage displays the first Import Web Wizard dialog box.

FrontPage will create the Lesson01 directory for you.

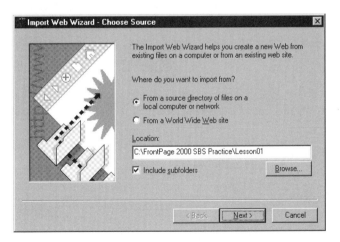

④ Click the From A Source Directory Of Files option, click the Include Subfolders check box, and click the Browse button.

⑤ Browse to the Lesson01 folder in the Web Publishing SBS Practice folder, and click OK.

6 Click Next twice, and then click Finish.

FrontPage creates a new Web based on the practice files and places it in the Lesson01 folder.

Explore FrontPage views

In this exercise, you explore different views of your new Web.

In the Folder List, an icon appears next to each filename, indicating the type of file (Web page, image file, and so forth).

1 If your Web is not already displayed in Page view, on the Views bar, click the Page icon.

2 In the Folder List, double-click the file Welcome.htm.

FrontPage displays the Welcome Web page.

On the status bar, FrontPage estimates the amount of time the current page will take to download over a 28.8-KB modem connection.

3 At the bottom of the FrontPage window, click the HTML tab.

FrontPage displays the HTML code for the current page.

4 At the bottom of the FrontPage window, click the Preview tab.

FrontPage displays a preview of how the page will look in a Web browser.

5 On the Views bar, click the Folders icon.

FrontPage displays a list of all folders and files in the current Web.

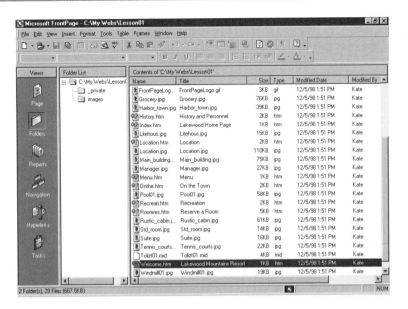

6   On the Views bar, click the Reports icon.

FrontPage displays a list of reports about the current Web.

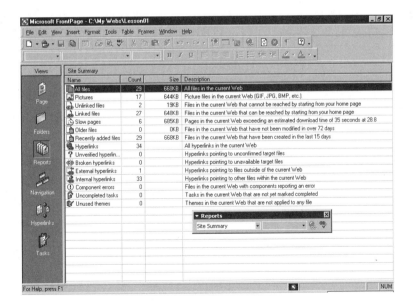

You can use the Reports toolbar to switch quickly between different report views.

In the Navigation view's tree diagram, you can drag Web pages to restructure your Web.

7   On the Views bar, click the Navigation icon.

FrontPage normally displays a tree diagram of the current Web. However, because you haven't yet created any Web pages, there is no tree diagram to display.

8   On the Views bar, click the Hyperlinks icon.

FrontPage displays a diagram of hyperlinks going to and from the page.

9   On the Views bar, click the Tasks icon.

Currently, there are no tasks to display.

Understanding FrontPage Folders

When you install FrontPage 2000, it creates a folder called "My Webs." This is the default folder in which FrontPage will store any Webs you create. Each separate Web you create gets its own subfolder in the My Webs folder in which FrontPage stores files specific to that Web.

When FrontPage creates a Web, it also creates at least three different folders in which to store Web pages and files. You don't have to worry about these folders: you can ignore them and your Web will still work perfectly. However, understanding these folders gives you insight into your Web and can help you organize your files.

Folder	Explanation
Main folder	Default folder for your Web page, image, and Java class files.
_private	FrontPage stores files used to organize and manage your Web in this folder. Should be left strictly alone.
Images	Folder into which you can move image files if desired. If you have a large number of image files, this helps remove clutter from your main folder.

(continued)

continued

In addition to the three default folders, you can also create your own folders to hold specific types or groups of files.

Create a folder

1 On the Views bar, click the Folders icon.

2 On the File menu, point to New, and then click Folder.

FrontPage creates a new folder. The default folder name is New Folder.

3 Delete the default folder name, type the desired name, and press Enter.

FrontPage renames the folder.

You can create a new folder for any purpose. The only thing you must remember is to use FrontPage—not the Windows Explorer—to move files into the folder. When you use FrontPage to move files, any hyperlinks to those files are automatically updated.

Close and reopen a Web

In this exercise, you close and reopen the Lesson01 Web.

1 On the File menu, click Close Web.

FrontPage closes the Lesson01 Web.

2 On the File menu, click Open Web.

FrontPage displays the Open Web dialog box.

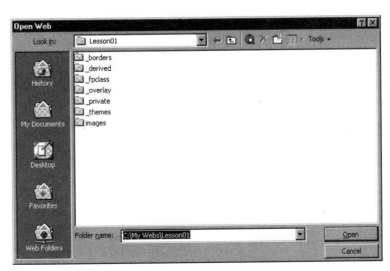

❸ If necessary, browse to the Lesson01 Web in the My Webs folder.

❹ If necessary, in the file list, click the Lesson01 folder.

❺ Click the Open button.

FrontPage opens the Web.

❻ On the Views bar, click the Page icon, and then in the Folder List, double-click the file History.htm.

FrontPage displays the History and Personnel Web page.

<table>
<tr><td>One
Step
Further</td><td># Getting Ideas
for a Web Site</td></tr>
</table>

You've tentatively decided to use frames in your Web for Lakewood Mountains Resort, but you'd like to get some more ideas for enhancing your Web. Your coworker suggests that the best place to look is the Web itself.

The first and most obvious place to look is Microsoft's own FrontPage Web site at *www.microsoft.com/frontpage*. Another place to look is CNet's Builder.com Web site at *www.builder.com*. This site has tutorials on Web design, HTML, scripting, and many other Web topics.

Finally, you should surf the Web to view as many Web pages as you can. Ideas are everywhere, and as long as you don't just copy the content of someone's Web site, the ideas are free. You'll often find some of the most innovative and appealing Web ideas at some of the most unusual—even bizarre—Web sites.

Get ideas for your Web site

In this exercise, you visit Web pages on the Internet to familiarize yourself with some of the places that offer ideas on Web design.

❶ Connect to the Internet, and then double-click the Web browser icon on the Windows desktop.

Your Web browser opens and displays your Internet home page.

❷ In the Address bar, type **microsoft.com/clipgallerylive**, and press Enter.

The End User License Agreement (EULA) is displayed.

❸ Read the license agreement, and then click the Accept button.

The Microsoft Clip Gallery Live Web page is displayed in your browser. From here you can download clip art, photo images, sounds, and videos.

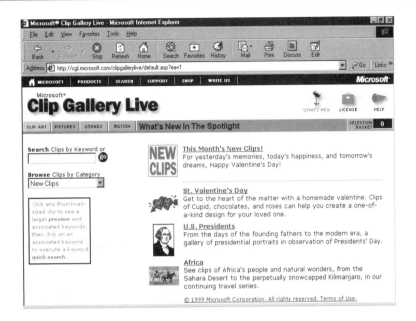

Microsoft's Clip Gallery Live page is continuously updated. If you visit the page on the Web, it will look different from the figure shown here.

④ In the Address bar, type **microsoft.com/frontpage**

Microsoft's FrontPage Web site is displayed in your browser.

⑤ In the Address bar, type **www.builder.com**, and then press Enter.

The CNet Builder.com Web page is displayed in your browser.

Finish the lesson

Close

① Click the Close button at the top-right corner of your Web browser window.

Your Web browser closes and FrontPage reappears.

② On the File menu, click Close Web.

③ For each page, if FrontPage prompts you to save changes, click Yes.

FrontPage saves your changes and closes the Lesson01 Web.

Lesson 1 Quick Reference

To	Do this	Icon
Plan a Web site	Decide on the purposes of the Web site, and then decide what Web pages are needed for the site.	
Start FrontPage	Click the Start button, point to Programs, and click Microsoft FrontPage.	
Create a new Web based on Web page files in a folder	On the File menu, point to New, and click Web. In the New dialog box, click the Import Web Wizard icon. In the Specify The Location Of The New Web text box, type the folder containing the files for the new Web. Click OK, click the From A Source Directory Of Files option, click the Include Subfolders check box, and click the Browse button. Browse to the folder that you want to import, click OK, click Next twice, and then click Finish.	
Open a Web	On the File menu, click Open Web. In the Open Web dialog box, browse to the folder containing the Web, and click the Open button.	
View or edit a Web page	Double-click the filename (with an .htm extension) in the Folder List.	
Preview the appearance of a Web page in Page view	Click the Page icon on the Views bar, and click the Preview tab at the bottom of the FrontPage window.	
View a tree diagram of a Web structure	Click the Navigation icon on the Views bar.	
View a diagram of hyperlinks to and from a Web page	Click the Web page filename in the Folder List, and then click the Hyperlinks icon on the Views bar.	
View a list of tasks required to complete a Web site	Click the Tasks icon on the Views bar.	
View a list of folders and files in a Web	Click the Folders icon on the Views bar.	
View reports about a Web	Click the Reports icon on the Views bar.	

LESSON

2

Creating a Web Site

ESTIMATED
TIME
40 min.

In this lesson you will learn how to:

✔ *Create a Web.*

✔ *Create a home page.*

✔ *Add and format Web page text.*

✔ *Add a scrolling marquee to a Web page.*

✔ *Preview a Web.*

✔ *Add pages to a Web.*

✔ *Change Web page properties.*

✔ *Organize a Web.*

Now that you've defined the purposes of the Lakewood Mountains Resort Web site and determined which pages it should include, it's time to start creating the Web site in Microsoft FrontPage 2000. That's the good news. But your boss just stuck his head in your office and announced that you're meeting with the client tomorrow afternoon. A first draft of the Web site has to be ready for presentation at the meeting.

In this lesson, you will learn about FrontPage tools that can help you create a Web site in record time. You will then create a Web and add a home page. You will enter and format text on the page, add a scrolling marquee, create another page, and import an existing page. You will change the properties of a Web page and preview your Web. Finally, you will learn how to organize your Web.

Creating a Web Site Using a Wizard

There are three ways to create a Web in FrontPage: use a wizard, use a template, or create the Web "from scratch." The method you choose depends on your specific needs and situation.

FrontPage wizards are best used for complex Web sites. Each wizard creates a different type of Web using a series of dialog boxes in which you select the specific options that fit your situation.

When you've made all your selections, the wizard creates the Web site based on your input. FrontPage includes the wizards described in the following sections.

Corporate Presence Wizard

The Corporate Presence Wizard creates a Web site for a company. The Web site includes a home page, a table of contents, a News Release page, a product and service directory, a Web page for each product or service, a Customer Feedback page, and a Web page that lets visitors search your site.

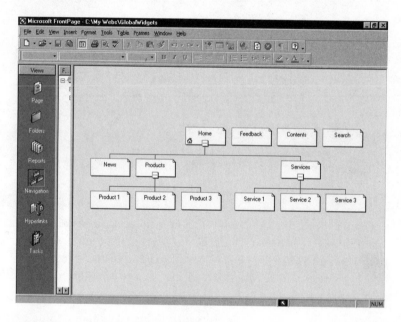

Discussion Web Wizard

The Discussion Web Wizard creates a Web site with a threaded message board, which allows visitors to view, post, and reply to messages on your Web site.

Import Web Wizard

The Import Web Wizard creates a new Web site based on existing Web files on your own computer or on a Web server. You can then modify the Web pages and Web structure as needed. You'll find this wizard especially useful for creating and testing updated versions of your own Web sites.

Create a Web site using a wizard

In this exercise, you create a Web site using the Corporate Presence Wizard.

❶ On the File menu, point to New, and then click Web.

FrontPage displays the New dialog box.

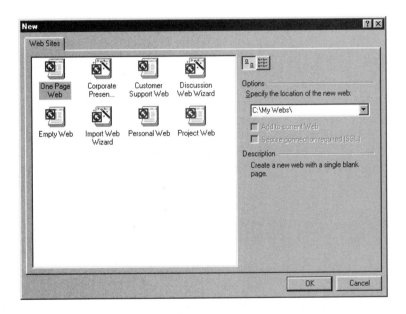

❷ In the Web Sites pane, click the Corporate Presence icon.

FrontPage will use the Corporate Presence Wizard to create the Web.

If your hard disk drive is not drive C, substitute the appropriate drive letter in step 3.

❸ In the Specify The Location Of The New Web text box, delete the default text and type **C:\My Webs\MyWizardDemo**.

FrontPage will create the C:\My Webs\MyWizardDemo folder. It will put all the Web files in that folder and its subfolders.

❹ Click OK, and then click Next.

FrontPage displays the first Corporate Presence Web Wizard dialog box, which explains the purpose of the wizard. It then displays the second dialog box, in which you can select pages to include in the Web.

The Corporate Web Wizard displays different dialog boxes depending on which pages you select for inclusion in your corporate Web.

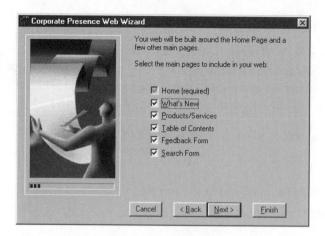

5 Click the What's New check box and the Search Form check box to clear them, and then click Next.

FrontPage will not include a What's New or a Search Form page in the Web. FrontPage displays the next dialog box, in which you select the information to be displayed on your corporate home page.

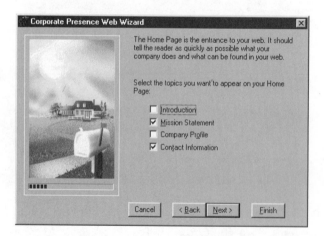

6 Click the Introduction check box to select it, and then click Next.

FrontPage will display an introduction on your corporate home page. FrontPage displays the next dialog box, in which you select how many pages the wizard should create to show information about products and services.

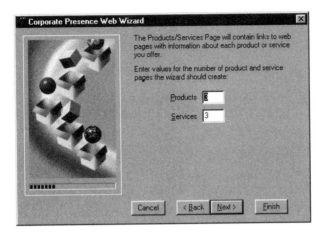

7   Click Next.

FrontPage accepts the default settings of three Product pages and three Services pages and displays a dialog box in which you can select the information you want displayed on each product or service Web page.

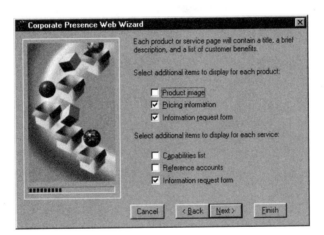

8   Click Next.

FrontPage accepts the default settings and displays a dialog box in which you can select the information you want to collect from Web site visitors who respond on your Feedback page.

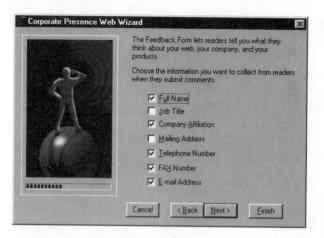

9 Click Next five times.

FrontPage displays a dialog box in which you enter the name and address of your company.

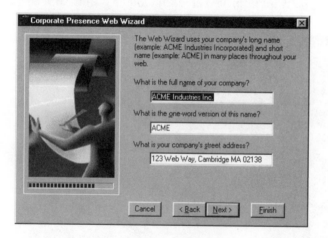

To keep this exercise brief, you skipped several dialog boxes you would normally complete, such as one in which you enter your company's phone number.

10 In the What Is The Full Name Of Your Company text box, type **Lakewood Mountains Resort**. Press Tab, type **Lakewood**, press Tab, type **1501 Bryant's Gap Trail, Erewhon, CA 94501**, and click Finish.

FrontPage creates a corporate presence Web based on the options you selected and the information you entered.

11 On the Views bar, click the Navigation icon, and in Navigation view, double-click the Home page icon.

FrontPage displays your corporate home page. You can now modify the page by entering additional information.

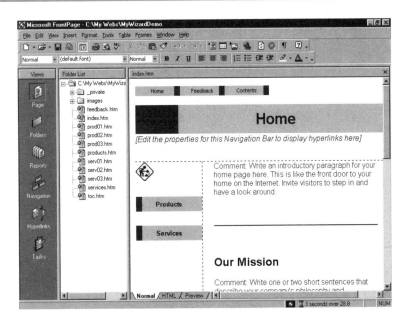

12 On the File menu, click Close Web.

FrontPage closes the Corporate Presence Web you just created.

tip

When you are creating Web filenames, get into the habit of creating names that do not contain spaces. Most Web servers do not recognize spaces in filenames. If you want to keep your Web filenames descriptive, you can separate words and still keep them connected by placing the underscore character (_) between words.

Corporate Presence Web Pages

The Corporate Presence Wizard can include several ready-to-use pages on your Web site. Even if you don't use the Corporate Presence Wizard, you can create these pages individually by using Web page templates. To use a template to create a page, click the Page icon on the Views bar. On the File menu, point to New, and click Page. FrontPage displays the New dialog box with a menu of page templates. Click the icon for the type of page you want to create, and then click OK.

(continued)

continued

Page template	Creates
Home	A home page containing information you specify.
What's New	A page with information about new pages or other updates on the Web site.
Products/Services	One or more pages about products or services offered by your company, with a description of each product or service, benefits, part numbers, and pricing.
Table of Contents	A list of all the pages in the Web site, with a hyperlink to each page.
Feedback Form	A form that allows Web site visitors to send feedback to an e-mail address you specify.
Search Form the Web site	A form that allows Web site visitors to search for pages containing words they specify.

Creating a Web Site Using a Template

Unlike wizards, which prompt you for input and then design a Web based on that input, templates are ready-made Web sites that you can modify for your own needs. FrontPage includes the following templates.

This template	Creates
Customer Support Web	A Web site in which a company can answer customer questions and get feedback. It combines a message board with several other features, such as a frequently asked questions list (FAQ), a suggestion form, and an area for downloading information and software.
Project Web	A Web site to share information about a project with members of the project team. It includes a page that lists team members, a schedule page, a project status page, a message board, and a search page.
Personal Web	A Web site to showcase the interests of an individual. It includes a home page, a photo album page, an interests page, and a Web page for links to other Web sites.
One Page Web	A Web site with only a home page.
Empty Web	A Web site that you build from scratch. It does not include any Web pages.

Create a Web site using a template

If you completed the previous exercise, notice that FrontPage has suggested MyWizardDemo2 as the name of your new Web because the last Web you created was named MyWizardDemo.

If your hard disk drive is not drive C, substitute the appropriate drive letter in step 3.

In this exercise, you create a Web using the Customer Support Web template.

1 On the File menu, point to New, and then click Web.

FrontPage displays the New dialog box.

2 In the Web sites pane, click the Customer Support Web icon.

FrontPage will use the Customer Support Web template. This creates a Web site designed to provide help and solve problems for users of a company's products.

3 In the Specify The Location Of The New Web text box, delete the default text and type **C:\My Webs\MyTempDemo**, and click OK.

FrontPage creates a new Web based on the Customer Support template.

4 In the Folder List, double-click the file Index.htm.

FrontPage displays the new Web's home page.

Unlike a wizard, which asks you a series of questions about your Web, a template is a blueprint used to create a particular kind of Web. Once you've created the Web, you can then modify it to suit your needs.

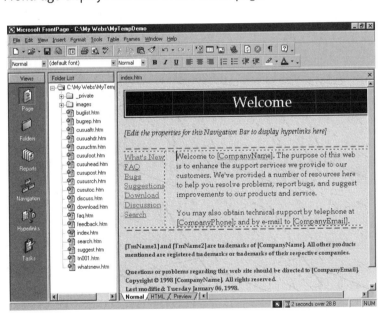

5 On the displayed Web page, select the text *[CompanyName]*, and then type **Lakewood Mountains Software**.

FrontPage replaces the selected text with the text you typed.

6 On the toolbar, click the Save button.

FrontPage saves the Web page with your changes.

Save

2

Creating a Web Site

❼ In the Folder List, double-click the file Bugrep.htm.

FrontPage displays the Web page that allows users to report problems in the company's products or services.

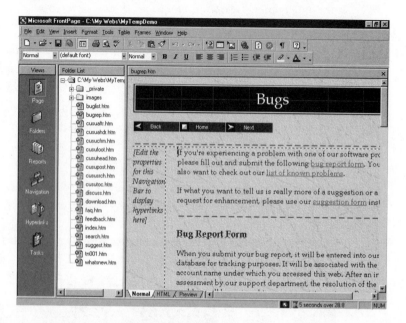

❽ In the Folder List, double-click the file Discuss.htm.

FrontPage displays the Web page that allows users to read and respond to messages in a discussion board.

❾ On the File menu, click Close Web.

FrontPage closes the Web you just created.

Creating and Importing Webs

Whether you use wizards or templates, there are essentially two ways to create a Web. The first way is to create the Web's pages and other files after you create the Web itself. The second way is to create a new Web based on existing files.

The second approach works especially well when you have a previous version of a Web—whether on your local hard disk drive or on a remote Web server—and you want to create a new version of the Web.

Create an empty Web

In this exercise, you create a new Web using the Empty Web template. You then close the empty Web.

❶   On the File menu, point to New, and then click Web.

FrontPage displays the New dialog box.

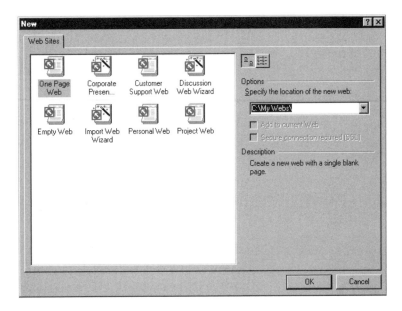

If your hard disk drive is not drive C, substitute the appropriate drive letter in step 2.

❷   Click the Empty Web icon. In the Specify The Location Of The New Web text box, delete the default text and type **C:\My Webs\Empty02**, and then click OK.

FrontPage creates a folder named Empty02 and places a new, empty Web in the folder.

❸   On the Views bar, click the Navigation icon.

FrontPage normally displays a tree diagram of the current Web. However, because you haven't yet created any Web pages, there is no tree diagram to display.

❹   On the File menu, click Close Web.

FrontPage closes the empty Web.

Import the Lesson 2 practice Web

In this exercise, you create a new Web based on the files in the Lesson02 folder in the Web Publishing SBS Practice folder. You will use this Web for all the remaining exercises in Lesson 2.

1 On the File menu, point to New, and then click Web.

FrontPage displays the New dialog box.

If your hard disk drive is not drive C, substitute the appropriate drive letter in step 2.

2 Click the Import Web Wizard icon. In the Specify The Location Of The New Web text box, type **C:\My Webs\Lesson02**, and then click OK.

FrontPage displays the first Import Web Wizard dialog box.

3 Click the From A Source Directory Of Files option, click the Include Subfolders check box, and click the Browse button.

4 Browse to the Lesson 02 folder in the Web Publishing SBS Practice folder, and click OK.

5 Click Next twice, and then click Finish.

FrontPage creates a new Web based on the practice files and places it in the Lesson02 folder.

Creating a Home Page and Adding Text

Once you've created a Web, the next step is to add Web pages. By default, the first page you add will be treated as your Web's home page. The filename for the home page is either Default.htm or Index.htm, although the Web page title can be anything you choose.

tip

Web servers don't all use the same conventions for naming home pages. Most require this file to be named either Default.htm or Index.htm. If your home page name is different from what the Web server you're publishing to requires, don't worry; FrontPage automatically renames the home page when you publish a Web to a server. (If you're uploading files manually instead of having FrontPage publish them for you—as you must with popular Web sites such as GeoCities or The Globe—you will have to rename the file yourself.)

FrontPage makes it easy to add text and other elements to Web pages. To add text, you simply type it on the page. You can then apply standard Web text styles to the text. You can also format text (and other Web page elements) with FrontPage's own formatting tools and styles for headings or body text. There's even a Formatting toolbar with the same buttons as those in Microsoft Word and other familiar Microsoft Office programs.

Create and title a Web page

If you are not working through this lesson sequentially, follow the steps in "Import the Lesson 2 Practice Web," earlier in this lesson.

In this exercise, you create a home page for Lakewood Mountains Resort.

❶ On the Views bar, click the Navigation icon.

❷ On the File menu, point to New, and then click Page.

FrontPage creates a new Web page and displays it as an icon.

You can also click the New button on the toolbar to create a new page.

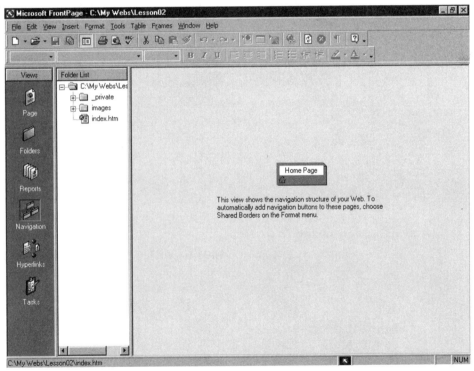

3 In the home page icon, click the text *Home Page* to select it, type **Lakewood Mountains Resort**, and then press Enter.

FrontPage retitles the Web page.

Add and format text

In this exercise, you open the Lakewood Mountains Resort home page for editing. You then add and format text on the page.

1 Make sure your Web is displayed in Navigation view. Double-click the Lakewood Mountains Resort home page icon.

FrontPage displays the home page in Page view.

2 Type **Lakewood Mountains Resort** (but do not press Enter).

3 The Text Style box at the left end of the Formatting toolbar currently says Normal. Click the drop-down arrow to expand the list.

The Text Style list shows available text styles.

Center

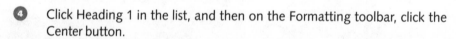

4 Click Heading 1 in the list, and then on the Formatting toolbar, click the Center button.

FrontPage formats the line in Heading 1 style and centers the heading horizontally on the Web page.

5 Press Enter twice, and type **1501 Bryant's Gap Trail, Erewhon, CA 94501**

tip

Notice that FrontPage underlines the word *Erewhon*. This indicates that the FrontPage spelling checker did not find the word in its word list and that it might be misspelled. However, you know that it is the proper name of a town and is spelled correctly. You'll learn how to use FrontPage's spelling checker in Lesson 9; just ignore the underlining for now.

6 Select the text in the address line.

Bold

Save

7 On the Formatting toolbar, click the Bold button.

FrontPage applies bold formatting to the selected text.

8 On the toolbar, click the Save button.

FrontPage saves your changes.

Adding, Formatting, and Previewing a Marquee

You can easily add an impressive feature to the Lakewood Mountains Resort home page. A scrolling *marquee* displays text that slowly moves across the screen. This provides an eye-catching way to showcase a marketing message for Web site visitors. But use marquees and other animations sparingly. Numerous studies of Web users have noted that many people find Web sites that have excessive motion, animation, and blinking to be annoying.

You can adjust the speed and direction of a marquee's text movement, as well as the font, size, and style of the text.

Add a marquee

If you are not working through this lesson sequentially, follow the steps in "Import the Lesson 2 Practice Web," earlier in this lesson, drag the file Index01.htm from the Folder List into the Navigation view, and double-click its icon.

In this exercise, you add a marquee to the Lakewood Mountains Resort home page. You then adjust the scrolling speed and format the text.

1 Click the line below the address line.

FrontPage moves the insertion point to the next line. Notice that the insertion point is now aligned with the Web page's left margin.

2 On the Insert menu, point to Component, and then click Marquee.

FrontPage displays the Marquee Properties dialog box.

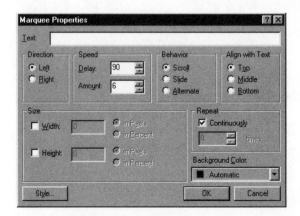

3 Type the following in the Text text box:

Welcome to Lakewood Mountains Resort, your luxury vacation retreat! Come home to: Spacious rooms. Fine food. Golf. Tennis. Swimming. Boating and fishing. Special programs for kids. And surprisingly low rates!

4 Click OK.

FrontPage places the marquee on your Web page. Only part of the text is visible, and it isn't scrolling. The text will scroll to the left when the page is displayed in a Web browser. You'll preview the marquee later in this lesson.

Customize the marquee

In this exercise, you change the width and background color of the marquee.

1 Right-click the marquee.

A shortcut menu appears.

②   On the shortcut menu, click Marquee Properties.

FrontPage displays the Marquee Properties dialog box.

③   In the Size section of the dialog box, click the Width check box, double-click the Width check box, type **400**, and verify that In Pixels is selected.

The marquee will now have a width of 400 pixels.

④   Click the Background Color drop-down arrow.

The Background Color palette expands.

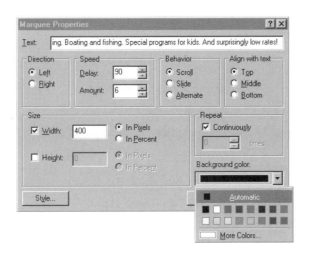

⑤   Click the Yellow color tile.

The Background Color palette closes.

⑥   Click OK.

FrontPage closes the Marquee Properties dialog box and changes the background color of the marquee to yellow.

Format the marquee text and save your work

In this exercise, you change the font and size of the marquee text.

1 Right-click the marquee, and then click Font on the shortcut menu.
FrontPage displays the Font dialog box.

In the Font dialog box, you can also click the Character Spacing tab to change the spacing or vertical position of the text in the marquee.

2 In the Font list, click Arial.
FrontPage displays a sample of the Arial font in the Preview pane.

3 In the Size list, click 4 (14 pt).
The preview text increases in size to 14 points.

tip
Points measure the height of text characters: there are 72 points per inch. Thus, 72-point type is one inch high, 12-point type is one-sixth of an inch high, and 14-point type is slightly less than one-fifth of an inch high.

4 Click OK.
FrontPage displays the marquee text in its new font and size.

5 On the toolbar, click the Save button.
FrontPage saves the Lakewood Mountains Resort home page.

Save

Preview your Web page

In this exercise, you preview the Lakewood Mountains Resort home page.

❶   Click the Preview tab at the bottom of the FrontPage window.

FrontPage displays a preview of the Web page. Although this provides you with a quick look at a Web page's appearance, it doesn't show how the page will look when loaded in a Web browser. Notice that the marquee text scrolls from right to left.

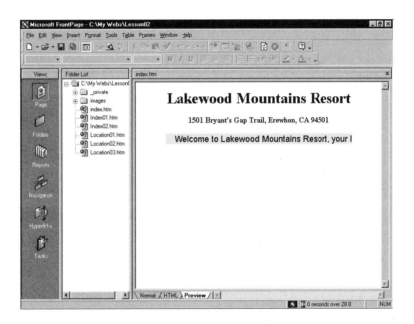

❷   On the toolbar, click the Preview In Browser button.

FrontPage displays the Web page in your default Web browser.

*Preview
In Browser*

❸   Click the Close button at the top-right corner of the Web browser window.

Your Web browser closes and FrontPage is redisplayed.

Close

❹   On the Views bar, click the Navigation icon.

FrontPage displays the Web structure.

Adding Web Pages

A Web can have just a single Web page. For a personal Web, you might consider this. But the Lakewood Mountains Resort Web needs several pages. You'll find that, with FrontPage, adding pages is easy to do.

To add a page, you can either create a new page or import an existing page. If you choose to create a new page, you can do so in most views. If you create a new page with your Web displayed in Navigation view (the view displayed when you click the Navigation icon on the Views bar), FrontPage creates a blank page and adds it to your Web.

There's an advantage in creating a page while your Web is shown in Page view (the view displayed when you click the Page icon on the Views bar). If you create a page in this view, you can use FrontPage's Web page wizards and templates. If you create a page in other views, it is a new blank page.

Just like the templates for Web sites, the templates for Web *pages* are pre-designed Web page blueprints for specific purposes. When you create a page with the Guest Book template, for example, the new page contains features and layout needed for a Web site guest book, as shown in the illustration. You simply add your own text and the page is ready to be used.

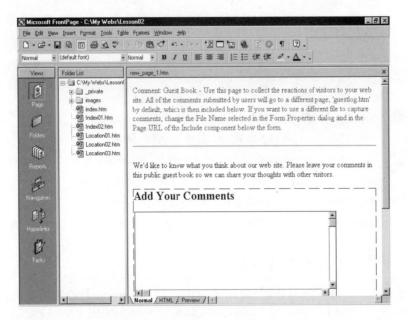

When creating the Web for Lakewood Mountains Resort, you'll create new pages in both Navigation and Page view, and you'll import an existing page.

Add a new Web page in Navigation view

If you are not working through this lesson sequentially, follow the steps in "Import the Lesson 2 Practice Web," earlier in this lesson, and drag the file Index01.htm from the Folder List into Navigation view.

In this exercise, you create a new page in Navigation view and then delete it from your Web.

❶ Make sure your home page is selected in Navigation view. On the File menu, point to New, and then click Page.

FrontPage creates a new Web page and adds it to the Web's tree diagram as a child of the home page.

❷ Click the new page, and then press Delete. If the Delete Page dialog box appears, click the Delete This Page From The Web option, and click OK.

FrontPage deletes the new Web page and its link to the home page.

Add a new Web page in Page view

FrontPage uses the terms "parent" and "child" to differentiate between upper-level and lower-level Web pages.

In this exercise, you switch to Page view and browse through page templates before creating a new Web page.

❶ On the Views bar, click the Page icon.

FrontPage displays the Web page in Page view.

❷ On the File menu, point to New, and then click Page.

FrontPage displays the New dialog box.

Frames Pages templates

Wizards and templates available

Preview of current template

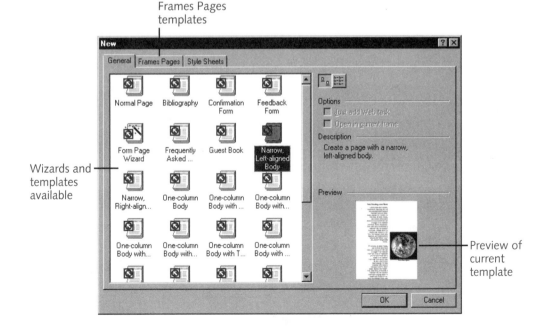

③ Click the icon for the Narrow, Left-Aligned Body template.

FrontPage displays the Web page layout in the Preview pane.

④ Click the Frames Pages tab at the top of the dialog box.

FrontPage displays available templates for frames pages.

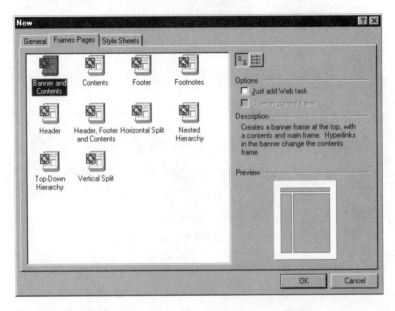

You'll learn how to create frames pages in Lesson 8, "Using Frames."

⑤ Click the General tab, click the Normal Page template, and then click OK.

FrontPage creates a new, blank Web page and displays it in Page view.

⑥ On the toolbar, click the Save button to display the Save As dialog box.

Save

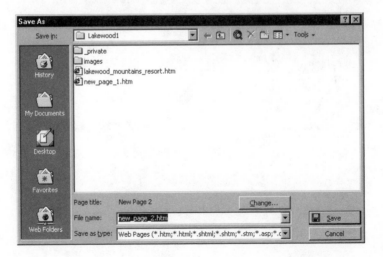

Save

⑦ In the File Name text box, type **Location.htm**, and then click Save.

FrontPage saves the new Web page and adds it to the Folder List.

⑧ On the toolbar, click the Save button.

FrontPage saves your changes to the Web.

New

tip

You can also create a new page by clicking the New button at the left end of the toolbar. Click the drop-down arrow to view a menu of options, including New Web.

Import a Web page

In this exercise, you import an existing Web page into the Lakewood Mountains Resort Web.

① On the Views bar, click the Navigation icon.

② On the File menu, click Import.

The Import dialog box appears.

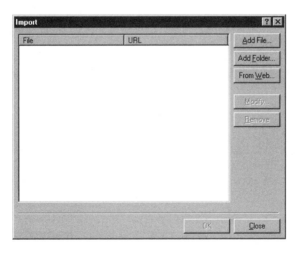

③ Click the Add File button.

FrontPage displays the Add File To Import List dialog box.

4 Click the Look In drop-down arrow, browse to the Web Publishing SBS Practice folder, double-click it, and then double-click the Extras folder.

The Extras folder opens and displays a file list.

5 Click the file named Recreati.htm, and then click the Open button.

FrontPage adds the file to the import list.

Press Ctrl while you click to select all three files.

6 Use the same method to add the files Boat_trips.jpg, Pool01.jpg, and Tennis_courts.jpg to the import list.

7 Click OK.

FrontPage imports the Web page and photo files into your Web. Notice that they now appear in the Folder List.

8 In the Folder List, double-click Recreati.htm.

FrontPage displays the Recreation Web page.

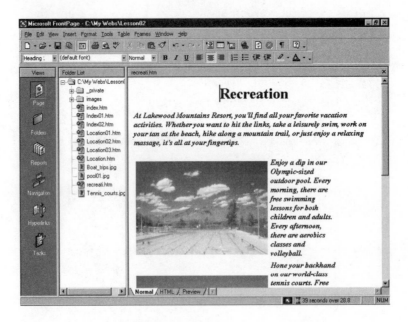

Save

9 On the toolbar, click the Save button.

FrontPage saves your changes.

Inserting a File into a Web Page

It's easy enough to enter Web page text in FrontPage. But what if you used Microsoft Word to write a description of Lakewood Mountains Resort? Of course, you could print the document and retype the text in FrontPage. But it's easier to insert the Word document's contents directly into a Web page.

Using FrontPage, you can insert the following types of files into Web pages.

- Microsoft Word documents.
- RTF (Rich Text Format) documents.
- TXT (plain text, or ASCII) files.
- Worksheets from Microsoft Excel and Lotus 1-2-3.
- WordPerfect 5.*x* and 6.*x* documents.
- HTML (Web page) files.

Insert a document into a Web page

In this exercise, you insert the contents of an existing Microsoft Word document into a Web page.

1 In the Folder List, double-click the file Location01.htm.

FrontPage displays the page (a blank Web page) in Page view.

2 On the Insert menu, click File.

FrontPage displays the Select File dialog box. Navigate to the Extras folder within the Web Publishing SBS Practice folder.

If an alert box is displayed notifying you that this feature is not installed, insert the Microsoft Office 2000 Premium CD 1 or FrontPage 2000 CD in your CD-ROM drive, and click Yes.

3 Click the Files Of Type drop-down arrow, and click Rich Text Format (*.rtf).

There is only one RTF document in the folder: Location.rtf.

4 Click Location.rtf, and then click the Open button.

FrontPage imports the text and inserts it on the Location01.htm page. Notice that the document's formatting, such as the bold type, has been preserved.

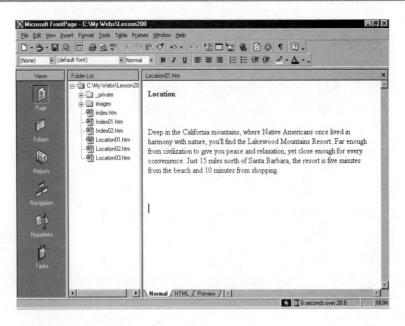

Save

5 On the toolbar, click the Save button.

FrontPage saves the Web page.

Changing Web Page Properties

Web page properties include a page's title, location, and summary. You can change a Web page's properties even after it has been created in FrontPage.

View and change the properties of a Web page

If you are not working through this lesson sequentially, follow the steps in "Import the Lesson 2 Practice Web," earlier in this lesson.

In this exercise, you view and change the properties of the Location Web page.

1 In the Folder List, right-click Location02.htm, and then click Properties on the shortcut menu.

FrontPage displays the Location02.htm Properties dialog box.

Creating a Web Site   2

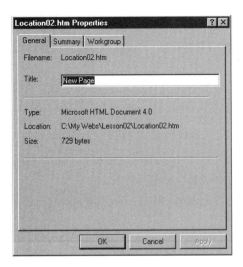

②   In the Title text box, type **Location**, and then click the Summary tab.

FrontPage displays the Summary section of the dialog box. In the Comments text box, you can type an explanation of the purpose of the current page.

③   Click OK.

FrontPage changes the title of the Web page.

Save

④   On the toolbar, click the Save button.

FrontPage saves the Location page with its new title.

<table>
<tr><td>**One
Step
Further**</td><td></td></tr>
</table>

Organizing Your Web

Although you now have three pages (the Index page, the Location page, and the Recreation page) in the Web site for Lakewood Mountains Resort, they aren't arranged in any particular structure. You know that the home page is the "starting" page, but beyond that, there's no organization.

In FrontPage, you can structure your Web by dragging Web page files into the Navigation view's tree diagram. There are many good reasons to do this. First, it makes your Web structure easier to understand. Instead of having to remember which Web pages link to which, you can simply look at the tree diagram.

Another reason has to do with designing your site. You can make FrontPage set up navigation bars to link all the pages displayed in Navigation view. Navigation bars use the information in the tree diagram to link pages. If the tree diagram of your Web isn't accurate, navigation bars won't work correctly.

Organize your Web

If you are not working through this lesson sequentially, follow the steps in "Import the Lesson 2 Practice Web," earlier in this lesson.

In this exercise, you create a navigation structure for the Lakewood Mountains Resort Web.

1 On the Views bar, click the Navigation icon.

Only the home page is displayed in Navigation view.

2 Drag the file Location01.htm from the Folder List into Navigation view below the home page.

A line connects the home page to the Location page.

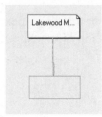

3 Release the mouse button.

FrontPage makes the Location page into a child page (lower-level page) of the home page.

Finish the lesson

1 On the File menu, click Close Web.

2 If FrontPage prompts you to save changes, click the Yes button.

FrontPage saves your changes and closes the Lesson02 Web.

Lesson 2 Quick Reference		
To	**Do this**	**Button**
Preview a Web page	Display the page in Page view and click the Preview tab at the bottom of the FrontPage window. *Or* click the Preview In Browser button on the toolbar.	

Lesson 2 Quick Reference

To	Do this
Create a Web	On the File menu, point to New, and click Web. Click the icon for the desired wizard or template. In the Specify The Location Of The New Web text box, type the name of the new Web and click OK. Use the Next button to work through the wizard dialog boxes, making selections as desired, and then click the Finish button.
Create a blank Web page	Display the Web in Navigation view. On the File menu, point to New, and then click Page.
Create a Web page using a wizard or template	Display the Web in Page view. On the File menu, point to New, and then click Page. In the dialog box, click the wizard or template you want to use, and click OK.
Enter and format text on a Web page	Double-click the Web page in the Folder List. In Page view, type and format text just as you would in Microsoft Word.
Add a marquee	Display the Web page in Page view and click the location where you want the marquee. On the Insert menu, point to Component, and then click Marquee. Type the marquee text, and then click OK.
Change marquee properties	Right-click the marquee and click Marquee Properties on the shortcut menu. Enter new properties as desired, and then click OK.
Change a Web page's properties	Right-click the Web page in the Folder List, and then click Properties. Use the General, Summary, or Workgroup tabs to enter or select new properties as desired. Click OK.
Import a Web page	On the File menu, click Import, and then click the Add File button. Browse to the file, click it, and click Open. Click OK.
Insert a file into a Web page	Display the Web page in Page view, and on the Insert menu, click File. Browse to the location of the file to insert, click the Files Of Type drop-down arrow, and then click the desired file type. Click the file to insert, and then click Open.
Organize a Web	Display the Web in Navigation view. Drag Web pages from the Folder List to form a tree diagram of the Web structure.

Creating a Web Site

2

3

Linking Web Pages

In this lesson you will learn how to:

✔ *Create text hyperlinks between Web pages.*

✔ *Link to Web pages on the Internet.*

✔ *Create electronic mail links.*

✔ *Edit hyperlinks.*

✔ *Create Web page bookmarks.*

✔ *Create image map hyperlinks.*

**ESTIMATED
TIME
30 min.**

Your client meeting with Lakewood Mountains Resort was a success: the resort manager was enthusiastic about the prototype Web site you created in Lesson 2. But she had a question: "Aren't the Web pages supposed to be linked together? I thought a user should be able to jump from one page to another by clicking text on the Web page."

You explain that Web pages can contain *hyperlinks,* which tell a Web browser to jump to another page on the Web site or on the Internet. She seems satisfied with that answer, which is lucky for you. Although you've used hyperlinks while surfing the Web, you have never created any. You'll soon learn that Microsoft FrontPage 2000 makes creating hyperlinks quick and easy.

In this lesson, you will learn how to create several kinds of hyperlinks. You will create text hyperlinks between Web pages, link to pages on the Internet, and create e-mail links. You will learn how to create and use bookmarks on your Web pages. Finally, you will create an image map hyperlink.

Creating Text Hyperlinks

A hyperlink is an HTML instruction embedded in a Web page. The instruction tells a Web browser to display another file or Web page when the visitor clicks the corresponding text or graphic. The newly displayed file can be a Web page on the World Wide Web, a Web page on a corporate intranet, or a file stored locally on the user's computer.

Pointing Hand

Each hyperlink has two parts: the hyperlink itself, and the *target,* which is the file displayed when a visitor clicks the hyperlink. When a visitor moves the mouse pointer over a hyperlink, it changes from its normal shape to a pointing hand. This tells the visitor that the pointer is over a hyperlink. The status bar at the bottom of the visitor's Web browser usually displays the address of the target. To create hyperlinks with Microsoft FrontPage, you just point and click. FrontPage takes care of the details.

Import the Lesson 3 practice Web

In this exercise, you create a new Web based on the files in the Lesson03 folder in the Web Publishing SBS Practice folder. You will use this Web for all the exercises in Lesson 3.

❶   On the File menu, point to New, and then click Web.

FrontPage displays the New dialog box.

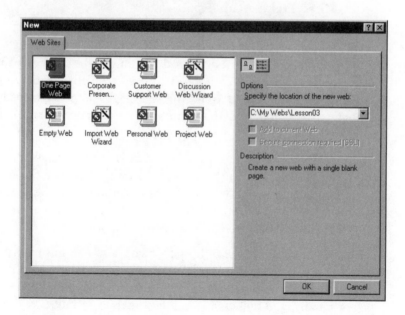

If your hard disk is not drive C, substitute the appropriate drive letter in step 2.

② Click the Import Web Wizard icon. In the Specify The Location Of The New Web text box, delete the default text and type **C:\My Webs\Lesson03**, and click OK.

FrontPage displays the first Import Web Wizard dialog box.

③ Click the From A Source Directory Of Files option, click the Include Subfolders check box, and click the Browse button.

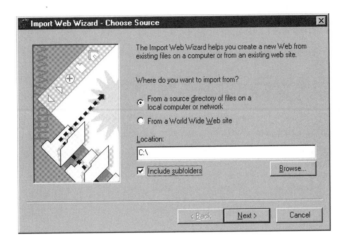

④ Browse to the Lesson03 folder in the Web Publishing SBS Practice folder, and click OK.

⑤ Click Next twice, and then click Finish.

FrontPage creates a new Web based on the practice files and places it in the Lesson03 folder.

New!
2000

tip

If you need to quit FrontPage before you finish these exercises, here's a quick way to open the Lesson03 Web again. On the File menu, point to Recent Webs, and then click Lesson03.

Link to a Web page in your current Web

In this exercise, you create a hyperlink between the Lakewood Mountains Resort home page and the Recreation page.

1 In the Folder List, double-click the file Index.htm.

FrontPage displays the home page in Page view.

2 On the home page, select the word *Recreation*.

3 On the Insert menu, click Hyperlink.

FrontPage displays the Create Hyperlink dialog box.

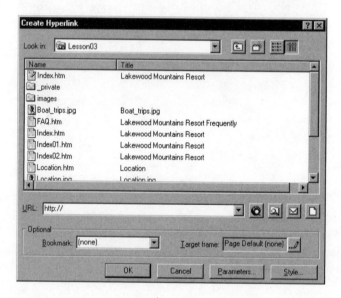

The shortcut key for inserting a hyperlink is Ctrl+K.

4 Click Recreati.htm in the file list.

FrontPage displays *Recreati.htm* in the URL text box. This is the Web page address for the hyperlink.

5 Click OK. Deselect the word *Recreation* by clicking any blank area of the home page.

FrontPage creates the hyperlink. Notice that the word *Recreation* is now underlined, indicating that it is a hyperlink.

Save

6 On the toolbar, click the Save button.

FrontPage saves your changes.

tip

When you move the pointer over a hyperlink, FrontPage displays the link target address on the status bar, at the lower-right corner of your screen. You can check the functioning of your hyperlink by holding down Ctrl and clicking the link. FrontPage then displays the target page. In a later exercise, you will preview your links in your Web browser.

Link by dragging

In this exercise, you create a hyperlink by dragging a Web page from the Folder List onto the Web page displayed in Page view.

1 In the Folder List, click Location.htm.

2 Drag Location.htm so that it is just above the Recreation hyperlink, and then
release the mouse button.

FrontPage creates a hyperlink to the Location page.

3 Press Ctrl and click the new Location link.

FrontPage displays the Location page.

Save

④   In the Folder List, double-click Index.htm.

FrontPage redisplays the home page.

⑤   On the toolbar, click the Save button.

FrontPage saves your changes.

Link to a Web page on the Internet

In this exercise, you create a hyperlink to a Web page on the Internet.

①   If necessary, connect to the Internet, and then switch back to FrontPage.

②   Select the word *Microsoft* in the last line on the home page, and then on the Insert menu, click Hyperlink.

FrontPage displays the Create Hyperlink dialog box.

Web Browser

③   Click the Web Browser button to link to a Web page on the Internet.

FrontPage opens your Web browser and instructs you to browse to the Web page you want to link.

④   In the Address bar of the Web browser, type **www.microsoft.com/frontpage** and press Enter.

Your Web browser connects to the Microsoft Web site and displays the FrontPage home page.

⑤   Press Alt+Tab on your keyboard to switch from your browser to FrontPage.

In the URL text box, FrontPage displays the Web address of the Microsoft FrontPage home page, as shown in the illustration.

6 Click OK.

FrontPage creates the hyperlink.

7 On the toolbar, click the Save button.

FrontPage saves your changes.

Save

Test your hyperlinks

In this exercise, you test the hyperlinks you created on the Lakewood Mountains Resort home page.

1 If necessary, connect to the Internet, and then switch back to FrontPage.

2 On the toolbar, click the Preview In Browser button.

FrontPage displays the home page in your Web browser.

Preview In Browser

3 Click the *Location* hyperlink.

Your Web browser displays the Location page.

4 On the toolbar of your Web browser, click the Back button.

Your Web browser returns to the Lakewood Mountains Resort home page.

Back

5 Click the *Recreation* hyperlink.

Your Web browser displays the Recreation page.

6 On the toolbar of your Web browser, click the Back button.

Your Web browser redisplays the Lakewood Mountains Resort home page.

Back

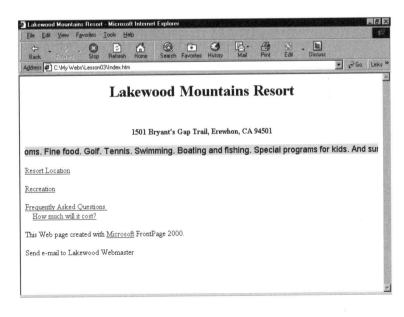

7 Click the *Microsoft* hyperlink.

FrontPage displays the Microsoft FrontPage home page in your Web browser.

X

Close

8 Click the Close button at the top-right corner of your Web browser window.

Your Web browser closes, and FrontPage is redisplayed.

Different Kinds of Hyperlinks

You can create several kinds of hyperlinks in the Create Hyperlinks dialog box.

You can also type the target address of the new hyperlink in the URL text box to create any kind of hyperlink.

Click	Name	To create a hyperlink
A file in the Folder List		To another page in your Web.
🔘	Web Browser	To a file on the Internet.
🔍	Local File	To a file on your own computer.
✉	E-mail	That sends e-mail.
🗋	New	To a new Web page and link to it.

Creating a Link to an Electronic Mail Address

Hyperlinks can do more than just display a Web page or file. They also provide a way for Web site visitors to send electronic mail to addresses specified in hyperlinks. When a visitor clicks an e-mail hyperlink, the Web browser launches the visitor's e-mail program and displays a message composition window with the e-mail address already entered. The visitor then writes and sends the e-mail message normally.

For the Lakewood Mountains Resort home page, you want to enable visitors to send e-mail to the resort's Web site administrator, so you'll create a link to the Web administrator's e-mail address.

Create an electronic mail link

If you are not working through this lesson sequentially, follow the steps in "Import the Lesson 3 Practice Web," earlier in this lesson, and in the Folder List, double-click Index01.htm.

In this exercise, you create a hyperlink that enables Web page visitors to send electronic mail to the Web site administrator.

1 Click the empty line below the Microsoft hyperlink.

2 Type **Send e-mail to Lakewood Webmaster**, and then select the words *Lakewood Webmaster*.

3 On the Insert menu, click Hyperlink.

FrontPage displays the Create Hyperlink dialog box.

4 In the Create Hyperlink dialog box, click the E-mail button.

FrontPage displays the Create E-mail Hyperlink dialog box.

E-mail

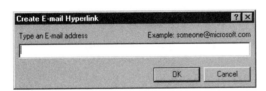

5 In the text box, type your own e-mail address, and then click OK.

The Create E-mail Hyperlink dialog box closes and the Create Hyperlink dialog box is again visible. Notice that the URL contains the text *mailto:* followed by your e-mail address.

6 Click OK.

FrontPage creates the new e-mail hyperlink.

Save

7 On the toolbar, click the Save button.

FrontPage saves your changes.

Editing Hyperlinks

Just like many other things in the modern world, hyperlinks often change. The name of a Web page file might change, it might be moved to a different Web site, or it might be deleted altogether. When such a change occurs, you need to change any hyperlinks that connect to the target file. Fortunately, changing a hyperlink in FrontPage is just as easy as creating it in the first place.

Change a hyperlink

If you are not working through this lesson sequentially, follow the steps in "Import the Lesson 3 Practice Web," earlier in this lesson, and in the Folder List, double-click Index01.htm.

In this exercise, you change the target Web page of the Lakewood Frequently Asked Questions hyperlink and then change the text of the Location hyperlink.

❶ Right-click the Frequently Asked Questions hyperlink.

FrontPage displays a shortcut menu.

❷ Click Hyperlink Properties.

FrontPage displays the Edit Hyperlink dialog box. Notice that the Frequently Asked Questions link has the Location page as its target in the URL text box. The Location page is an incorrect target for this link.

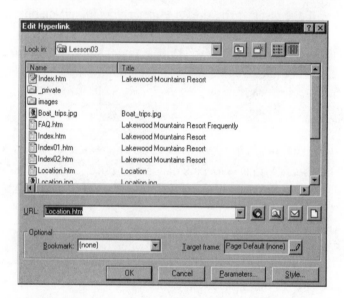

❸ Click FAQ.htm in the file list, and then click OK.

FrontPage changes the target page to FAQ.htm.

❹ Click any blank area of the page to deselect the link, and then check the Frequently Asked Questions link by pressing Ctrl and clicking the link.

FrontPage displays the Frequently Asked Questions page.

Close

❺ Click the Close button at the top-right corner of the FAQ page.

FrontPage closes the FAQ page and displays the Index page.

❻ Double-click the Location hyperlink, and then type **Resort Location**.

The new text replaces the old text, leaving the hyperlink intact.

Save

❼ On the toolbar, click the Save button.

FrontPage saves your changes.

Delete a hyperlink

In this exercise, you delete a hyperlink but leave its Web page text intact.

1 Right-click the Lakewood Webmaster hyperlink.

FrontPage displays a shortcut menu.

2 On the shortcut menu, click Hyperlink Properties.

FrontPage displays the Edit Hyperlink dialog box. The URL text is selected.

3 Press Delete.

FrontPage deletes the URL text from the text box.

4 Click OK.

FrontPage deletes the hyperlink from the Web page text. Notice that the text is no longer underlined.

5 On the toolbar, click the Save button.

FrontPage saves your changes.

Save

tip

You can also delete a hyperlink by deleting the text on the Web page that contains the hyperlink.

Creating Bookmarks on a Web Page

Normally, when visitors click a hyperlink to a Web page, their browsers display only as much of the page as will fit in the browser window. If the Web page is longer than will fit on the screen, visitors must scroll down the page to see the rest of its content. For long Web pages, this can get to be a considerable chore.

Bookmarks can help with this problem. In FrontPage, a bookmark is a link to a specific location on a Web page. Lakewood Mountains Resort's Frequently Asked Questions (FAQ) page is very long, so you decide to insert a few bookmarks to make things easier for Web site visitors.

Create bookmarks

If you are not working through this lesson sequentially, follow the steps in "Import the Lesson 3 Practice Web," earlier in this lesson.

In this exercise, you create bookmarks on the Lakewood Mountains Resort's Frequently Asked Questions (FAQ) Web page.

1 In the Folder List, double-click the file FAQ.htm.

FrontPage displays the FAQ page in Page view.

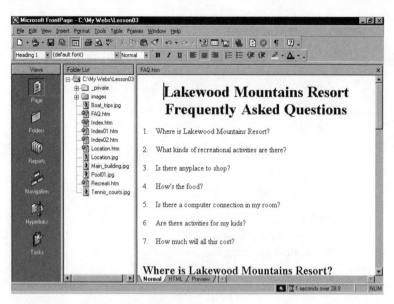

2   Scroll down to the end of the FAQ page.

FrontPage displays the question *How much will all this cost?* and its answer.

3   Select the question text *How much will all this cost?*

tip

You aren't required to select text for a bookmark. You can simply place the insertion point where you want the bookmark, click Bookmark on the Insert menu, type a name for the bookmark, and click OK.

4   On the Insert menu, click Bookmark.

FrontPage displays the Bookmark dialog box.

⑤ Click OK, and then deselect the question text by clicking any blank area of the FAQ page.

FrontPage creates the bookmark. Notice that the text is now underlined with a broken line. The broken underline distinguishes it from the solid underline displayed by a hyperlink.

⑥ Scroll up to the paragraph with the heading *How's the food?*, and select the question *How's the food?* On the Insert menu, click Bookmark.

FrontPage displays the Bookmark dialog box.

⑦ In the Bookmark dialog box, click OK.

FrontPage inserts another bookmark on the FAQ page.

Save

⑧ Deselect the question text by clicking any blank area of the FAQ page, and then on the toolbar, click the Save button.

FrontPage saves the FAQ page with the new bookmarks.

Link to a bookmark on the same Web page

In this exercise, you link from one location on a Web page to a bookmark at another location on the same Web page.

❶ Scroll to the numbered list of questions at the top of the FAQ page.

❷ Select the text *How's the food?*

❸ On the Insert menu, click Hyperlink, and then click FAQ.htm in the dialog box's file list.

❹ Click the Bookmark drop-down arrow, click *How's the food?*, and click OK.

FrontPage inserts the hyperlink.

Save

❺ On the toolbar, click the Save button.

FrontPage saves your changes.

Link from another Web page to a bookmark

In this exercise, you create a link from a Web page to a bookmark on another Web page.

❶ In the Folder List, double-click the file Index.htm.

FrontPage displays the home page in Page view.

❷ Select the text *How much will it cost?*

❸ On the Insert menu, click Hyperlink.

FrontPage displays the Create Hyperlink dialog box.

④ In the file list, click FAQ.htm, and then click the Bookmark drop-down arrow at the bottom of the dialog box.

FrontPage displays a list of bookmarks on the FAQ page.

⑤ In the Bookmark list box, click *How much will all this cost?* and click OK.

The URL text box displays the target address and FrontPage inserts the hyperlink.

Save

⑥ On the toolbar, click the Save button.

FrontPage saves your changes.

Test your bookmarks

In this exercise, you test the bookmarks you created in the previous exercises.

Preview In
Browser

① On the toolbar, click the Preview In Browser button.

FrontPage opens the home page in your Web browser.

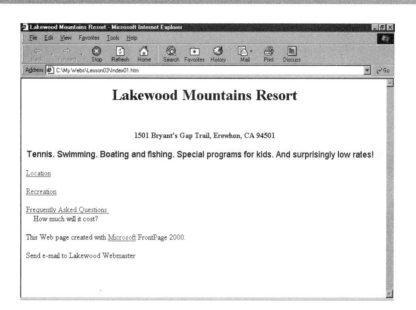

2   Click the *How much will it cost?* hyperlink.

Your Web browser jumps down to the final question on the FAQ Web page.

3   Scroll to the top of the FAQ page.

4   Click the *How's the food?* hyperlink.

Your Web browser jumps down to the *How's the food?* bookmark.

Close

Save

⑤ Click the Close button at the top-right corner of your Web browser window.

Your Web browser closes, and FrontPage is redisplayed.

⑥ On the toolbar, click the Save button.

FrontPage saves your changes.

Delete a bookmark

In this exercise, you delete a bookmark from the FAQ page.

① In the Folder List, double-click the file FAQ.htm.

FrontPage displays the FAQ page in Page view.

② If necessary, scroll to display the *How's the food?* bookmark (not the hyperlink).

③ Right-click the bookmark text.

A shortcut menu is displayed.

④ On the shortcut menu, click Bookmark Properties.

FrontPage displays the Bookmark dialog box.

You can also right-click the bookmark text, click Bookmark Properties, and press Delete to delete a book-mark.

⑤ In the Other Bookmarks On This Page box, click *How's the food?*, and then click the Clear button.

FrontPage deletes the bookmark.

Save

⑥ On the toolbar, click the Save button.

FrontPage saves your changes.

One Step Further	**Creating Image Map Hyperlinks**

So far, you've created text hyperlinks for the Lakewood Mountains Resort Web site. The resort manager, however, would like the Web site to have more visual excitement. She's seen Web sites in which a visitor can click part of an image and be taken directly to the Web page connected with that part of the image.

You've heard about that feature. It's called an *image map*. FrontPage makes it easy to create image maps. All you have to do is insert an image on a Web page, draw *hotspots*, create a few hyperlinks, and you've got an image map.

Insert an image on a Web page

If you are not working through this lesson sequentially, follow the steps in "Import the Lesson 3 Practice Web," earlier in this lesson.

In this exercise, you insert an image of the hotel building on the Lakewood Mountains Resort home page in preparation for creating an image map.

1 In the Folder List, double-click the file Index.htm.

FrontPage displays the Lakewood Mountains Resort home page.

2 Click the line below the text *Lakewood Mountains Resort* and above the resort's address.

3 On the Insert menu, point to Picture, and then click From File.

FrontPage displays the Picture dialog box.

4 In the file list, click Main_building.jpg.

FrontPage displays a preview of the image in the preview pane.

Save

⑤ Click OK.

FrontPage inserts the image at the location you selected.

⑥ On the toolbar, click the Save button.

FrontPage saves your changes.

Create an image map

In this exercise, you draw hotspots on the resort image to create an image map.

① Click the resort image to select it.

FrontPage displays the Image toolbar along the bottom of the screen.

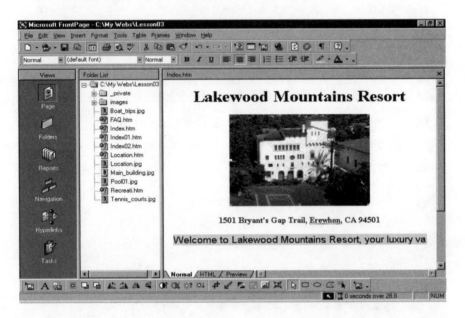

Rectangular Hotspot

② On the Image toolbar, click the Rectangular Hotspot button.

③ Hold down the mouse button, drag the mouse pointer to draw a rectangle on the grassy area in front of the hotel building, and release the mouse button.

FrontPage displays the Create Hyperlink dialog box.

④ In the file list, click Recreati.htm, and then click OK.

FrontPage inserts a hyperlink for the image area you selected.

⑤ Click the Rectangular Hotspot button, draw another rectangle on the hotel building, and then release the mouse button.

FrontPage displays the Create Hyperlink dialog box.

Save

6 In the file list, click Location.htm, and then click OK.

FrontPage inserts another hyperlink for the image area you selected.

7 On the toolbar, click the Save button.

FrontPage saves your changes.

Test the image map

In this exercise, you test the image map you created in the previous exercise.

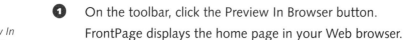
Preview In Browser

1 On the toolbar, click the Preview In Browser button.

FrontPage displays the home page in your Web browser.

Pointing Hand

2 Move the mouse pointer over the image.

Over the hotspots, the mouse pointer changes from an arrow into a pointing hand, indicating the presence of hyperlinks.

3 Click the grassy area hotspot.

Your Web browser displays the Recreation page.

Back

4 On the toolbar of your Web browser, click the Back button, and then click the hotel building hotspot.

Your Web browser displays the Location page.

Finish the lesson

Close

① Click the Close button at the top-right corner of your Web browser window. Your Web browser closes and FrontPage reappears.

② On the File menu, click Close Web.

③ For each page, if FrontPage prompts you to save changes, click Yes. FrontPage saves your changes and closes the Lesson03 Web.

Lesson 3 Quick Reference

To	Do this
Import a Web	On the File menu, point to New, and click Web. Click the Import Web Wizard icon, type the name of the folder for the new Web, and click OK. Click the From A Source Directory Of Files option to select it, click the Include Subfolders check box, and then click the Browse button. Browse to the folder that contains the files you want to import, and click OK. Click Next, click Next again, and then click Finish.
Create a text hyperlink	Select the hyperlink text, and on the Insert menu, click Hyperlink. If necessary, browse to the target file. Select the target file, and click OK.
Create a hyperlink by dragging	Display the Web page that will have the hyperlink in Page view. Drag a file from the Folder List to the desired location on the Web page and release the mouse button.
Change a hyperlink target	Right-click the hyperlink and click Hyperlink Properties. In the Edit Hyperlink dialog box, select the new hyperlink target, and click OK.
Change hyperlink text	Select the hyperlink text, and type the new text.
Delete a hyperlink	Right-click the hyperlink text, click Hyperlink Properties, and then press Delete. Click OK.
Create a bookmark	Select the bookmark text, on the Insert menu, click Bookmark, and then click OK.
Create a hyperlink to a bookmark	Select the hyperlink text, and then click Hyperlink on the Insert menu. If necessary, browse to the target file. Select the target file, click the Bookmark drop-down arrow, click the desired bookmark, and then click OK.

Lesson 3 C...

To	...s	Button
Delete a bookmark	Right-click the bookmark text, click Bookmark Properties, and then click the Clear button.	
Create an e-mail hyperlink	Select the hyperlink text, and then on the Insert menu, click Hyperlink. Click the E-mail button, type the e-mail address, and click OK twice.	
Insert an image on a Web page	Place the insertion point in the desired location. On the Insert menu, point to Picture, and then click From File. If needed, browse to the location of the image file. Click the image file, and then click OK.	
Create an image map	Click the image on the Web page. On the Image toolbar, click the Rectangular Hotspot button and draw a hotspot on the image. In the Create Hyperlink dialog box, select the target file, and then click OK.	

4

Adding Style to Web Pages

**ESTIMATED
TIME
30 min.**

In this lesson you will learn how to:

✔ *Apply a FrontPage theme.*

✔ *Modify a FrontPage theme.*

✔ *Use FrontPage components.*

✔ *Modify component properties.*

✔ *Use Web page style sheets.*

The prototype Web site for Lakewood Mountains Resort is a big hit at your next meeting, but the client has a few requests. First, all Web pages on the Web site should have a nice color scheme and a consistent style or "look" for text, hyperlinks, buttons, banners, and other Web page elements. Second, each Web page should have a banner at the top, and the home page should show how many *hits*, or visitors, the Web site has received. Finally, each Web page should have a copyright notice.

You assure the client that Microsoft FrontPage 2000 makes it easy to add these features to the Web site. In this lesson, you will learn how to apply FrontPage *themes* to give a consistent look to all of your Web pages. You will also learn how to use FrontPage components to display hit counters, Web page banners, and other features. Finally, you will learn how to use Web page style sheets. Armed with themes and components, you prepare to make the changes requested by the client.

Understanding FrontPage Themes

FrontPage themes provide ready-to-use arrangements of stylish backgrounds and graphics for Web pages. You can apply a theme to an entire Web or just to an individual page. When you apply a theme to an entire Web, it gives a consistent look to all of the pages in your Web.

When you select a theme, all Web pages get the same color scheme, background, navigation bars, buttons, and other Web page elements. This gives your Web a polished, professional look with minimal time and effort. When you add new pages to your Web, FrontPage automatically creates them using the same theme.

Import the Lesson 4 practice Web

In this exercise, you create a new Web based on the files in the Lesson04 folder in the Web Publishing SBS Practice folder. You will use this Web for all the exercises in Lesson 4.

1 On the File menu, point to New, and then click Web.

FrontPage displays the New dialog box.

If your hard disk has a drive letter other than C, substitute the appropriate drive letter in step 2.

2 Click the Import Web Wizard icon. In the Specify The Location Of The New Web text box, delete the default text and type **C:\My Webs\Lesson04**, and then click OK.

FrontPage displays the first Import Web Wizard dialog box.

3 Click the From A Source Directory Of Files option, click the Include Subfolders check box, and then click the Browse button.

4 Browse to the Lesson 04 folder in the Web Publishing SBS Practice folder, and click OK.

5 Click Next twice, and then click Finish.

FrontPage creates a new Web based on the practice files and places it in the Lesson04 folder.

Apply a theme to a single Web page

In this exercise, you view the themes included with FrontPage and apply the Expedition theme to a single page of your Web.

1 In the Folder List, double-click the file Welcome.htm.

FrontPage displays the Web page.

② On the Format menu, click Theme.

FrontPage displays the Themes dialog box.

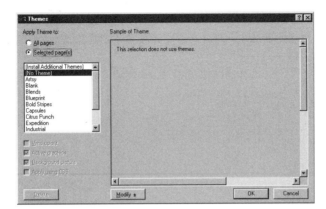

③ In the Themes list at the left, click Artsy.

FrontPage displays a sample of how Web page elements look with the Artsy theme.

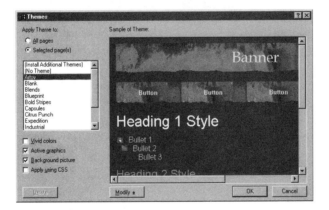

④ In the Themes list, click Rice Paper.

FrontPage displays a sample of how Web page elements look with the Rice Paper theme.

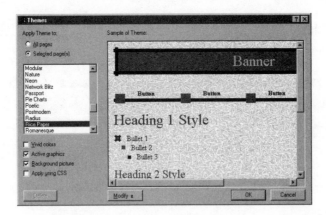

5 In the Themes list, click Expedition.

FrontPage displays a sample of how Web page elements look with the Expedition theme.

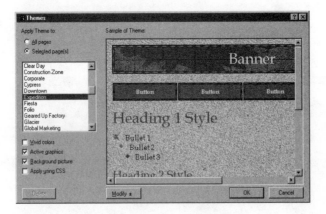

6 Click the Background Picture check box.

FrontPage displays a sample of the page without the background picture.

7 Click the Background Picture check box again.

FrontPage restores the background picture.

8 Click OK, and then click Yes.

FrontPage applies the Expedition theme to the Welcome Web page, with the options you selected.

Save

9 On the toolbar, click the Save button.

FrontPage saves your changes to the Web page.

tip

You can apply a background image to a Web page without using a theme. To do so, display the Web page in Page view and click Background on the Format menu. In the Page Properties dialog box, click the Background tab, click the Background Picture check box, and click the Browse button. Browse to the image you want, and then click OK twice. Note that the image you select will appear as a repeating tile in the background of your Web page.

Apply a theme to a Web

In this exercise, you apply the Expedition theme to all the pages of the Lakewood Mountains Resort Web.

1 On the Format menu, click Theme.

FrontPage displays the Themes dialog box with the Expedition theme selected.

2 At the top-left corner of the dialog box, click the All Pages option, and then click OK.

FrontPage applies the Expedition theme to all the Web pages in the Lesson04 Web.

tip

To remove a theme from a Web page, display the Web page in Page view, and click Theme on the Format menu. In the Themes dialog box, click the Selected Pages option, click No Theme in the Themes list, and click OK. To remove a theme from an entire Web, click Theme on the Format menu, click the All Pages option, click No Theme in the Themes list, and then click OK.

Modify a theme

In this exercise, you modify the theme of the Lakewood Mountains Resort Web.

1 On the Format menu, click Theme.

FrontPage displays the Themes dialog box with a preview of the Web's current theme.

2 Click the Modify button.

The dialog box now displays a row of buttons labeled *What Would You Like To Modify?*

3 Click the Colors button, click the Custom tab, and then click the Item drop-down arrow.

The Item box expands and displays a list of Web page items whose color you can change.

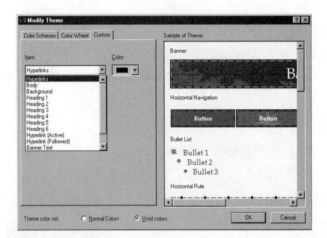

4 Click any blank area of the dialog box to close the drop-down list. Click Cancel, click the Graphics button, and then click the Item drop-down arrow.

FrontPage displays the Modify Theme dialog box with a list of graphic elements whose appearance you can change.

5 Click any blank area of the dialog box to close the drop-down list. Click Cancel, and then click Text.

FrontPage displays the Modify Theme dialog box with a list of the textual theme elements whose appearance you can change.

6 Click the Item drop-down arrow, click Heading 1, scroll down the Font list, and then click Comic Sans MS. Click OK.

FrontPage changes the font of the Heading 1 style to Comic Sans MS.

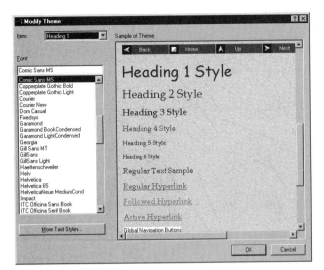

❼ Click OK, and then click No so you don't permanently modify the theme.

FrontPage closes the dialog box without saving your changes.

Delete a theme from a Web page

In this exercise, you delete a theme from the Welcome Web page.

❶ If necessary, double-click Welcome.htm in the Folder List.

FrontPage displays the Welcome page in Page view.

❷ On the Format menu, click Theme.

FrontPage displays the Themes dialog box. The Expedition theme is selected.

❸ In the Apply Theme To section of the dialog box, if the Selected Page(s) option is not selected, click it.

FrontPage will apply any changes only to the currently displayed Web page.

❹ In the Themes list, click No Theme, and then click OK.

FrontPage removes the theme from the Welcome page.

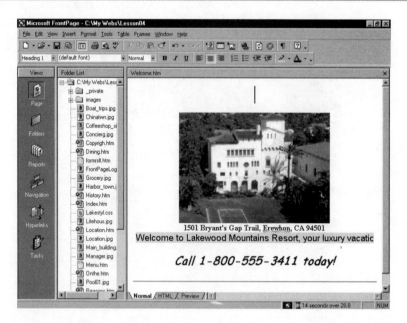

Save

Close

⑤ On the toolbar, click the Save button, and then click the Close button at the top-right corner of the Welcome page.

FrontPage saves your changes and closes the Welcome page.

Delete a theme from an entire Web

In this exercise, you delete a theme from an entire Web rather than a single page.

① On the Format menu, click Theme.

FrontPage displays the Themes dialog box. Expedition is selected.

② In the Apply Theme To section of the dialog box, make sure the All Pages option is selected.

FrontPage will apply any changes to all pages in the Web.

③ In the Themes list, click No Theme, and then click OK.

FrontPage removes the theme from the entire Web.

Adding FrontPage Components

FrontPage components are ready-to-use programs that are activated when a user loads a page into a Web browser. They provide a quick and easy way to build features into Web pages without having to learn Web page scripting or ActiveX and Java programming. Some components included with FrontPage are summarized in the following table.

Component	Explanation
Comment	Inserts a comment into a Web page's HTML code to explain some aspect of the coding or design. The comment is invisible when the page is viewed in a browser, though it is visible in Page view. Useful for annotating the page as you work on it.
Page Banner*	Inserts a graphical banner at the top of a Web page.
Banner Ad Manager	Rotates the display of multiple images at specified intervals. Allows you to select the type of transition between banners (dissolve, horizontal blinds, and so on) and link banners to a Web page.
Hit Counter*	Displays the number of times a page has been visited, or "hit."
Hover Button	Inserts a link that displays a visual effect when the mouse pointer "hovers," or is positioned over it. Effects include changing color and appearing to be pressed like a button.
Marquee	Displays text that scrolls horizontally on the Web page.
Confirmation Field*	Confirms a user's entry on a Web page form.
Include Page	Inserts a Web page at a specified location inside another page. For example, you might insert a copyright page at the bottom of every page in your Web.
Scheduled Picture*	Displays a picture for a specified period of time and optionally replaces it with another picture. Useful for displaying time-critical information, such as a "New" icon on a new page.
Scheduled Include Page*	Inserts a Web page inside another page for a specified period of time and optionally replaces it at a specified time. Useful for displaying time-critical information, such as notification of a seasonal sale.
Substitution	Replaces a section of text with a specified value, such as another text string.
Categories	Inserts links to pages by category. Useful for creating tables of contents for pages of a certain type, such as Expense Reports or Planning.
Search Form*	Allows visitors to search the site for specified text. When you save a page with a Search form, FrontPage builds an index of the site. When users perform a search, FrontPage uses the index to create a list of hyperlinks to pages containing the word or phrase.
Table of Contents	Creates a table of contents for the Web site.

*Requires a Web server that has the FrontPage Server Extensions.

Adding Style to Web Pages

4

Add a Web page banner

If you are not working through this lesson sequentially, follow the steps in "Import the Lesson 4 Practice Web," earlier in this lesson.

In this exercise, you add a banner to the Welcome page of the Lakewood Mountains Resort Web site.

1 In the Folder List, double-click the file Welcome.htm.

FrontPage displays the Welcome page in Page view.

2 On the Format menu, click Theme. Click Expedition, and then click OK.

FrontPage applies the Expedition theme to the Welcome page.

3 If necessary, click the line above the hotel photo.

The insertion point moves to the line above the photo.

tip

To display banners properly, a Web page must meet two requirements. First, it must be included in a Web page hierarchy that you create in Navigation view. Second, the page must have a theme applied; otherwise the banner will appear as plain text.

4 On the Insert menu, click Page Banner.

FrontPage displays the Page Banner Properties dialog box.

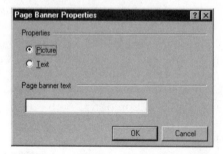

5 Click OK.

FrontPage displays the banner at the top of the Web page, but the banner text is not yet displayed.

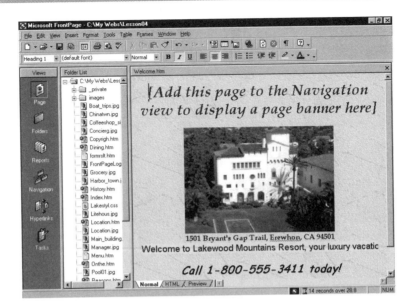

6 On the Views bar, click the Navigation icon.

FrontPage displays the Web in Navigation view. At present, only the Web's home page is shown in the hierarchy diagram.

7 Drag Welcome.htm from the Folder List into Navigation view until a line connects it to the home page, and release the mouse button.

The Welcome page is now linked to the home page.

8 In the Folder List, double-click the file Welcome.htm.

FrontPage displays the page. The banner text is now displayed correctly.

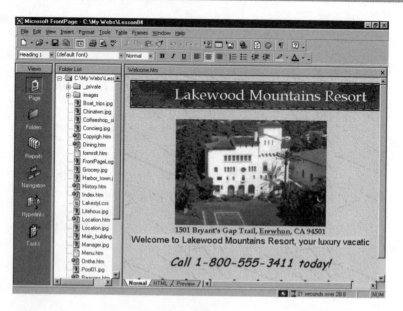

Save

9   On the toolbar, click the Save button.

FrontPage saves your changes.

tip

If page banner text is not being displayed correctly, first right-click the banner and click Page Banner Properties on the shortcut menu. If the banner text in the dialog box is correct and the Picture option is selected, click Cancel, and then click the Navigation icon on the Views Bar. Verify that the Web page is linked into the Web hierarchy diagram.

Add a hit counter

In this exercise, you add a hit counter to the Welcome page. The hit counter will display the number of visitors to your site since it was installed or reset.

important

To publish and display a hit counter on your local computer, you must be running Microsoft Personal Web Server, which you can download from the Microsoft Web site. If you do not have the Personal Web Server installed, you can insert a hit counter on a page, but you cannot display it until you publish your Web to a Web server.

1 Click at the right end of the line *Call 1-800-555-3411 today!* and press Enter.

The insertion point moves to a new line below the phone number.

2 On the toolbar, click the Font Size drop-down arrow, and click 3 (12pt).

FrontPage changes the current text size to 12 points.

3 Type **You are visitor number**, and then press the Spacebar.

FrontPage inserts a caption for the hit counter.

4 On the Insert menu, point to Component, and then click Hit Counter.

FrontPage displays the Hit Counter Properties dialog box.

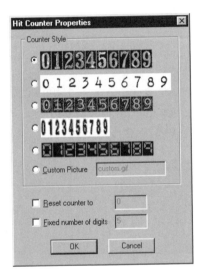

5 Click the option for the style you like best, click the Fixed Number Of Digits check box, and then click OK.

FrontPage inserts the hit counter at the selected location. However, the hit counter will not be displayed until you publish the Web.

6 On the toolbar, click the Save button.

FrontPage saves your changes.

7 On the File menu, click Publish Web, and then click the Options button.

FrontPage displays the Publish Web dialog box with the Options area visible.

Save

If you have not downloaded and installed the Microsoft Personal Web Server, stop after step 6.

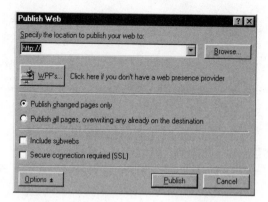

8   In the Specify The Location To Publish Your Web To text box, type **http:// localhost**.

This tells FrontPage that you want to publish your Web to your local hard disk drive.

9   Click the Publish All Pages option, and then click the Publish button.

FrontPage displays a dialog box indicating that you successfully published your Web to your local hard disk drive.

Depending on the speed of your computer and hard disk drive, publishing your Web could take a minute or two.

10   In the dialog box, click the text *Click Here to View Your Published Web Site*.

FrontPage opens the published Web site in your Web browser. Notice that the hit counter is partially visible at the bottom of the browser window.

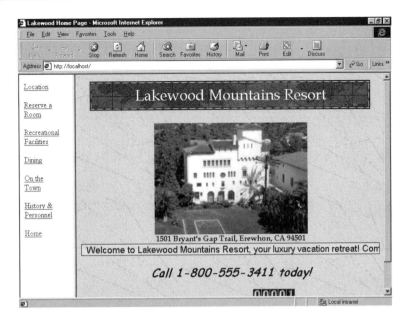

(11) Scroll down in your Web browser to view the bottom of the Welcome page.

You can now see the hit counter and its caption.

Close

(12) Click the Close button at the top-right corner of your Web browser window.

Your Web browser closes and the dialog box reappears in FrontPage.

(13) Click the Done button.

The dialog box closes.

important

Once you publish your Web to a server, components such as the hit counter will require that the Web server have the FrontPage Server Extensions in order to work properly.

Include one Web page inside another

In this exercise, you include the Copyright page in the Lakewood Mountains Resort Welcome page.

(1) Scroll down if necessary, and then click the line below the horizontal line at the bottom of the Web page.

FrontPage moves the insertion point to the bottom of the Web page.

② On the Insert menu, point to Component, and then click Include Page.

FrontPage displays the Include Page Properties dialog box.

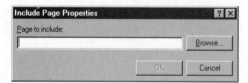

③ Click the Browse button, and in the file list, click Copyrigh.htm (the Copyright Web page).

④ Click OK twice.

The dialog boxes close and the Copyright page is inserted at the bottom of the Welcome page.

⑤ If necessary, scroll down to view the included Web page.

The included page contains copyright information, an e-mail link, and the "Site Created With Microsoft FrontPage" logo.

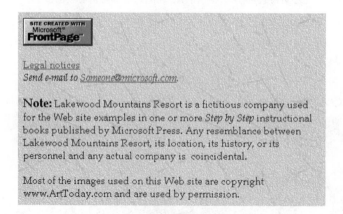

Save

⑥ On the toolbar, click the Save button.

FrontPage saves your changes.

One Step Further

Using Web Page Style Sheets

Themes are just one way you can customize the appearance of your Web pages. Another way is to use *styles* and *style sheets*. A style is a set of characteristics (such as size, spacing, and color) that you apply to a Web page element, such as a heading. A style sheet is a collection of styles that you apply to an entire page.

Elements such as headings and text have a default appearance that depends partly on the user's Web browser and partly on the fonts installed on the user's computer. By applying styles or style sheets, you can often override these defaults and display the page precisely as you want.

FrontPage gives you three ways to apply styles. First, you can simply right-click a specific Web page element, click Properties on its shortcut menu, and change its appearance in the Properties dialog box. (This is called applying an inline style.) It applies the style changes only to the Web page element you selected; if you change the style of one body text paragraph, all other paragraphs on the page will remain unchanged.

Another way of applying styles is to create a page header style sheet. When you apply a style to an element (such as a heading or the body text) in a Web page header style sheet, it affects all elements of that type on the current page. For example, you might create a style for body text to make it 36 points in size, centered, red-colored, and using the Arial font. When you apply this style to a Web page, all of the body text on the page turns into 36-point, centered, red Arial text. To create a header style sheet, you click Style on the Format menu and then make the desired changes in the Style dialog box.

The third and most powerful way to apply styles is to create an external style sheet and link it to one or more Web pages on your Web site. This enables you to make the same style changes to multiple Web pages, but it is more difficult than the other methods. You can learn more about creating external style sheets on the Help menu or on the World Wide Web Consortium's site at *www.w3.org*.

tip
You'll sometimes hear style sheets called "Cascading Style Sheets" (CSS). This means that you can apply multiple style sheets to the same Web page, so that styles in a higher layer override styles in lower layers.

Create a header style sheet

If you are not working through this lesson sequentially, follow the steps in "Import the Lesson 4 Practice Web," earlier in this lesson.

In this exercise, you create a header style sheet for a Web page.

1 In the Folder List, double-click the file Reasons.htm.

FrontPage displays the Web page.

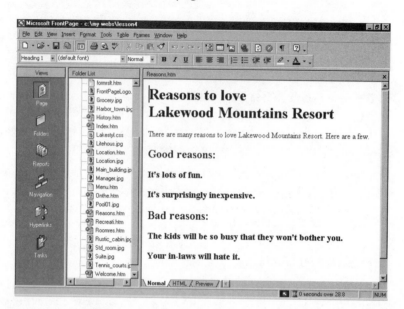

2 On the Format menu, click Style.

FrontPage displays the Style dialog box.

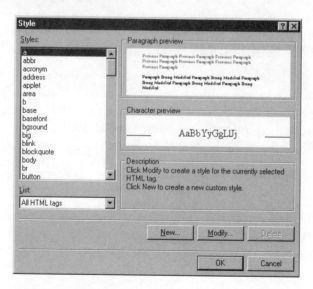

❸ In the Styles list, scroll down and click H1, and then click the Modify button.

The Modify Style dialog box appears.

❹ Click the Format button, and then click Font on the shortcut menu.

The Font dialog box appears.

❺ Click the Color drop-down arrow, click one of the Blue color tiles, and click OK twice.

FrontPage creates an H1 style and sets the text color to blue. The Style dialog box reappears.

❻ Click the List drop-down arrow and click All HTML Tags.

FrontPage redisplays the full list of Web page styles.

❼ In the Styles list, click H2, click the Modify button, click the Format button, and click Font on the shortcut menu.

FrontPage displays the Font dialog box.

❽ Click the Color drop-down arrow, click the Red color tile, click the All Caps check box to select it, and then click OK three times.

The dialog boxes close and FrontPage displays the style changes. Notice that the Heading 1 text is now blue, and the Heading 2 text is red and all uppercase.

Finish the lesson

1 On the File menu, click Close Web.

2 For each page, if FrontPage prompts you to save changes, click Yes.

FrontPage saves your changes and closes the Lesson04 Web.

Lesson 4 Quick Reference

To	Do this
View FrontPage themes	On the Format menu, click Theme. In the Themes dialog box, click the desired theme and view it in the sample pane.
Apply a theme to an individual Web page	Display the page in Page view. On the Format menu, click Theme. In the Themes dialog box, click the Selected Pages option, and click the desired theme. Check the desired check boxes, and then click OK.
Apply a theme to an entire Web	On the Format menu, click Theme, click the All Pages option, and click the desired theme. Check the desired check boxes, and click OK.
Modify a theme	On the Format menu, click Theme. In the Themes dialog box, click the Modify button, and then click the button for the theme characteristic you want to modify. Make the desired changes in the Modify Theme dialog box, and then click OK. Click the Save As button, type a new theme name if desired, and click OK.
Insert a FrontPage component	Click the desired location for the component. On the Insert menu, point to Component, and click the desired component. Adjust the component properties as needed.
Insert a Web page banner	Display the Web page in Page view. On the Insert menu, click Page Banner. Type the Web page banner text, and click OK. Click the Navigation icon on the Views Bar and drag the Web page into the Web hierarchy diagram.
Insert a hit counter	Display the Web page in Page view and click at the desired location for the hit counter. Type a caption and press the Spacebar. On the Insert menu, point to Component, and then click Hit Counter. Adjust the hit counter style and properties, and then click OK.

Lesson 4 Quick Reference

To	Do this
Include a page in another Web page	If necessary, create the Web page you want to include. In Page view, display the Web page in which the included Web page will be inserted, and click the desired location. On the Insert menu, point to Component, and then click Include Page. Click Browse, browse to the Web page to be included, and click OK twice.
Create a header style	Display the desired Web page in Page view. On the Format menu, click Style. If needed, click the List drop-down arrow and click All HTML Tags to display all Web page styles in the Styles list. Click the style you want to modify, click the Modify button, click the Format button, and click the desired style attribute on the shortcut menu. Make the desired changes, and click OK three times.

Adding Style to Web Pages
4

5

Formatting Web Pages

In this lesson you will learn how to:

✔ *Create bulleted and numbered lists.*

✔ *Format bulleted and numbered lists.*

✔ *Use tables to arrange Web page elements.*

✔ *Format tables and table cells.*

✔ *Change Web page properties.*

**ESTIMATED
TIME
40 min.**

As you refine your Web site for Lakewood Mountains Resort, you think about how you should format some information on its Web pages. Some of the information can be put into lists, such as bulleted or numbered lists. In other cases, when you want to show text side by side with photos of the resort, you realize that lists won't do. In such situations, you've heard that tables can be used to arrange elements on the Web page. You're a little worried that it might be difficult, but your coworker reassures you that with Microsoft FrontPage 2000, it's going to be a snap.

In this lesson, you will learn how to create and format bulleted and numbered lists. You will then learn how to create tables on Web pages, insert text in table cells, format cell text, change the size of rows and columns, and make table borders invisible. Finally, you will learn how to change Web page properties.

Import the Lesson 5 practice Web

In this exercise, you create a new Web based on the files in the Lesson05 folder in the Web Publishing SBS Practice folder. You will use this Web for all the exercises in Lesson 5.

1 On the File menu, point to New, and then click Web.

FrontPage displays the New dialog box.

If your hard disk has a drive letter other than C, substitute the appropriate drive letter in step 2.

2 Click the Import Web Wizard icon. In the Specify The Location Of The New Web text box, delete the default text and type **C:\My Webs\Lesson05**, and then click OK.

FrontPage displays the first Import Web Wizard dialog box.

3 Click the From A Source Directory Of Files option, click the Include Subfolders check box, and click the Browse button.

4 Browse to the Lesson05 folder in the Web Publishing SBS Practice folder, and click OK.

5 Click Next twice, and then click Finish.

FrontPage creates a new Web based on the practice files and places it in the Lesson05 folder.

Creating Lists

If the filename is too long to be completely visible in the Folder List, hold the mouse pointer over the filename for a moment. A ScreenTip will display the complete filename.

You've heard that FrontPage makes it easy to create and format lists. You decide to start by creating two list pages: one with a bulleted list of special programs for kids, and the other with a numbered list of directions to the resort.

Create a bulleted list

In this exercise, you create a bulleted list that describes hotel services and activities for kids.

If you are not working through this lesson sequentially, follow the steps in "Import the Lesson 5 Practice Web," earlier in this lesson.

1 In the Folder List, double-click the file Special_programs_for_kids01.htm.

FrontPage opens the Web page in Page view.

2 Click the line below the heading, and click the Bullets button on the toolbar.

FrontPage inserts a bullet.

3 Type **State-certified daycare for toddlers** and press Enter.

FrontPage creates the first bullet item and moves the insertion point down to the next line, adding a second bullet.

4 Type **Junior lifesaving classes at the pool for ages 12–15** and press Enter.

FrontPage creates the second bullet item and moves the insertion point down to the next line, adding a third bullet.

5 Type **Pony rides from 10 A.M. to 3 P.M. every day** and press Enter.

FrontPage creates the last bullet item and moves the insertion point down to the next line, adding a bullet.

Bullets

6 On the toolbar, click the Bullets button.

FrontPage removes the bulleted list format from the bottom line.

You can convert existing text to a bulleted list by selecting the text and clicking the Bullets button on the toolbar.

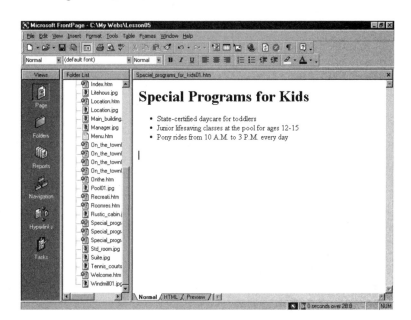

7 On the toolbar, click the Save button.

FrontPage saves your changes.

Save

tip

To change a bulleted list to another style of list, right-click one of the bullets, click List Properties, click the Other tab, click the list style you want, and then click OK. You can change the bulleted list to a numbered list, definition list, directory list, or menu list.

Format a bulleted list

In this exercise, you change the bullet symbol used in a bulleted list.

1 Right-click one of the bullets in the list, and on the shortcut menu, click List Properties.

FrontPage displays the List Properties dialog box. Various bullet styles are displayed.

To quickly change a bulleted list to a numbered list, open the List Properties dialog box, click the Numbers tab, click the numbering style you want, and click OK.

2 Click the lower-right sample box, which displays a square bullet style, and then click OK.

FrontPage changes the bullet style to square bullets.

3 On the toolbar, click the Save button.

FrontPage saves your changes.

Save

tip

To change the style of only one item in a list, right-click the item you want to change, and on the shortcut menu, click List Item Properties. In the dialog box, make the desired changes and click OK.

Create a numbered list

In this exercise, you create a numbered list of driving directions.

Numbering

1 In the Folder List, double-click the file Directions_to_lakewood01.htm.

FrontPage opens the Web page in Page view.

2 Click the line below the heading, and click the Numbering button.

FrontPage inserts the number 1.

3 Type **Take the highway up from Santa Barbara.** and press Enter.

FrontPage moves the insertion point down to the next line, adding the number 2.

You can convert existing text to a numbered list by selecting the text and clicking the Numbering button on the toolbar.

4 Type **Turn left at the scarecrow.** and press Enter.

FrontPage moves the insertion point down to the next line, adding the number 3.

5 Type **Go two miles, and you're here!** and press Enter.

FrontPage moves the insertion point down to the next line, adding the number 4.

Numbering

6 On the toolbar, click the Numbering button.

FrontPage removes the numbered list format from the bottom line.

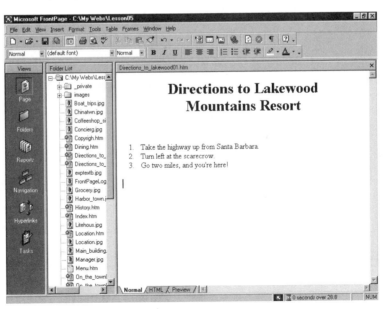

Save

7 On the toolbar, click the Save button.

FrontPage saves your changes.

tip
You can also remove bulleted or numbered list formatting after the last list item by pressing Enter twice or by pressing Enter once and then pressing Backspace.

Format a numbered list

In this exercise, you format the numbers used in a numbered list.

❶ Right-click one of the numbers in the list, and on the shortcut menu, click List Properties.

FrontPage displays the List Properties dialog box. Various numbering styles are shown.

❷ Click the lower-right sample box, which displays a lowercase Roman numeral numbering style. Click OK.

FrontPage changes the numbering style to lowercase Roman numerals.

Save

❸ On the toolbar, click the Save button.

FrontPage saves your changes.

tip
To change a numbered list to another style of list, right-click one of the numbers, click List Properties, click the Other tab, click the list style you want, and then click OK. You can change the numbered list to a bulleted list, definition list, directory list, or menu list.

Using Tables to Arrange Page Elements

Many Web pages present data in single-column format. They have text or graphic elements left-aligned, right-aligned, or centered, but Web page elements are still displayed one after another down the page—not side by side. To display a photo and explanatory text side by side, you can use tables.

In addition to their more conventional use of presenting information in a row and column format, tables let you position elements side-by-side on a Web page. You've planned several pages in the Lakewood Mountains Resort Web site that would benefit from using tables. You decide to experiment by creating and formatting a table.

Insert a table

If you are not working through this lesson sequentially, follow the steps in "Import the Lesson 5 Practice Web," earlier in this lesson.

In this exercise, you insert a table on a Web page and specify the table size.

1. In the Folder List, double-click the file On_the_town01.htm.

   FrontPage displays the Web page in Page view.

2. Click the line below the explanatory paragraph. On the Table menu, point to Insert, and then click Table.

   FrontPage displays the Insert Table dialog box. The insertion point is in the Rows text box.

❸ In the Rows text box, delete the default value of 2, type **3**, and in the Specify Width text box type **100**, and then click OK.

FrontPage inserts a table with three rows and two columns.

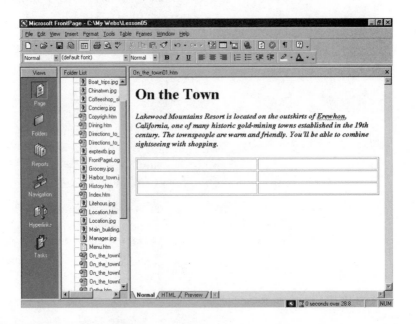

Save

❹ On the toolbar, click the Save button.

FrontPage saves your changes.

tip

Insert Table

Another way to create a table is to click the Insert Table button on the toolbar and drag to select the desired number of rows and columns.

Insert and format text in a table cell

In this exercise, you insert text into a table cell and format the cell contents by changing text alignment and font attributes.

❶ Click in the top-right table cell, and then type **Visit the original Erewhon power plant, which generated electricity for miners during the California gold rush.**

FrontPage inserts the text into the table cell.

2 Press the Tab key twice, and then type **Visit the Erewhon harbor, where fishing boats go out to sea.**

FrontPage moves the insertion point and inserts the text into the cell.

3 Select the two cells containing text.

To move the insertion point to the right and down in a table, press Tab. To move the insertion point to the left and up in a table, press Shift+Tab.

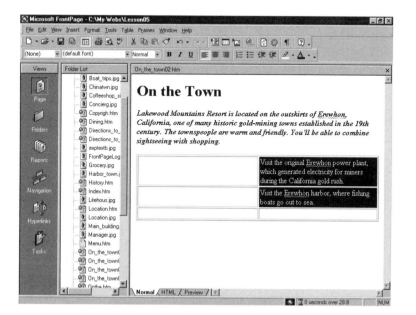

4 Right-click the selected area, and on the shortcut menu, click Cell Properties.

FrontPage displays the Cell Properties dialog box.

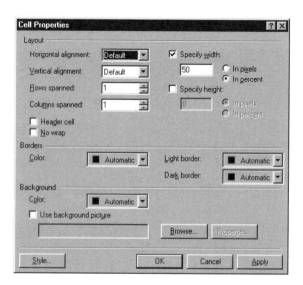

⑤ Click the Horizontal Alignment drop-down arrow, click Right, and click OK.
The text is right-aligned within the cell.

⑥ Right-click the selected area again, and on the shortcut menu, click Font.
FrontPage displays the Font dialog box.

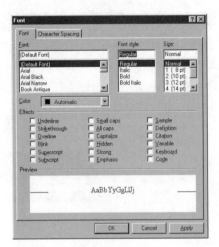

⑦ Click Arial in the Font list, click Bold Italic in the Font Style list, and click OK.
FrontPage changes the font and style of the text in the selected cells.

⑧ On the toolbar, click the Save button.
FrontPage saves your changes.

Save

Format a table

In this exercise, you format a table by changing its column width, row height, and border style.

Vertical Double Arrow

❶ Position the mouse pointer over the horizontal border below the text *California gold rush*.
The mouse pointer changes to a vertical double arrow.

❷ Drag the border down approximately ½ inch.
FrontPage makes the row taller and vertically centers the text.

	Visit the original _Erewhon_ power plant, which generated electricity for miners during the California gold rush.
	Visit the _Erewhon_ harbor, where fishing boats go out to sea.

Horizontal Double Arrow

❸ Position the mouse pointer over the vertical border in the center of the table.

The mouse pointer changes to a horizontal double arrow.

❹ Drag the border approximately ¼ inch to the left.

FrontPage resizes the table columns.

❺ Right-click one of the table borders, and on the shortcut menu, click Table Properties.

FrontPage displays the Table Properties dialog box.

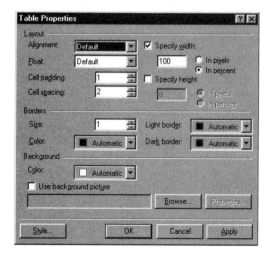

❻ Click in the Borders Size text box, delete the default value of 1, and type **0**. Click OK.

FrontPage makes the table borders invisible.

Save

You will learn how to insert images in table cells in Lesson 6, "Adding Multimedia to Web Pages."

❼ On the toolbar, click the Save button.

FrontPage saves your changes.

❽ In the Folder List, double-click the file On_the_town04.htm.

FrontPage displays a completed version of the table in Page view.

One Step Further Understanding Page Properties

In the section "Changing Web Page Properties" in Lesson 2, you learned how to use the Page Properties dialog box to change the title of a Web page. Now that you've begun formatting Web pages, your coworker informs you that Web page properties include more than just the titles of your pages. In fact, you can use the following page properties to control the appearance of your Web pages.

- Background pictures and colors.
- Margin widths and heights.
- Hyperlink colors.

Change Web page properties

If you are not working through this lesson sequentially, follow the steps in "Import the Lesson 5 Practice Web," earlier in this lesson.

In this exercise, you add a background picture to a Web page and change the layout of the page.

1 In the Folder List, double-click the file Special_programs_for_kids03.htm.

FrontPage displays the Web page in Page view.

2 Right-click a blank area of the Web page, and on the shortcut menu, click Page Properties.

FrontPage displays the Page Properties dialog box.

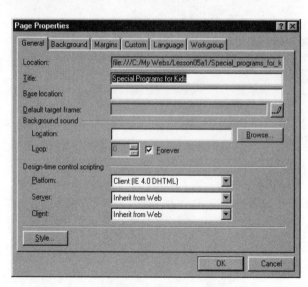

❸ Click the Background tab.

❹ Click the Background Picture check box and click Browse.

FrontPage displays the Select Background Picture dialog box.

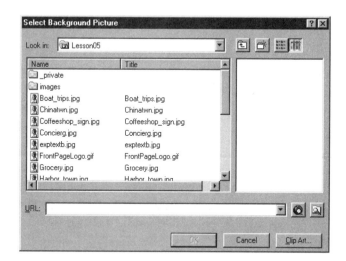

You can use any image file as a background picture. It need not be in the same folder as your Web, and it need not be an image that came with FrontPage.

❺ In the file list, click the file Exptextb.jpg and click OK.

FrontPage selects the image file as the Web page's background picture.

❻ Click the Margins tab.

FrontPage displays the Margins section of the dialog box.

❼ Click the Specify Left Margin check box, type **40** in the Specify Left Margin text box, and click OK.

FrontPage adds a background image to the Web page and moves the page text 40 pixels to the right.

Save

❽ On the toolbar, click the Save button.

FrontPage saves your changes.

tip

To copy a background from another Web page to the current page, right-click the current page in Page view, click Page Properties, click the Background tab, and click the Get Background Information From Another Page check box. Click Browse, browse to the location of the file that contains the background you want to copy, and then click OK twice.

Finish the lesson

❶   On the File menu, click Close Web.

❷   For each page, if FrontPage prompts you to save changes, click Yes.
FrontPage saves your changes and closes the Lesson05 Web.

Lesson 5 Quick Reference

To	Do this	Button
Create a bulleted list	Click the page location where you want to start the list. On the toolbar, click the Bullets button, and type the list items, pressing Enter after each item.	
Format bullets in a bulleted list	Right-click one of the bullets, click List Properties on the shortcut menu, choose a style, and click OK.	
Convert existing text to a bulleted list	Select the text and click the Bullets button on the toolbar.	
Create a numbered list	Click the page location where you want to start the list. On the toolbar, click the Numbering button, and type the list items, pressing Enter after each item.	
Format numbers in a numbered list	Right-click one of the numbers, click List Properties on the shortcut menu, choose a style, and click OK.	
Change the starting number of a list	Right-click one of the numbers, click List Properties, type the desired number in the Start At text box, and click OK.	
Convert existing text to a numbered list	Select the text and click the Numbering button on the toolbar.	
Insert a table	Click the desired page location. On the Table menu, point to Insert, click Table, enter the number of rows and columns, and click OK.	
Insert text in a table cell	Click in the cell, and then type the desired text.	

Lesson 5 Quick Reference

To	Do this
Format text in one or more table cells	Select the text in the cell(s), right-click the selected text, click Cell Properties, Font, or Paragraph, make the changes, and click OK.
Resize a table row or column	Drag a border of the row or column to the appropriate location, and then release the mouse button.
Change a table's border	Right-click a border, click Table Properties on the shortcut menu, make the desired changes, and click OK.
Change Web page properties	Right-click a blank area of the page, click Page Properties, make the changes, and click OK.

Formatting Web Pages

5

LESSON

6

Adding Multimedia to Web Pages

ESTIMATED TIME 30 min.

In this lesson you will learn how to:

- ✔ *Insert photos and clip art on a Web page.*
- ✔ *Create thumbnails of Web page images.*
- ✔ *Edit Web page images.*
- ✔ *Add a background sound to a Web page.*
- ✔ *Add a motion clip to a Web page.*
- ✔ *Create hover buttons on a Web page.*

So far, the managers of Lakewood Mountains Resort have been very happy with your work on the resort's Web site. However, you'd like to impress them even more by incorporating pictures, sounds, and motion clips on their Web pages. After all, the Web is a graphically oriented way to send information over the Internet. A state-of-the-art Web site should make use of that feature.

Your coworker tells you that Microsoft FrontPage 2000 makes it simple to put all kinds of multimedia on Web pages, so you decide to give it a try. In this lesson, you will learn how to insert photos and clip art images on Web pages, insert images in table cells on a Web page, and create thumbnails. You will also learn how to add a background sound to a Web page and insert a motion clip on a Web page. Finally, you will learn how to create *hover buttons* that change in appearance when a mouse pointer is positioned over them.

Import the Lesson 6 practice Web

In this exercise, you create a new Web based on the files in the Lesson06 folder in the Web Publishing SBS Practice folder. You will use this Web for all the exercises in Lesson 6.

1 On the File menu, point to New, and then click Web.

FrontPage displays the New dialog box.

If your hard disk drive has a letter other than C, substitute the appropriate drive letter in step 2.

2 Click the Import Web Wizard icon. In the Specify The Location Of The New Web text box, type **C:\My Webs\Lesson06**, and then click OK.

FrontPage displays the first Import Web Wizard dialog box.

3 Click the From A Source Directory Of Files option, click the Include Subfolders check box, and click the Browse button.

4 Browse to the Lesson06 folder in the Web Publishing SBS Practice folder, and click OK.

5 Click Next twice, and then click Finish.

FrontPage creates a new Web based on the practice files and places it in the Lesson06 folder.

Using Images on Web Pages

Your first task is to learn how to insert different kinds of images on Web pages. There are essentially two kinds of static images you'll use on Web pages: photo files and clip art. Photo files come in many different file formats, but they're usually either GIF (Graphics Interchange Format) files or JPEG (Joint Photographic Experts Group) files. GIF and JPEG files compress the image, allowing a smaller file size than other formats. This allows GIF and JPEG files to download faster to a Web site visitor's computer.

Likewise, clip art images come in a variety of formats, including GIF, JPEG, BMP (Windows bitmap), and PNG (Portable Network Graphics). However, GIF and JPEG are still the most common formats for clip art files. FrontPage includes an extensive Clip Art Gallery with hundreds of ready-to-use images, including buttons, cartoons, pictures, backgrounds, and many other images. The Clip Art Gallery even includes sound and motion clip files.

Regardless of the file format, you insert photo and clip art images on a Web page in much the same way. In FrontPage, it's just a matter of making a few menu selections. An especially valuable FrontPage feature creates *thumbnails*, which are small versions of images that download very quickly. To create a thumbnail, you first insert a full-sized image file on a Web page. Then you select the image and click the Auto Thumbnail button on the Image toolbar.

On the Web page, FrontPage replaces the original full-sized image with a thumbnail version. By clicking the thumbnail, a Web site visitor can display the full-sized image.

Insert a photo on a Web page

If you are not working through this lesson sequentially, follow the steps in "Import the Lesson 6 Practice Web," earlier in this lesson.

In this exercise, you insert a photo on the Lakewood Mountains Resort Welcome page.

1 In the Folder List, double-click the file Welcome01.htm.

FrontPage displays the Lakewood Welcome page in Page view.

2 Click the blank line underneath the text *Lakewood Mountains Resort* and above the resort's address.

The insertion point is centered on the line.

3 On the Insert menu, point to Picture, and then click From File.

FrontPage displays the Picture dialog box.

4 In the file list, click Main_building.jpg.

FrontPage displays a preview of the image in the preview pane.

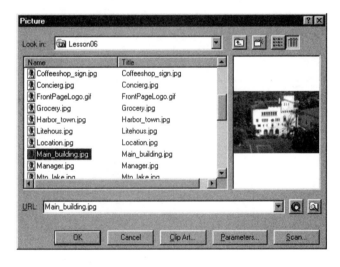

5 Click OK.

FrontPage inserts the image at the location you selected.

Save

6 On the toolbar, click the Save button.

FrontPage saves your changes.

> ### tip
> By reducing the size of image files, you reduce the time it takes to download them to the Web site visitor's computer. Apart from reducing the size of the image itself, a good way to shrink file size is to use an image-editing program such as Paint Shop Pro or Microsoft PhotoDraw to reduce the number of colors in the image.

Explore the Clip Art Gallery

In this exercise, you explore the FrontPage Clip Art Gallery.

❶   In the Folder List, double-click the file Sights01.htm.

     FrontPage displays the Web page.

❷   On the Insert menu, point to Picture, and then click Clip Art.

     FrontPage displays the Clip Art Gallery window. On the Pictures tab, you can select clip art to insert on Web pages.

❸   Click the Sounds tab.

     On the Sounds tab, you can select sound effects to insert on Web pages.

❹   Click the Motion Clips tab.

     On the Motion Clips tab, you can select motion clips and animated GIF files to insert on Web pages.

⑤ In the Categories pane, click the Academic icon.

FrontPage displays the motion clips available in this category.

If there are no motion clips displayed, you can download clips from the Microsoft Clip Gallery Live.

⑥ Click one of the motion clip pictures.

FrontPage displays the pop-up menu for the motion clip. The clip is an animated GIF file.

An animated GIF file contains a short sequence of images. When a Web site visitor views the GIF file, the images are displayed in rapid sequence, producing an animated picture.

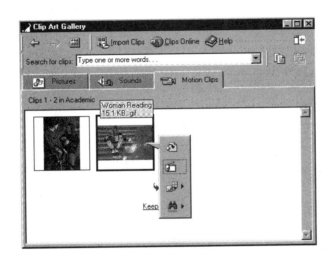

Play Clip

⑦ On the pop-up menu, click the Play Clip button.

FrontPage plays the motion clip in the GIF Player window.

⑧ Click the Close button at the top-right corner of the GIF Player window.

FrontPage closes the GIF Player window.

⑨ On the Clip Art Gallery toolbar, click the Back button.

FrontPage redisplays the Motion Clips tab of the Clip Art Gallery window.

Back
The Forward and Back buttons work just as they do in Microsoft Internet Explorer.

⑩ Click the Close button at the top-right corner of the Clip Art Gallery window.

FrontPage closes the window.

tip

To download additional clip art, sounds, and motion clips from the Web, connect to the Internet, and click the Clips Online button on the toolbar in the Clip Art Gallery window. FrontPage connects to the Microsoft Clip Gallery Live site on the World Wide Web, from which you can download additional clip art images for your Web pages. You can also download clip art, sounds, and motion clip files from newsgroups on the Internet, such as *alt.binaries.sounds.midi*.

Adding Multimedia

6

Search the Clip Art Gallery

In this exercise, you search for clip art in the Clip Art Gallery.

1 On the Sights01 Web page, click the blank line below the heading and above the table.

FrontPage moves the insertion point to the line below the heading.

2 On the Insert menu, point to Picture, and then click Clip Art.

FrontPage displays the Clip Art Gallery window.

3 Click in the Search For Clips text box, type **arrow**, and then press Enter.

FrontPage searches the Clip Art Gallery for arrow images and displays the search results on the Pictures tab.

The window on your screen might differ slightly from the one shown in the illustration.

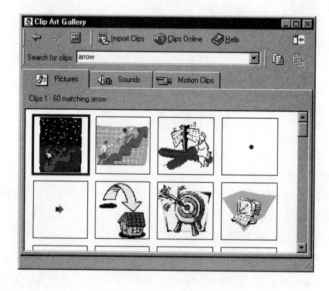

Insert clip art on a Web page

If your window does not contain the globe-arrow image, just use any clip art image you like.

In this exercise, you select a clip art image, insert it on a Web page, and then save the Web page.

1 Click the globe-arrow image.

FrontPage displays the pop-up menu for the clip art image.

2 On the pop-up menu, click the Insert Clip button.

FrontPage inserts the globe-arrow clip art at the selected location on the Web page and closes the Clip Art Gallery window.

Insert Clip

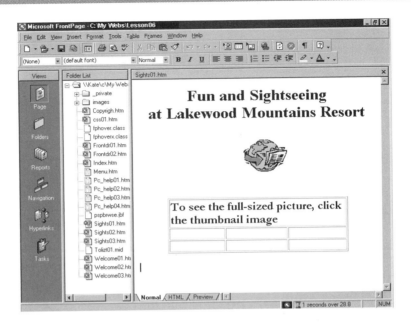

Save

③ On the toolbar, click the Save button, and then click OK in the Save Embedded Files dialog box.

FrontPage saves the Web page with your changes.

tip

You can make almost any image on a Web page a hyperlink, including clip art. To make a clip art image a hyperlink, right-click the image, and click Hyperlink on the shortcut menu. In the Create Hyperlink dialog box, browse to the file that will be the link target, click the file, and click OK.

Insert images in table cells and create thumbnails

In this exercise, you arrange images on a Web page by inserting them in table cells. You then shrink the images by converting them to thumbnails that link to the full-sized images.

① In the Folder List, double-click the file Sights02.htm.

FrontPage opens the Web page in Page view.

② Click in the top-left cell of the first empty row in the table. On the Insert menu, point to Picture, and click From File.

FrontPage displays the Picture dialog box.

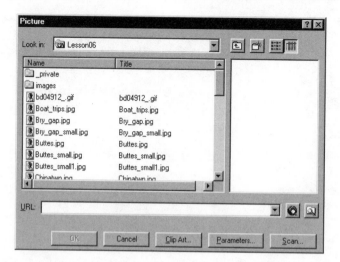

❸ In the file list, click Bry_gap.jpg, and then click OK.

FrontPage inserts the image into the table cell. Notice that the image is too large to fit in the table cell.

❹ Click the image in the table cell.

FrontPage displays the Image toolbar along the bottom of your screen.

Auto Thumbnail

❺ On the Image toolbar, click the Auto Thumbnail button.

FrontPage converts the table image into a much smaller thumbnail that contains a hyperlink to the full-sized image.

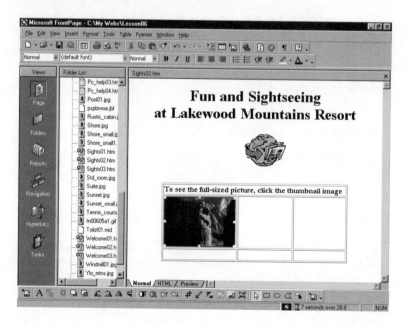

6 Click in the middle cell of the same row. On the Insert menu, point to Picture, click From File, click Shore.jpg, and then click OK.

FrontPage inserts an image into the middle cell of the row.

Auto Thumbnail

7 Click the image in the middle cell, and on the Image toolbar, click the Auto Thumbnail button.

FrontPage creates a thumbnail image and links it to the full-sized image.

Save

8 On the toolbar, click the Save button, and click OK in the Save Embedded Files dialog box.

FrontPage saves your changes.

Move image files to the images folder

When you create a Web, FrontPage automatically includes an images folder. If your Web has a large number of images, moving all image files to the images folder makes your Web easier to manage. In this exercise, you move image files from your Web's main folder to its images folder and observe how FrontPage updates the images' hyperlinks.

1 On the Views bar, click the Folders icon.

FrontPage displays a list of all files and folders in the Lesson06 Web.

2 Click the Type button at the top of the file list.

FrontPage displays the files in alphabetical order by type.

If files are displayed in reverse order, click the Type button one more time.

3 In the file list, click Boat_trips.jpg. Scroll down until you see Ylo_mtns_small.jpg, hold down Shift, and click that file.

4 Drag the selected files to the images subfolder in the Folder List.

FrontPage moves all the JPEG image files to the images subfolder and updates all hyperlinks between Web pages and JPEG files to reflect the files' new location.

5 In the file list, click FrontPageLogo.gif, hold down the Ctrl key, and click any other GIF files.

The GIF image files are selected.

The Sights03.htm page is a completed version of the Sights01.htm page that you worked on earlier.

6 Drag the GIF image files to the images subfolder.

FrontPage moves all the GIF image files to the images subfolder and updates the hyperlinks.

7 On the Views bar, click the Page icon, and then double-click Sights03.htm in the Folder List.

FrontPage displays the Web page in Page view.

Adding Multimedia

6

8 Right-click the picture in the top-left table cell, and then on the shortcut menu, click Hyperlink Properties.

FrontPage displays the Edit Hyperlink dialog box. Notice that the hyperlink's target (in the URL text box) has been updated and is in the images folder.

9 Click the Cancel button in the Edit Hyperlinks dialog box.

FrontPage closes the Edit Hyperlinks dialog box.

Editing Images on Web Pages

Placing an image on a Web page is easy, but often the image is too large or too small to fit properly on the Web page. Moreover, some Web site visitors set up their Web browsers to download Web pages without embedded images: this makes the pages download more quickly, but leaves gaps where images would otherwise appear. FrontPage enables you to specify "alternative text" that is displayed when images aren't downloaded. Instead of the image, visitors see your alternative text description at the page location where the image would have appeared.

Resize an image

If you are not working through this lesson sequentially, follow the steps in "Import the Lesson 6 Practice Web," earlier in this lesson.

In this exercise, you resize an image on a Web page.

1 In the Folder List, double-click Welcome02.htm.

FrontPage displays the Welcome02.htm Web page in Page view. The hotel image is so large that it pushes the address and phone number off the bottom of the screen.

2 Click the hotel image, and then scroll to the lower-right corner of the image.

A small square (a resize handle) appears at the corner of the image.

3 Move the mouse pointer over the resize handle.

The mouse pointer changes into a diagonal double arrow.

Double Arrow

4 Drag the mouse pointer upward and to the left to shrink the image.

FrontPage resizes the hotel image, retaining the original proportions, as shown in the illustration on the following page.

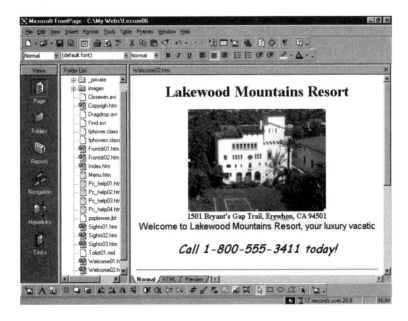

Specify alternative text for an image

In this exercise, you specify alternative text for an image on a Web page.

1 Right-click the hotel image, and then on the shortcut menu, click Picture Properties.

FrontPage displays the Picture Properties dialog box.

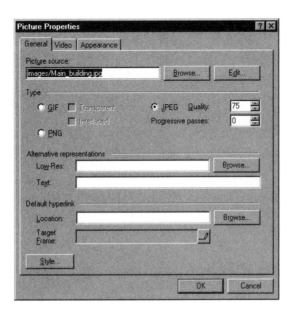

Adding Multimedia

6

② Click in the Text text box under Alternative Representations, type **Lakewood Mountains Resort main building**, and click OK.

FrontPage inserts the text to be displayed if a Web site visitor's browser does not display Web page images.

③ On the toolbar, click the Save button.

FrontPage saves your changes.

Save

Adding Sound Effects and Music to Web Pages

Most Web page content is informative, but there's more to the Web surfing experience than just getting information. You want the Lakewood Mountains Resort Web site to be a pleasant place to visit. One way to make the site interesting is to add a background sound to the home page. This background sound will play as long as the home page is displayed in a Web browser.

important

When you use these steps to insert a sound file on a Web page, the sound file will play only if the page is loaded in Microsoft's Internet Explorer Web browser—but not if the user loads it into Netscape's Navigator Web browser. Netscape Navigator uses different HTML coding to play a background sound.

Add a background sound

If you are not working through this lesson sequentially, follow the steps in "Import the Lesson 6 Practice Web," earlier in the lesson.

In this exercise, you add a background sound to a Web page and preview the sound in your Web browser.

① In the Folder List, double-click Welcome03.htm.

FrontPage displays the Welcome03.htm Web page in Page view.

② Right-click a blank area of the page, and then click Page Properties.

FrontPage displays the Page Properties dialog box.

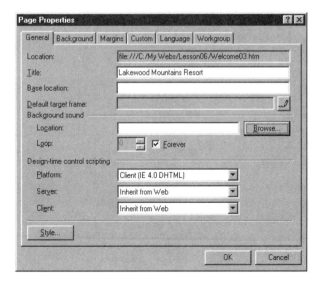

③ Click the Browse button.

FrontPage displays the Background Sound dialog box.

④ Click Tolizt01.mid, and click OK twice.

FrontPage inserts the file as a background sound that will play as long as the page is displayed in a visitor's Web browser.

⑤ On the toolbar, click the Save button, and then click the Preview In Browser button.

FrontPage saves the page and displays it in your Web browser. If you are using Microsoft Internet Explorer, the background sound plays automatically.

⑥ Click the Close button at the top-right corner of your Web browser window.

Your Web browser closes and FrontPage reappears.

Save

*Preview In
Browser*

Close

tip

By default, a background sound continues to play as long as the Web page is displayed in a visitor's Web browser. However, you can specify that the sound play a certain number of times and then stop. In the Page Properties dialog box, clear the Forever check box. In the Loop text box, enter the number of times the background sound should repeat, and then click OK.

Adding Video to Web Pages

So far, you've had great success using FrontPage to insert static pictures on Web pages. What's even more impressive, however, is that you can just as easily insert motion clips on Web pages. When Web site visitors load a page with an embedded motion clip, the video will automatically play both motion and sound. You can also create hyperlinks that lead to motion clip files.

Insert a motion clip

If you are not working through this lesson sequentially, follow the steps in "Import the Lesson 6 Practice Web," earlier in this lesson.

In this exercise, you insert a motion clip on a Web page and preview the video in your Web browser.

❶ In the Folder List, double-click Pc_help01.htm.

FrontPage displays the Web page in Page view.

❷ Click the empty line just below the page text. On the Insert menu, point to Picture, and then click Video.

FrontPage displays the Video dialog box.

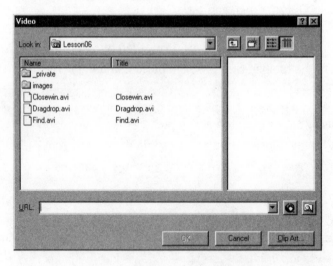

The file Pc_help02.htm is the completed version of the page you edit in this exercise.

❸ Click Closewin.avi in the Lesson06 folder, and then click OK.

FrontPage inserts the motion clip directly on the Web page. When a Web site visitor displays the page, the video will play once.

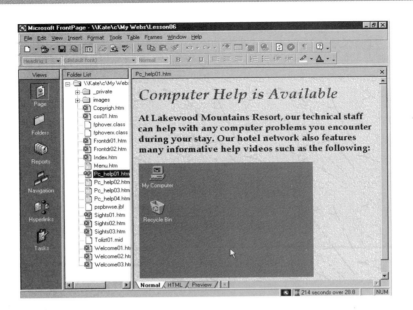

Save

*Preview
In Browser*

Close

④ On the toolbar, click the Save button, and then click the Preview In Browser button.

FrontPage saves the page and displays it in your Web browser. The motion clip plays automatically.

⑤ Click the Close button at the top-right corner of your Web browser window.

Your Web browser closes and FrontPage reappears.

Link to a motion clip

In this exercise, you create a hyperlink to a motion clip file instead of inserting the file directly on a Web page.

❶ In the Folder List, double-click Pc_help03.htm.

FrontPage displays the Web page in Page view.

❷ Select the text *How to drag and drop*.

❸ Right-click the selected text, and on the shortcut menu, click Hyperlink.

FrontPage displays the Create Hyperlink dialog box.

Adding Multimedia *6*

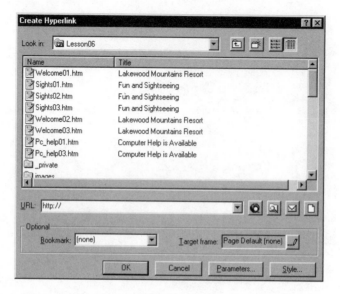

The file
Pc_help04.htm
is the com-
pleted version
of the page you
edit in this ex-
ercise.

4 In the file list, click Dragdrop.avi, and then click OK.

FrontPage inserts the hyperlink.

Save

5 On the toolbar, click the Save button, and then click the Preview In Browser button.

FrontPage saves the Web page and displays it in your Web browser.

Preview
In Browser

6 Click the hyperlink How To Drag And Drop.

The Windows Media Player opens and plays the motion clip.

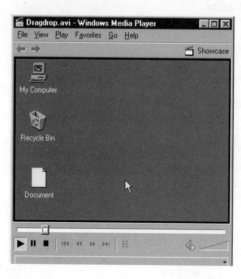

Close

❼   Close the Media Player and your Web browser.

FrontPage is redisplayed.

Using Style Sheets to Position Web Page Items

One of the exciting but somewhat advanced techniques supported by FrontPage 2000 is the ability to use Web page *style sheets* to control the appearance of your Web pages. A Web page style sheet is a separate text file in which you specify how various elements of your Web page should look. Techniques for creating style sheets—called *cascading style sheets* (CSS) because you can apply multiple style sheets to a single Web page—are defined by the World Wide Web Consortium (*www.w3.org*).

FrontPage makes it easy to use one of the most powerful style sheet features to be added in the latest CSS version: absolute and relative positioning of Web page elements. Previously, you've seen how you can use tables to place items in specific locations on your Web pages. That's how it's been done for most of the Web's history. With style sheets, however, you can position Web page items exactly where you want them *without* using tables.

With FrontPage, you don't have to write any style sheet code to position Web page items. You simply use menu choices and dialog boxes to specify the position you want for an item. FrontPage does all the work of creating the style sheet code; you never even have to see it.

Use a style sheet to position an image

If you are not working through this lesson sequentially, follow the steps in "Import the Lesson 6 Practice Web," earlier in this lesson.

❶   On the Views bar, click the Page icon.

FrontPage displays the Web in Page view.

❷   On the toolbar, click the New button.

FrontPage creates a new Web page and displays it in Page view.

❸   On the Insert menu, point to Picture, and then click From File.

FrontPage displays the Picture dialog box.

New

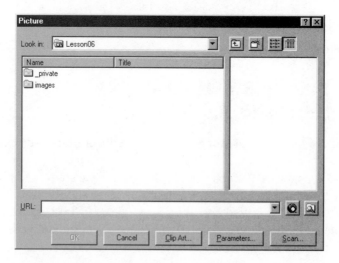

4 Double-click the Images folder, click Bry_gap_small.jpg, and click OK.

FrontPage inserts the picture at the top-left corner of the Web page.

5 On the Insert menu, point to Picture, and then click From File.

FrontPage displays the Picture dialog box.

6 In the dialog box's file list, click Shore_small.jpg, and click OK.

FrontPage inserts the new picture just to the right of the first picture.

7 Right-click the second picture (Shore_small.jpg). On the shortcut menu, click Picture Properties. Click the Style button, click the Format button, and in the drop-down menu, click Position.

FrontPage displays the Position dialog box.

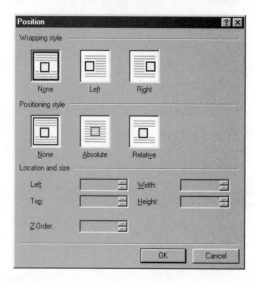

8 In the Positioning Style section of the dialog box, click the Absolute icon. Type **300** in the Left text box and type **50** in the Top text box.

FrontPage will position the picture 300 pixels from the left edge of the Web page and 50 pixels from the top of the Web page.

9 Click OK three times.

FrontPage closes all the dialog boxes and positions the picture at the location you specified.

10 Right-click the first picture (Bry_gap_small.jpg). On the shortcut menu, click Picture Properties. Click the Style button, click the Format button, and in the drop-down menu, click Position.

FrontPage displays the Position dialog box.

11 In the Positioning Style section, click the Absolute icon. Type **50** in the Left text box and type **50** in the Top text box.

FrontPage will position the picture 50 pixels from the left edge of the Web page and 50 pixels from the top of the Web page.

12 Click OK three times.

FrontPage closes all the dialog boxes and positions the picture at the location you specified.

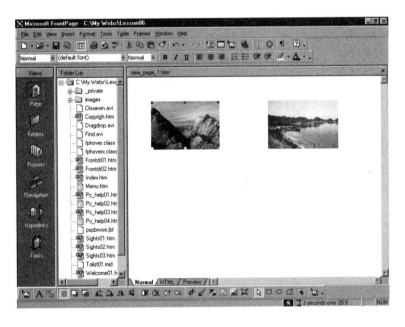

Save

13 On the toolbar, click the Save button, type **CSS01.htm** in the File Name text box, and click Save.

FrontPage saves your changes.

tip

You can use style sheets to position items on a Web page with *absolute* or *relative* positioning. Absolute positioning, which you used in the previous exercise, places the item at exactly the distance you specify from the top and left edges of the page—even if there's another item in that location. Relative positioning moves the item the specified distance down and to the right from the point at which it would normally appear, not from the edges of the page. Thus, relative positioning is slightly safer but doesn't give you as much control.

One Step Further   # Creating Hover Buttons

Motion clips aren't the only kind of animation you can create with FrontPage. Another popular multimedia effect is the *hover button*, whose appearance changes if a Web site visitor points to it with the mouse—that is, when the mouse pointer "hovers" over the button.

A hover button is actually a Java applet created by FrontPage. You can use a hover button to link to another Web page. When a Web site visitor points to the hover button, the button displays a hover effect such as changing color or appearing to have been pushed. When a Web site visitor clicks the hover button, the linked Web page is displayed.

Create a hover button

If you are not working through this lesson sequentially, follow the steps in "Import the Lesson 6 Practice Web," earlier in this lesson.

In this exercise, you create a hover button and set its properties.

1   In the Folder List, double-click Frontdr01.htm.

FrontPage opens the Web page and displays it in Page view.

2   Click the line below the *Welcome* text. On the Insert menu, point to Component, and then click Hover Button.

FrontPage displays the Hover Button Properties dialog box. The default text in the Button Text box is already selected.

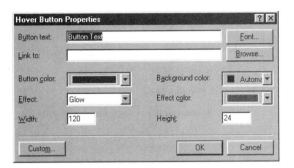

*The file
Frontdr02.htm
is a completed
version of the
file you edit in
this exercise.*

❸ Type **Enter the Web Site** in the Button Text text box. Type **300** in the Width text box and **50** in the Height text box.

FrontPage sets the button caption and size.

❹ Click the Effect drop-down arrow.

FrontPage displays a list of animation effects you can use with hover buttons.

❺ Click Bevel In.

FrontPage sets the button to look as if it has been pressed when the mouse pointer is on it.

❻ Click the Browse button.

FrontPage displays the Select Hover Button Hyperlink dialog box.

❼ Scroll down in the file list, click Index.htm, and click OK twice.

FrontPage creates a hover button with the properties you specified.

Save

❽ On the toolbar, click the Save button, and then click the Preview In Browser button.

FrontPage saves your changes and displays the page in your Web browser.

*Preview
In Browser*

❾ Move the mouse pointer over the hover button.

The hover button text moves slightly, as if the button has been pressed inward.

❿ Click the hover button.

Your Web browser loads the Web's home page.

tip

Another way to create a hyperlink hover button is to right-click the button and click Hover Button Properties on the shortcut menu. The Hover Button dialog box will be displayed. In the Link To text box, browse to the file that will be the link target, click the file, and click OK.

Finish the lesson

Close

❶   Click the Close button at the top-right corner of your Web browser window.
      Your Web browser closes and FrontPage reappears.

❷   On the File menu, click Close Web.

❸   For each page, if FrontPage prompts you to save changes, click Yes.
      FrontPage saves your changes and closes the Lesson06 Web.

Lesson 6 Quick Reference

To	Do this	Button
Insert a photo on a Web page	Click the desired location on the Web page. On the Insert menu, point to Picture, and click From File. Browse to the desired file, click it, and click OK.	
Search the Clip Art Gallery	On the Insert menu, point to Picture, and click Clip Art. In the Search For Clips text box, type the search text, and press Enter.	
Insert clip art on a Web page	Click the desired location on the Web page. On the Insert menu, point to Picture, and click Clip Art. Click a category, click the desired clip art, and click the Insert Clip button.	
Insert an image in a table cell	Click in the desired table cell. On the Insert menu, point to Picture, and click From File. In the file list, click the desired image, and click OK.	
Move image files to the images folder	Click the Folders icon on the Views bar, and click the Type button at the top of the file list. Select the image files, and drag them to the images folder in the Folder List.	
Create image thumbnails	Click the image on the Web page, and then click the Auto Thumbnail button on the Image toolbar.	

Lesson 6 Quick Reference

To	Do this
Resize an image	Click the image to select it, and then drag one of its resize handles to resize the image.
Add a background sound to a Web page	Right-click a blank area of the Web page, and on the shortcut menu, click Page Properties. Click the Browse button, select the desired sound file, and click OK twice.
Specify alternative text for an image	Right-click the image, and on the shortcut menu, click Picture Properties. Click in the Text text box, type the alternative text, and then click OK.
Insert a motion clip directly on a Web page	Click the desired location on the Web page. On the Insert menu, point to Picture, and click Video. Select the desired motion clip, and then click OK.
Link to a motion clip	Select and right-click the text or image for the link. On the shortcut menu, click Hyperlink. Select the desired video file, and then click OK.
Create a hover button	Click the desired location on the Web page. On the Insert menu, point to Component, and click Hover Button. Enter the button text and dimensions, click the Effect drop-down arrow, select an effect from the list box, and click the Browse button. Browse to the file you want the hover button to link to, and click OK twice.

6

Adding Multimedia

7

Creating Forms for User Feedback

ESTIMATED TIME
35 min.

In this lesson you will learn how to:

✔ *Use the Form Page Wizard.*

✔ *Create a form from scratch.*

✔ *Add fields and text to forms.*

✔ *Modify form fields.*

✔ *Send form data to a text file or e-mail address.*

✔ *Create a guest book page.*

So far, you've created a fairly impressive Web site to showcase the attractions of Lakewood Mountains Resort. But as Web users become more sophisticated, it's not enough merely to present static information on the Web. Web site visitors often want to be able to send information or comments to a Web site and get a reply from the site's owner. The manager of Lakewood Mountains Resort would like you to make it possible for Web site visitors to send their contact information and vacation plans, to reserve a room, or to request more information about the resort.

In this lesson, you will learn how to create Web page forms that let visitors send data to the Web site. You'll also learn how to create forms with the Form Page Wizard; how to create forms "from scratch" on an existing Web page; how to add fields and text to a form; and how to route form data to a Web page, an e-mail address, a database, or a Web server program. Finally, you will learn how to create a guest book page that allows visitors to sign in and leave comments.

Import the Lesson 7 practice Web

In this exercise, you create a new Web based on the files in the Lesson07 folder in the Web Publishing SBS Practice folder. You will use this Web for all the exercises in Lesson 7.

1 On the File menu, point to New, and then click Web.

FrontPage displays the New dialog box.

If your hard disk drive has a drive letter other than C, substitute the appropriate drive letter in step 2.

2 Click the Import Web Wizard icon. In the Specify The Location Of The New Web text box, delete the default text and type **C:\My Webs\Lesson07**, and click OK.

FrontPage displays the first Import Web Wizard dialog box.

3 Click the From A Source Directory Of Files option, click the Include Subfolders check box, and click the Browse button.

4 Browse to the Lesson07 folder in the Web Publishing SBS Practice folder, and click OK.

5 Click Next twice, and then click Finish.

FrontPage creates a new Web based on the practice files and places it in the Lesson07 folder.

Understanding Forms

Forms are everywhere. You fill out a form at the bank to get money from your account, at the Motor Vehicle Department to get your driver's license, and even at some pizza restaurants to place your order. Most paper forms have a common structure: a list of questions accompanied by areas in which you can write your answers. Some forms also include check boxes that let you select from multiple predetermined options. When you've filled out the form, you hand it to the salesperson, bank teller, or clerk, who takes actions based on the information you provided.

Web page forms work in the same way. When Web site visitors load a page containing a form, they can type information into text boxes. They can also click check boxes and radio buttons, make choices from drop-down menus, and type free-form text into scrolling text boxes that can hold more text than they display on the screen. And instead of physically handing a paper form to someone, Web site visitors just click a Submit button to send the form data to the Web server where it can be sent to a file, an e-mail address, or a server program for further processing.

Label

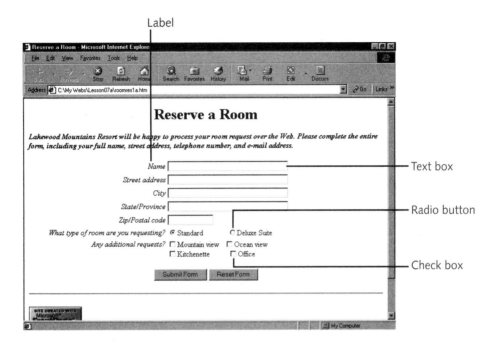

Text box

Radio button

Check box

Creating Forms in FrontPage

To create a form without FrontPage, you would need a pretty good understanding of HTML, as well as how to use its various form tags, such as <FORM>, <INPUT>, and so on. With FrontPage, however, you need no HTML knowledge to create a form. All you need is the keyboard or the mouse.

There are three ways to create a form: use the Form Page Wizard, use a form page template, or create your form from scratch. When you create a form with the Form Page Wizard, FrontPage asks you a series of questions about what you want on your form. It creates a form based on your answers. You can then modify the form to fit your exact needs. Using a template is slightly simpler: instead of asking you questions, FrontPage just creates a form based on a particular design—say, for a Guest Book page. Then you can modify the form to suit your particular needs.

When you create a form from scratch, you first create a Web page and then insert a form area on the page. Inside the form border, FrontPage has already inserted a Submit Form button, as well as a Reset Form button. You just insert the text and form fields that you need. You can also create a new form by inserting any form field on the page, outside of any existing forms.

Types of Form Controls

Web page forms use controls that are defined in the HTML language. FrontPage's form controls are summarized in the following table.

Form control	Explanation
Form	Inserts a form area on a Web page.
One-line text box	Inserts a one-line text box on a form (that is, inside the form border on a Web page).
Scrolling text box	Inserts a scrolling text box on a form. Web site visitors can type as much text as they wish.
Check box	Inserts a check box on a form. Visitors can click multiple check boxes to select from pre-defined alternatives.
Radio button	Inserts a radio button (option button) on a form. Visitors can click only one of a group of radio buttons to select from a group of predefined alternatives.
Drop-down menu	Inserts a drop-down menu on a form—similar to a group of radio buttons. Visitors can (by default) click only one of a group of predefined alternatives. Better than radio buttons for presenting a large number of alternatives; also can be set to allow multiple selections.
Push button	Inserts a push button on a form. Visitors click the button to perform an action. Not usually needed because FrontPage automatically creates Submit Form and Reset Form buttons when you create a form. You can insert push buttons to display message boxes, execute Web page scripts, and perform other tasks not directly related to the submission of form data to a server.
Picture	Inserts a picture on a form. You can use a picture in the same way you use a button.
Label	When a form field and its label are both selected, makes the label "clickable" to activate the form field.

Create a form with the Form Page Wizard

If you are not working through this lesson sequentially, follow the steps in "Import the Lesson 7 Practice Web," earlier in the lesson.

In this exercise, you create a form to collect a visitor's contact information using the FrontPage Form Page Wizard.

1 Make sure your Web is displayed in Page view, and then on the File menu, point to New, and click Page.

The New dialog box appears.

2 Click the Form Page Wizard icon, and then click OK.

FrontPage displays the first Form Page Wizard dialog box.

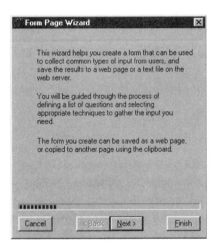

3 Click the Next button.

FrontPage displays the second Form Page Wizard dialog box.

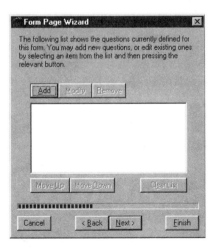

4 Click the Add button to add information to the form.

The dialog box lists the different types of information the wizard can set up the form to collect.

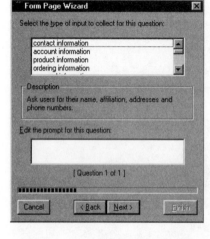

Notice that as you create your form, a progress bar appears at the bottom of the Form Page Wizard dialog box. The progress bar shows how far along you've come in creating your form.

If you accept the default question text, you can always change it later.

5 In the Select The Type Of Input To Collect For This Question box, click Contact Information. In the Edit The Prompt For This Question text box, delete the default text, and then type **Please enter your full name and street address:**. Click the Next button.

The wizard asks what contact information the form should collect.

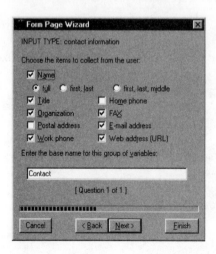

6 In the dialog box, clear the check boxes for Title, Organization, Work Phone, Fax, E-mail Address, and Web Address. Click the check boxes for Postal Address and Home Phone, and then click the Next button.

The dialog box displays the list of questions that will appear on the form.

Add radio buttons with the Form Page Wizard

In this exercise, you use the Form Page Wizard to add radio buttons, which will allow visitors to select the type of room they would like.

1 In the Form Page Wizard dialog box, click the Add button.

The dialog box lists the different types of information the wizard can set up the form to collect.

2 In the Select The Type Of Input To Collect For This Question box, scroll down and click One Of Several Options. Delete the default text in the Edit The Prompt For This Question text box, and then type **What type of room would you like?** and click the Next button.

The wizard displays a dialog box that you can use to create a list of radio buttons.

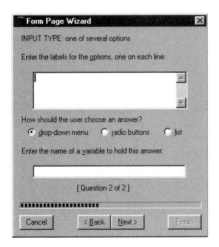

3 In the Enter The Labels For The Options text box, type the following list, pressing Enter at the end of each line:

Standard Room

Deluxe Suite

Honeymoon Suite

4 Click the Radio Buttons option. In the Enter The Name Of A Variable To Hold This Answer text box, type **roomtype**.

A variable is like a little box in which you can store a value, such as a number or a text string. Later, when needed, your Web site can retrieve the value from the box.

The dialog box should look like the following illustration.

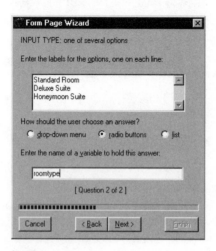

5 Click the Next button.

The wizard redisplays the list of questions that will appear on the form.

tip

FrontPage enables you to use exclusive alternatives in three different ways: in a drop-down menu, in a group of radio buttons, or in a list. These three methods all let a Web site visitor select only one of a group of options. The method you choose is a matter of taste. However, if you need to display a large number of options, a drop-down menu is best because it requires little space on the form.

Add check boxes with the Form Page Wizard

In this exercise, you add check boxes (which will allow visitors to select features they would like in their rooms) with the Form Page Wizard.

1 In the Form Page Wizard dialog box, click the Add button.

The dialog box lists the different types of information that the wizard can set up the form to collect.

2 In the Select The Type Of Input To Collect For This Question box, scroll down and click Any Of Several Options. Delete the default text in the Edit The Prompt For This Question text box, type **What extra features would you**

like?, and click the Next button.

The Form Page Wizard displays a dialog box that you can use to create a list of check boxes.

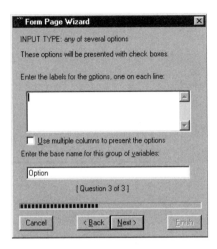

③   In the Enter The Labels For The Options text box, type the following list, pressing Enter at the end of each line:

Kitchenette

Office

Internet Connection

④   Click the Use Multiple Columns To Present The Options check box. In the Enter The Base Name For This Group Of Variables text box, delete the default text, and type **Extras**

The dialog box should look like the illustration on the following page.

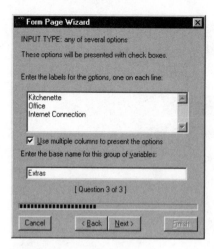

⑤   Click the Next button.

The wizard redisplays the list of questions that will appear on the form.

Choosing Between
Radio Buttons and Check Boxes

Radio buttons and check boxes look similar, but they differ in a vital way. Radio buttons are used to present a group of mutually exclusive alternatives; the Web site visitor is allowed to select only one of the alternatives. For example, if you want a visitor to specify what day of the week he or she will arrive at the resort, the visitor must specify only one day. Check boxes present a set of choices; the visitor can select one or more of them. If you want a Web site visitor to specify his or her favorite recreational activities, multiple selections should be allowed: liking tennis doesn't exclude liking swimming, boating, or bungee jumping.

Finish creating a form with the Form Page Wizard

In this exercise, you title and save a form.

❶   In the Form Page Wizard dialog box, click the Finish button.

The Form Page Wizard creates a form based on your input.

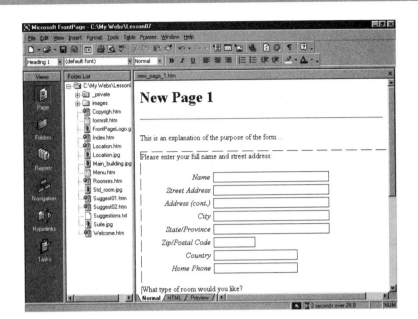

The dotted line on the Web page shows the form border. Anything inside the border is on the form; anything outside the border is not. Although it's unusual, you can have more than one form on the same Web page.

2 On the File menu, click Save As.

FrontPage displays the Save As dialog box.

3 In the File Name text box, type **Roomres01.htm**.

4 Click the Change button.

FrontPage displays the Set Page Title dialog box.

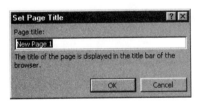

5 In the Page Title text box, type **Room Request Form**, click OK, and click the Save button.

FrontPage saves the form page.

6 Scroll down to view the bottom part of the form, and then scroll back to the top of the form.

The Form Page Wizard created radio buttons and check boxes as you instructed. At the bottom of the page, the wizard inserted a Submit Form button and a Reset Form button.

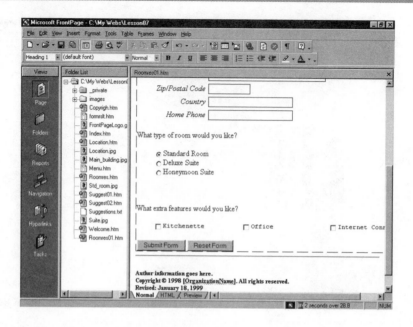

Edit form text

If you insert a Page Banner component on a page, the page title is displayed in the banner at the top of the page.

In this exercise, you edit the placeholder text on a form created with the Form Page Wizard.

1 Select the New Page heading, and type **Request a Room**

The new text replaces the selected text.

2 Just above the form border, delete the text *This is an explanation of the purpose of the form...*, and type the following:

Lakewood Mountains Resort will be happy to process your room request over the Web.

3 Click the first line inside the form border just after the words *full name*. Type a comma and then type **phone number** so that the prompt now reads:

Please enter your full name, phone number, and street address:

Save

4 On the toolbar, click the Save button.

FrontPage saves your changes to the form page.

Create a form from scratch

In this exercise, you create a blank Web page and then create a form on it.

New

1 On the toolbar, click the New button.

FrontPage creates a blank Web page and displays it in Page view.

2   On the left side of the toolbar, click the Style drop-down arrow. Click Heading 1, type **Give us your suggestions**, and then press Enter.

FrontPage creates a heading for the form page and moves the insertion point to the next line.

3   On the Insert menu, point to Form, and then click Form.

FrontPage creates a form on the Web page. The form has Submit and Reset buttons.

4   Press Enter five times, and click the line below the top border of the form.

This creates space to insert form controls.

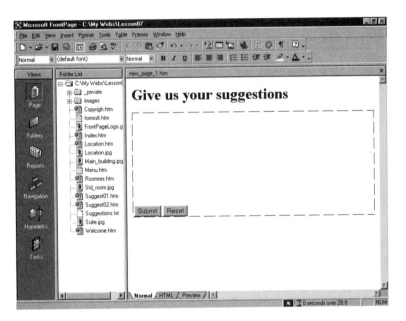

Save

5   On the toolbar, click the Save button. Type **Suggest.htm** in the File Name text box and click the Save button in the dialog box.

FrontPage saves the new form page.

Modifying Forms

Once you've created a form—whether you've used the Form Page Wizard or created the form from scratch—you can modify the form in any way you like. You can add new input fields or explanatory text, change the form properties, add new items to drop-down menus, add new check boxes or radio buttons, and change where the form data will be sent.

Add explanatory text and an input field

If you are not working through this lesson sequentially, follow the steps in "Import the Lesson 7 Practice Web," earlier in this lesson, and in the Folder List, double-click Suggest01.htm.

In this exercise, you add explanatory text and a scrolling text box to a form.

1 Click the top line inside the form border, type **We always like to hear from you!** and then press Enter.

FrontPage inserts the new text on the top line of the form.

2 Type **What's most important about a resort?** and press the Spacebar.

3 On the Insert menu, point to Form, and then click Scrolling Text Box.

FrontPage inserts a scrolling text box to the right of your question. Web site visitors will be able to enter as much text as they like in the text box.

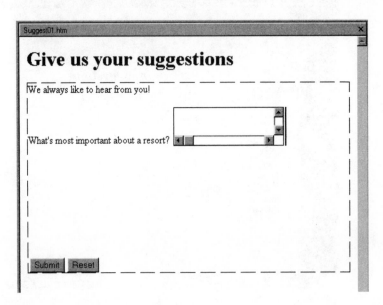

Add a drop-down menu

In this exercise, you add a drop-down menu to a form.

1 Click the line under the scrolling text box, type **I really like:** and then press the Spacebar.

2 On the Insert menu, point to Form, and then click Drop-Down Menu.

FrontPage inserts a drop-down menu to the right of your new text.

3 Right-click the drop-down menu, and on the shortcut menu, click Form Field Properties.

FrontPage displays the Drop-Down Menu Properties dialog box.

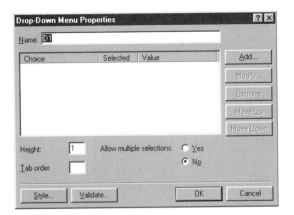

❹   Click the Add button.

FrontPage displays the Add Choice dialog box. You use this dialog box to add items to the drop-down menu.

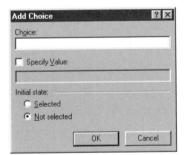

❺   In the Choice text box, type **Fine food**, and then click OK.

FrontPage adds the item to the drop-down menu.

If you want one of the drop-down menu items to be selected by default, click the Selected option in the Initial State section of the Add Choice dialog box.

❻   Using the same method, add Hiking, Swimming, and Snoozing to the drop-down menu.

FrontPage adds the three new items to the menu.

❼   In the menu list, click Snoozing, and click the Remove button.

FrontPage removes the item from the menu list.

❽   In the menu list, click Swimming, and click the Move Up button twice.

FrontPage moves Swimming to the top of the drop-down menu.

❾   Click OK.

FrontPage displays the drop-down menu with its new contents on the form.

You cannot open the drop-down menu in Page view. It can be opened only when the Web page is loaded or pre-viewed in a Web browser.

tip

By default, drop-down menus work the same as radio buttons; the visitor can select only one item. However, you can modify a drop-down menu to allow the visitor to select multiple items. Just right-click the drop-down menu, click Form Field Properties, and in the Drop-Down Menu Properties dialog box, click the Yes option next to Allow Multiple Selections.

Add check boxes

In this exercise, you add check boxes to the form.

1 Click the line below the drop-down menu, type **Indoor Pastimes:** and press the Spacebar.

FrontPage moves the insertion point just to the right of your new text.

2 On the Insert menu, point to Form, and then click Check Box.

FrontPage inserts a check box to the right of the prompt text.

3 Type **Bingo** and press the Spacebar twice.

FrontPage inserts a label for the first check box.

4 On the Insert menu, point to Form, click Check Box, and type **Bridge**

FrontPage inserts another check box and label.

5 Drag the mouse to select both the word *Bridge* and the check box next to it.

The check box and its label are selected.

6 On the Insert menu, point to Form, and then click Label.

FrontPage makes the selected text into a clickable label for the check box. Now a form user can click either the check box itself or the label to check or uncheck the check box. If you like, you can use the same method to make the word *Bingo* a clickable label.

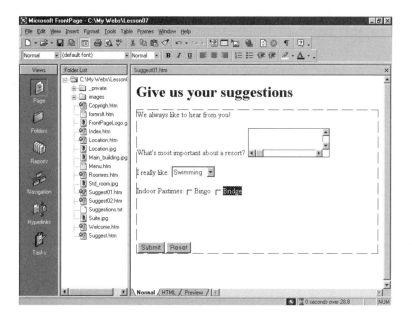

Delete form fields

In this exercise, you delete fields and their labels from a form.

1 Select the entire line containing the check boxes.

2 Press Delete.

The check boxes and text are deleted.

Save

3 On the toolbar, click the Save button.

FrontPage saves your changes.

Sending Form Data to an E-mail Address or a File

Once you have set up a form on your Web page, you need to know how to retrieve the information (the form data) entered by visitors to your Web site. By default, FrontPage sets up forms to send their data to a text file or Web page on the server. To retrieve the form data, you simply open the Web page in FrontPage. This page has the default filename of Form_results.txt.

However, you can change these defaults. You can route the form data to a different file on the Web server, to an e-mail address, to both a file and an e-mail address, to a database residing on the Web server, or to a Web server program.

Send form data to an e-mail address

If you are not working through this lesson sequentially, follow the steps in "Import the Lesson 7 Practice Web," earlier in this lesson, and in the Folder List, double-click the file Suggest02.htm.

In this exercise, you route form data to your e-mail address.

important

This exercise shows the steps you perform in FrontPage to route form data to an e-mail address. However, your Web server must be configured to support this operation. Ask your system administrator or Webmaster to set it up for you.

❶ Right-click a blank area of the form, and on the shortcut menu, click Form Properties.

FrontPage displays the Form Properties dialog box.

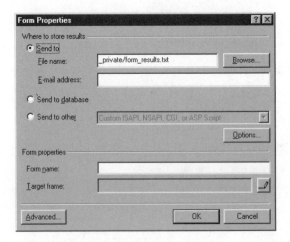

❷ In the E-mail Address text box, type your own e-mail address.

If you clicked OK at this point, the form data would be sent both to a text file on the Web server and to your e-mail address.

❸ Click in the File Name text box, delete the text, and then click OK.

FrontPage displays a dialog box explaining that your Web server must be configured before you can send form data to e-mail. The dialog box asks if you want to delete the e-mail address from the form.

❹ Click No.

Once your Webmaster or system administrator has configured the Web server, form data will be routed to your e-mail address.

> **tip**
> FrontPage also allows you to route form data to a database or a Web server program. However, these actions require that a database or server program be set up by your Webmaster. Web server programs are often used to process and summarize large amounts of data gathered from many Web site visitors.

Send form data to a text file

In this exercise, you send form data to a text file other than the default.

1 Right-click a blank area inside the form border, and on the shortcut menu, click Form Properties.

FrontPage displays the Form Properties dialog box.

2 In the File Name text box, delete any text currently in the text box.

3 Type **Suggestions.txt,** delete the contents of the E-mail Address text box, and click the Options button.

4 Click the File Format drop-down arrow, select Formatted Text, and click OK.

When a Web site visitor clicks the Submit Form button, data will be sent to a file named Suggestions.txt on the Web server. If the file does not yet exist, it will be automatically created the first time a Web site visitor uses the form.

Save

5 On the toolbar, click the Save button.

FrontPage saves your changes.

Test your form

In this exercise, you test the form you just created.

*Preview
In Browser*

1 On the toolbar, click the Preview In Browser button.

FrontPage starts your Web browser and displays the form page.

2 In the What's Most Important text box, type **The golf course!**

3 Click the Submit button.

Your Web browser displays a page indicating that your form will work when you publish your Web to a FrontPage-compliant Web server, as shown on the following page.

④ Click the Close button at the top-right corner of your Web browser window. Your Web browser closes and FrontPage reappears.

After you've published your Web to a FrontPage-compliant Web server, you'll be able to test your form pages "live." When you click the Submit button, the Web server will display a confirmation page.

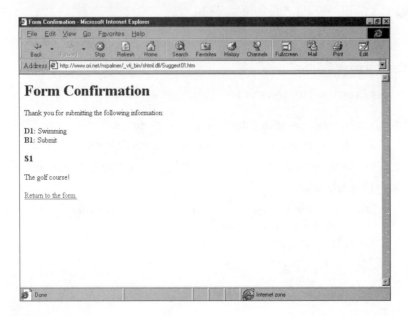

One Step Further

Creating a Guest Book

One of the most popular Web site features is the Guest Book page, which allows visitors to leave their names, e-mail addresses, and comments about a Web site. FrontPage provides a template that makes it easy for you to create a guest book page for your Web site. To create a guest book page, you simply create a new Web page based on the template, and then modify the default text as you wish.

Create a guest book

In this exercise, you create a guest book page, which will allow visitors to send feedback on the Web site.

1 On the File menu, point to New, and then click Page.

FrontPage displays the New dialog box.

2 Click the Guest Book icon, and then click OK.

FrontPage creates a guest book page and displays it in Page view. Web site visitors can type their comments in the scrolling text box, and then click the Submit Comments button to send their comments to the Web server.

You can add fields to the guest book form just as you would to any other form. Position the insertion point at the desired location, and on the Insert menu, point to Form, and click the desired field.

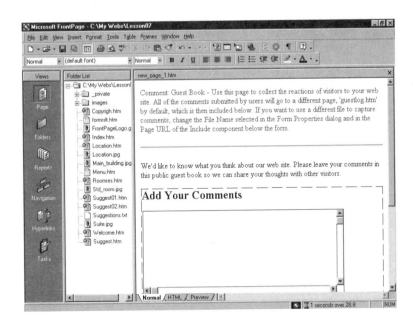

Creating Forms

3 Select everything above the form border, and then press Enter.

FrontPage deletes the comment and the default text, and creates a blank line above the form.

4 Type **Your feedback about the Web site is welcome!**

FrontPage adds the new text above the form.

Save

5 On the toolbar, click the Save button. Type **Feedback.htm** as the filename, and click the Save button in the dialog box.

FrontPage saves your guest book page.

tip

As you've probably guessed, a guest book page is just a special kind of form. By default, the data that Web site visitors enter on the guest book page is sent to the file Guestlog.htm on the Web server. You can create a link from your home page to Guestlog.htm so that other visitors can read the comments. You can also change the data's destination in the same way as you would with any other form: by right-clicking a blank area of the form, clicking Form Properties on the shortcut menu, and using the Form Properties dialog box to specify the new destination.

Finish the lesson

1 On the File menu, click Close Web.

2 For each page, if FrontPage prompts you to save changes, click Yes.

FrontPage saves your changes and closes the Lesson07 Web.

Lesson 7 Quick Reference

To	Do this
Create a form with the Form Page Wizard	On the Views bar, click the Page icon. On the File menu, point to New, and then click Page. In the New dialog box, click the Form Page Wizard icon, click OK, and follow the wizard's instructions to add form fields. When the form is complete, click the Finish button.

Lesson 7 Quick Reference

To	Do this
Add radio buttons with the Form Page Wizard	In the Form Page Wizard dialog box, click Next, and then click the Add button. In the type of input list, click One Of Several Options. In the Edit The Prompt For This Question text box, delete the default text, type your question, and click the Next button. Type a list of radio button labels, click the Radio Buttons option, type the name of the variable to hold the data the visitor enters, and click the Next button.
Add check boxes with the Form Page Wizard	In the Form Page Wizard dialog box, click the Add button. In the type of input list, click Any Of Several Options. In the Edit The Prompt For This Question text box, delete the default text, type your question, and click the Next button. Type a list of check box labels, type the name of the variable to hold the data the visitor enters, and click the Next button.
Edit form text	Open the Web page containing the form. Add and delete text just as you normally would.
Create a form from scratch	Create or open the Web page that will contain the form, and position the insertion point at the desired location. On the Insert menu, point to Form, and then click Form.
Add a form field to a form	Open the Web page containing the form, and position the insertion point at the desired location. On the Insert menu, point to Form, and click the type of field you want to insert.
Add choices to a drop-down menu	Insert the menu on a form, right-click the menu, and click Form Field Properties. Click the Add button, add a choice, and click OK. Repeat the process to add other menu choices.
Delete a form field	Drag the mouse to select the form field and its label, and press Delete.

7

Creating Forms

Lesson 7 Quick Reference

To	Do this
Change the destination of form data	Right-click a blank area of the form, click Form Properties, type the desired data destination, and click OK.
Create a guest book page	Click the Page icon on the Views bar. On the File menu, point to New, and then click Page. Click the Guest Book icon, and then click OK.

LESSON

8

Using Frames

ESTIMATED TIME 40 min.

In this lesson you will learn how to:

✔ *Design a Web site with frames.*
✔ *Create frames pages.*
✔ *Create no-frames pages.*
✔ *Create a front door page.*
✔ *Use shared borders.*

So far, everyone is pleased with your work on the Lakewood Mountains Resort Web site. You've used Microsoft FrontPage 2000 to create many impressive Web page features. But when you first planned the site back in Lesson 1, you decided that you would use frames to make the Web site easier to navigate. That feature is still on your to-do list. Both your boss and the Lakewood management are eager to see frames in action.

In this lesson, you will learn how to use frames on a Web site. You will learn how to create a frames page, how to create a contents frame, and how to create a no-frames alternative for people who either can't view frames in their Web browsers or just prefer not to. Finally, you will learn how to create frames and hyperlink menus using two of FrontPage's popular shortcuts: shared borders and navigation bars.

Import the Lesson 8 practice Web

In this exercise, you create a new Web based on the files in the Lesson08 folder in the Web Publishing SBS Practice folder. You will use this Web for all the exercises in Lesson 8.

1 On the File menu, point to New, and then click Web.

FrontPage displays the New dialog box.

If your hard drive is not drive C, substitute the appropriate letter in step 2.

2 Click the Import Web Wizard icon. In the Specify The Location Of The New Web text box, type **C:\My Webs\Lesson08**, and click OK.

FrontPage displays the first Import Web Wizard dialog box.

3 Click the From A Source Directory Of Files option, click the Include Subfolders check box, and click the Browse button.

4 Browse to the Lesson08 folder in the Web Publishing SBS Practice folder, and click OK.

5 Click Next twice, and then click Finish.

FrontPage creates a new Web based on the practice files and places it in the Lesson08 folder.

6 If the Folder List shows no file named Welcome.htm, right-click the file index.htm. On the shortcut menu, click Rename, type **Welcome.htm**, and press Enter.

FrontPage displays the Rename dialog box, asking if you want it to adjust hyperlinks to reflect the page's new filename.

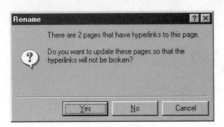

7 Click Yes.

FrontPage adjusts the hyperlinks.

Understanding Frames

Frames provide a way to divide a Web site visitor's screen into two or more areas, each of which contains a separate, independently scrolling Web page. FrontPage lets you create any of 10 different frame layouts, as shown in the Frames Pages section of the New dialog box.

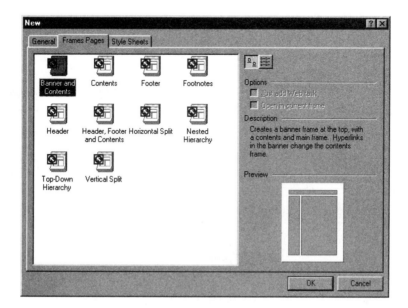

Frames earned a bad reputation when they were first introduced because they were overused and misused. Web page creators would put frames at the top of their Web sites, at the bottom, in the middle, and six ways around the ends. Web page visitors sometimes couldn't figure out what was going on.

The point of frames is to make a Web site easier, not more complicated, to view and navigate. Using too many frames or using them in ways that don't fit the content can confuse Web site visitors. A good rule of thumb is to use only as many frames as you really need. The most popular frame layout—a contents or menu frame on the left with a main frame on the right—uses only two frames. Another popular layout adds a banner frame at the top of the screen for a total of three frames. FrontPage lets you create these and eight other frame layouts.

Create a frames page

If you are not working through this lesson sequentially, follow the steps in "Import the Lesson 8 Practice Web," earlier in this lesson.

In this exercise, you create a frames page as the home page for the Lakewood Mountains Resort Web site.

1 On the Views bar, click the Page icon. On the File menu, point to New, and then click Page.

FrontPage displays the New dialog box.

2 Click the Frames Pages tab, click the Contents icon, and then click OK.

FrontPage creates a frames page and displays it in Page view.

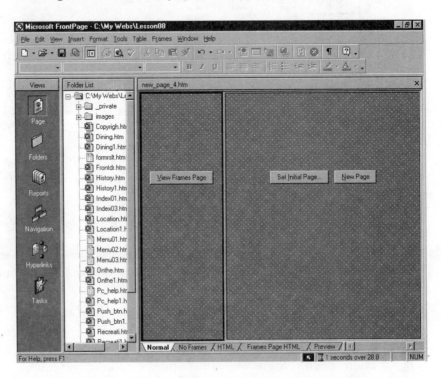

Assign Web pages to frames

In this exercise, you assign Web pages to frames in the frames page, save the frames page, and then preview the frames page in your Web browser.

1 Click Set Initial Page in the left frame. In the Create Hyperlink dialog box, scroll down until you see Menu01.htm, click Menu01.htm, and click OK.

FrontPage inserts the menu Web page in the contents frame on the left.

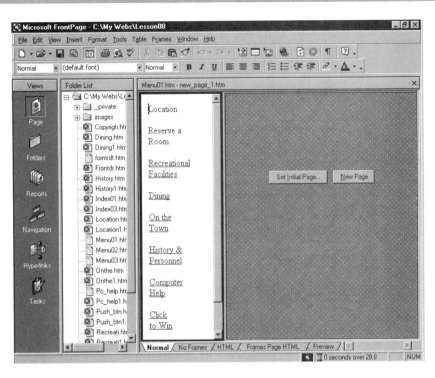

② Click Set Initial Page in the right frame. In the Create Hyperlink dialog box, scroll down the file list until you see Welcome.htm, click Welcome.htm, and click OK.

FrontPage inserts the Welcome page in the main frame at the right.

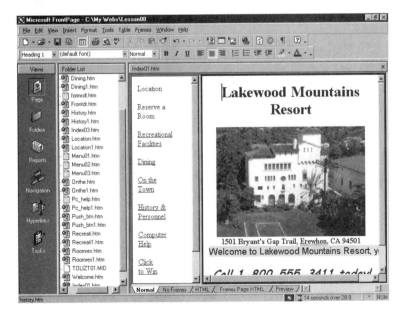

In the Save As dialog box, you can enter or change the page's title (which is different from its filename) by clicking the Change button.

Close

New

❸ On the File menu, click Save As, and then in the File Name text box, type **Index01a.htm**, and click the Save button.

FrontPage saves the frames page as the Web's home page.

❹ On the toolbar, click the Preview In Browser button.

FrontPage starts your Web browser and displays the frames page.

❺ Click the Close button at the top-right corner of your Web browser window.

Your Web browser closes and FrontPage reappears.

tip

When you're creating a frames page, you can either use existing pages to fill the frames, or you can create new pages to put in the frames. To create a new page and insert it in a frame, click the New button.

Create hyperlinks in the contents frame

In this exercise, you create hyperlinks in the contents frame and verify the result in your Web browser.

❶ In the contents frame on the left, double-click the word *Location*, right-click the selected text, and on the shortcut menu, click Hyperlink.

FrontPage displays the Create Hyperlink dialog box.

❷ Scroll down the file list, click the file Location.htm, and click OK.

FrontPage inserts the hyperlink in the selected text.

❸ In the contents frame on the left, select the text *Reserve a Room*, right-click the selected text, and on the shortcut menu, click Hyperlink.

FrontPage displays the Create Hyperlink dialog box.

❹ Scroll down the file list, click Roomres.htm, and click OK.

FrontPage inserts the hyperlink in the selected text.

Save

Preview In Browser

❺ On the toolbar, click the Save button.

FrontPage saves the frames page, the menu page, and the main frame page with your changes.

❻ On the toolbar, click the Preview In Browser button.

FrontPage starts your Web browser and displays the frames page.

❼ In the contents frame, click the Location hyperlink.

The Lakewood Mountains Resort Location page is redisplayed in the main frame.

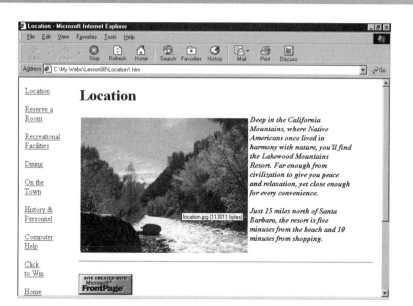

8   In the contents frame, click the Reserve a Room hyperlink.

The Reserve a Room page is displayed in the main frame.

9   Click the Close button at the top-right corner of your Web browser window.

Your Web browser closes and FrontPage reappears.

Close

Providing No-Frames Alternatives

Not everyone likes to use frames, and some older Web browsers can't display frames. For these reasons, it's wise to create a no-frames alternative for Web site visitors who either can't use frames or prefer not to do so.

There are essentially three approaches to providing a no-frames alternative for your Web site. The first is to do nothing. When you create a frames page, FrontPage creates a default no-frames page for Web site visitors whose browsers won't display frames. The page simply informs visitors that the Web site uses frames, that their browser won't display frames, and, therefore, that they are "out of luck" if they want to view the site. Because the no-frames message is all that the visitor sees, this is not a practical alternative for most serious Web sites. Certainly, you don't want Lakewood Mountains Resort to lose potential guests—even if only a small number of potential guests—just because their Web browsers won't display frames.

Using Frames

The second approach is to create a parallel Web hierarchy with pages that do not use frames. You then set up your Web site with a *front door* page that lets visitors select the frames or no-frames version of the Web site. This involves a certain amount of extra work, but with FrontPage, it's not as difficult as it sounds.

The third approach is somewhere in the middle. You still create a parallel hierarchy that contains no-frames versions of your Web pages. However, instead of creating a front door page, you put a no-frames version of your home page in the no-frames page that was automatically created by FrontPage. This lets visitors with older, no-frames Web browsers view your site, but does not allow visitors to choose whether they want to use frames. No-frames browsers get the no-frames Web pages; frames-capable browsers get the frames pages.

important

If you're creating a Web for a company intranet, federal law might require you to create a no-frames alternative for employees protected under the Americans with Disabilities Act (ADA).

Create a no-frames page

If you are not working through this lesson sequentially, follow the steps in "Import the Lesson 8 Practice Web," earlier in this lesson.

New

In this exercise, you create a no-frames home page for the Lakewood Mountains Resort Web site.

① On the Views bar, click the Page icon. On the toolbar, click the New button.

FrontPage creates a new Web page and displays it in Page view.

② On the Table menu, point to Insert, and click Table.

FrontPage displays the Insert Table dialog box.

③ Type **1** in the Rows text box, and type **100** in the Specify Width text box, if necessary. Verify that In Percent is selected, and click OK.

FrontPage inserts a two-column, one-row table on the page.

④ Verify that the insertion point is in the left table cell and on the Insert menu, click File. In the Select File dialog box, browse to the Lesson08 Web in the My Webs folder, click Menu02.htm, and then click the Open button.

FrontPage inserts the contents of the hyperlinks menu page into the left table cell. The hyperlinks, however, still point to frames pages. You will re-target the hyperlinks in the next exercise.

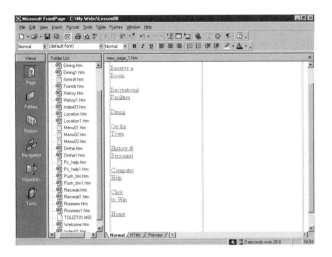

⑤ Use the mouse to drag the table column's right border to the left until the column is just wide enough for the longest line of hyperlink text.

⑥ Right-click the right column of the table, and on the shortcut menu, click Cell Properties.

FrontPage displays the Cell Properties dialog box.

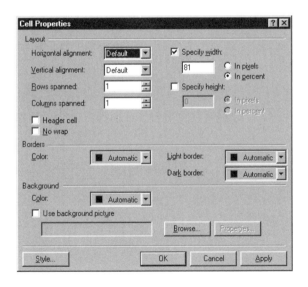

7 Click the Vertical Alignment drop-down arrow, click Top, and click OK.

FrontPage will align any content with the top of the cell.

8 On the Insert menu, click File. In the Select File dialog box, click Welcome.htm, and click the Open button.

FrontPage inserts the content of the Welcome page into the right column of the table.

9 On the File menu, click Save As to display the Save As dialog box. In the File Name text box, type **Index02.htm** and click the Save button.

FrontPage saves the no-frames home page.

Retarget hyperlinks to no-frames pages

In this exercise, you retarget hyperlinks in the no-frames page's menu column and then preview the page in your Web browser.

1 In the left column of the table, right-click the Location hyperlink, and on the shortcut menu, click Hyperlink Properties.

FrontPage displays the Edit Hyperlink dialog box.

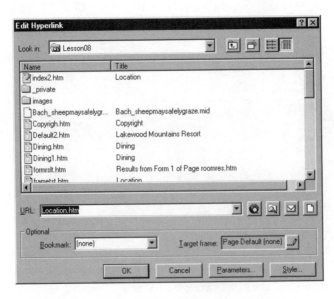

You would normally have had to create Location1.htm; in this exercise, it has been created for you.

2 In the file list, click Location1.htm, and click OK.

FrontPage retargets the hyperlink to a no-frames version of the Location Web page.

❸ Right-click the Reserve a Room hyperlink, and click Hyperlink Properties. In the Edit Hyperlink dialog box, click Roomres1.htm, and click OK.

FrontPage retargets the hyperlink to a no-frames version of the Reserve a Room page.

tip
If you wish, you can retarget the rest of the hyperlinks. The no-frames pages all end in "1.htm," such as Location1.htm, Push_btn1.htm, and so forth.

Save

*Preview
In Browser*

❹ On the toolbar, click the Save button, and then click the Preview In Browser button.

FrontPage saves your changes and opens the page in your Web browser.

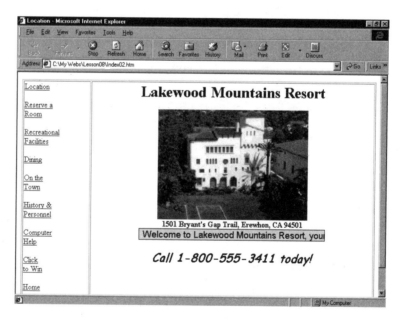

❺ Click the Location hyperlink in the left column.

Your Web browser displays Location1.htm. Notice that this page is designed so that the left column of the table displays a Web site menu, giving the appearance of a contents frame.

Close

❻ Click the Close button at the top-right corner of your Web browser window.

Your Web browser closes and FrontPage is redisplayed.

Create a front door Web page

In this exercise, you create a front door page for the Web site, which lets visitors choose whether they want to view frames or no-frames Web pages.

1 In the Folder List, double-click the file Frontdr.htm.

FrontPage displays the Frontdoor Web page in Page view. A page heading and photo have already been inserted for you.

2 Click the line below the hotel photo. On the Table menu, point to Insert, and click Table.

FrontPage displays the Insert Table dialog box.

3 Type **1** in the Rows text box, type **50** in the Specify Width text box, and click OK.

FrontPage inserts a table under the photo.

Center

4 On the Table menu, point to Select, and click Table. On the Formatting toolbar, click the Center button.

FrontPage centers the table under the photo.

5 Click in the left cell of the table, type **Use Frames**, and select the cell's text.

6 Right-click the selected text, and on the shortcut menu, click Hyperlink. In the file list, select Index01.htm, and click OK.

FrontPage inserts a hyperlink to the frames page.

7 Click in the right cell of the table, type **No Frames**, and select the cell's text.

8 Right-click the selected text and on the shortcut menu, click Hyperlink. In the file list, select Index03.htm, and click OK.

FrontPage inserts a hyperlink to the no-frames home page.

Save

9 On the toolbar, click the Save button.

FrontPage saves your changes.

Test the front door page

In this exercise, you test the front door page that lets visitors choose whether they view a frames or no-frames version of the Web site.

Preview In Browser

1 On the toolbar, click the Preview In Browser button.

FrontPage starts your Web browser.

2 Click the No Frames hyperlink.

Your Web browser displays the no-frames home page.

❸ Click the Location hyperlink.

Your Web browser displays a no-frames version of the Location page.

Back

❹ Click the Web browser's Back button twice.

Your Web browser redisplays the front door page.

❺ Click the Use Frames hyperlink.

Your Web browser displays the frames home page.

Close

❻ Click the Close button at the top-right corner of your Web browser window.

Your Web browser closes and FrontPage reappears.

Fill in FrontPage's default no-frames page

In this exercise, you add content to a no-frames page.

❶ In the Folder List, double-click the file Index03.htm.

FrontPage displays the no-frames version of the home page in Page view.

❷ On the Table menu, point to Select, and then click Table.

FrontPage selects the table containing the hyperlink menu and the home page content.

❸ On the Edit menu, click Copy.

FrontPage copies the table to the Windows Clipboard.

❹ In the Folder List, double-click the file Index01.htm.

FrontPage displays the frames version of the Lakewood Mountains Resort home page in Page view.

❺ Click the No Frames tab at the bottom of the FrontPage window.

Click here

FrontPage displays the default no-frames page.

❻ Select the default text. On the Edit menu, click Paste.

FrontPage deletes the default text and pastes the no-frames home page into the no-frames page.

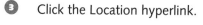

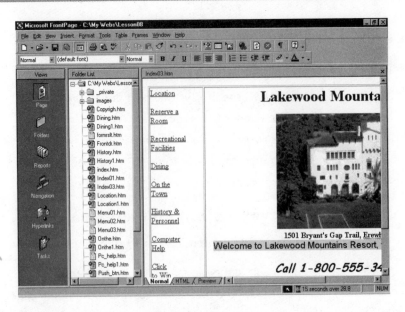

Save

❼   On the toolbar, click the Save button.

FrontPage saves your changes.

<table>
<tr><td>One
Step
Further</td><td></td></tr>
</table>

Using Shared Borders and Navigation Bars

FrontPage makes it easy to create a Web site with frames, but there's an even easier method than you've seen so far. Instead of creating a frames page and assigning a page to each separate frame, you can just apply *shared borders* either to your whole Web site or to individual Web pages. A shared border is a frame that appears along the top, left, or bottom of a Web site visitor's screen. The shared border contains a FrontPage component called a *navigation bar* that automatically creates and displays hyperlinks to selected pages of your Web site.

In spite of the ease with which shared borders and navigation bars can be set up, they do have two minor disadvantages. First, navigation bars offer less flexibility than you can get if you create a frame and insert hyperlinks manually. A navigation bar will display only certain hyperlinks; you can customize it, but not much. Second, navigation bars won't work until you create a hierarchy in Navigation view—something that requires that your Web server have the FrontPage Server Extensions.

Create a Web hierarchy

If you are not working through this lesson sequentially, follow the steps in "Import the Lesson 8 Practice Web," earlier in this lesson.

In this exercise, you create a three-page Web hierarchy so that FrontPage's navigation bars will work correctly.

1   On the Views bar, click the Navigation icon.

FrontPage displays the Web in Navigation view. At present, only the home page (Welcome.htm, titled Lakewood Mountains Resort) is displayed in the Web hierarchy.

2   In the Folder List, click the file Location.htm, and drag it below the home page until a line connects it to the home page.

FrontPage inserts the Location page as a child of the home page.

3   In the Folder List, click the file Onthe.htm, and drag it below the Location page until a line connects it to the Location page.

FrontPage inserts the On the Town page as a child of the Location page.

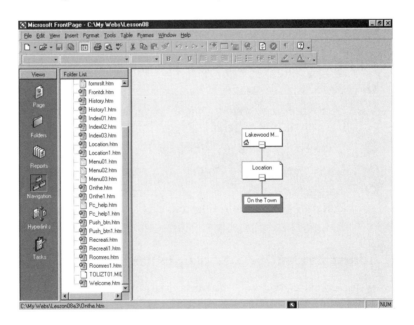

Create shared borders

In this exercise, you create shared borders for the pages in your Web hierarchy.

1   In Navigation view, double-click the Location page icon.

FrontPage opens the Location page in Page view.

❷ On the Format menu, click Shared Borders.

FrontPage displays the Shared Borders dialog box.

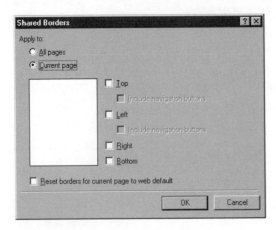

❸ Make sure the Current Page option is selected, and click the Left check box to select it.

Notice that the dialog box displays a preview of the shared border layout.

❹ Click OK.

FrontPage creates a left shared border for the Location page. A navigation bar with default hyperlinks appears at the top of the shared border.

❺ In the Folder List, double-click the file Onthe.htm.

FrontPage opens the On the Town page in Page view.

❻ On the Format menu, click Shared borders. In the dialog box, make sure the Current Page option is selected, click the Left check box, and click OK.

FrontPage creates a left shared border for the On the Town page.

Adjust navigation bar properties

In this exercise, you will adjust navigation bar properties to include links to the home page and the On the Town page.

❶ Right-click the On the Town page's navigation bar, and on the shortcut menu, click Navigation Bar Properties.

FrontPage displays the Navigation Bar Properties dialog box. Notice that the Child Level option is selected.

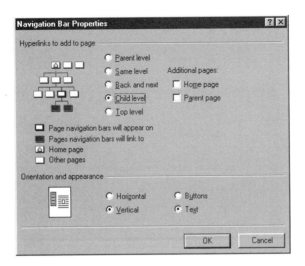

❷ Click the Parent Page check box, and click the Home Page check box.

The navigation bar will include a link to the page just above the On the Town page (its "parent page") in the Web hierarchy. It will also include a link to the home page.

❸ Click OK.

FrontPage adjusts the navigation bar properties. The navigation bar now shows two links: Home, leading to the home page, and Up, leading to the parent page.

Save

Close

❹ On the toolbar, click the Save button, and then click the Close button at the top-right corner of the On the Town page.

FrontPage saves your changes, closes the On the Town page, and redisplays the Location page.

❺ Right-click the navigation bar and click Navigation Bar Properties on the shortcut menu.

FrontPage displays the Navigation Bar Properties dialog box.

❻ If necessary, click the Home Page and Parent Page check boxes, make sure the Child Level option is selected, and click OK.

The navigation bar now shows two links: Home, leading to the home page, and On the Town, leading to the On the Town page. There is no separate link for a parent page because the home page is the Location page's parent page in the Web hierarchy.

Save

❼ On the toolbar, click the Save button.

FrontPage saves your changes.

Test shared borders and navigation bars

In this exercise, you test the shared borders and navigation bars in your Web browser.

Preview In Browser

1 On the toolbar, click the Preview In Browser button.

FrontPage starts your Web browser and displays the Location page. Notice the navigation bar links at the left side of the page.

Navigation bar links →

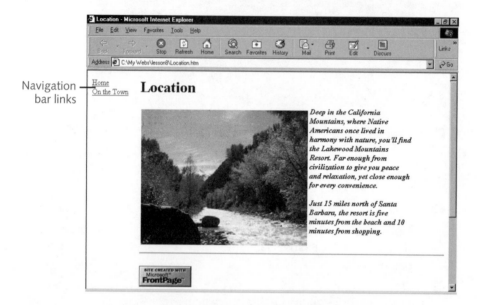

2 On the navigation bar, click the On the Town hyperlink.

Your Web browser displays the On the Town page.

3 On the navigation bar, click the Home hyperlink.

Your Web browser displays the home page.

Finish the lesson

Close

1 Click the Close button at the top-right corner of your Web browser window.

Your Web browser closes and FrontPage reappears.

2 On the File menu, click Close Web.

3 For each page, if FrontPage prompts you to save changes, click Yes.

FrontPage saves your changes and closes the Lesson08 Web.

Lesson 8 Quick Reference

To	Do this
Create a frames page	On the Views bar, click Page. On the File menu, point to New, click Page, and click the Frames Pages tab. Click the desired frame layout, and click OK.
Assign Web pages to frames	Click Set Initial Page, click the Web page to assign, and click OK. Repeat for other frames in the frames page.
Create hyperlinks in the contents frame	Type and select the text for the link, right-click the selected text, and on the shortcut menu, click Hyperlink. Click the target file, and then click OK.
Create a no-frames version of a frames page	Create a new, blank page. On the Table menu, point to Insert and click Table. Enter the appropriate number of rows and columns, set height and width, and click OK. Click in a table cell. On the Insert menu, click File, navigate to the desired folder, click the desired file, and click OK. Repeat for each table cell.
Retarget a hyperlink to a no-frames page	Right-click the hyperlink, click Hyperlink Properties, click the target file, and click OK.
Create a front door Web page	Create a new, blank page. On the new page, insert the desired content and two hyperlinks. One link should lead to the frames home page, and the other to the no-frames home page.
Fill in the default no-frames page	Display the framed home page in Page view and click the No Frames tab. Delete the default text and insert or paste the desired content.
Create shared borders and navigation bars	Click the Navigation icon on the Views bar and create a Web hierarchy. On the Format menu, click Shared Borders. Click either the All Pages or Selected Pages option, click the check box for the desired border layout, and click OK.
Adjust navigation bar properties	Display a page in Page view and right-click the navigation bar. In the dialog box, click the desired check boxes and options, and then click OK.

9

Publishing a Web

**ESTIMATED
TIME
30 min.**

In this lesson you will learn how to:

✔ *Check spelling on Web pages.*

✔ *Publish a Web locally.*

✔ *Publish a Web to a Web server.*

✔ *Update a Web on a Web server.*

✔ *Maintain a Web.*

✔ *Delete a Web.*

✔ *Publish a Web to a non–FrontPage-compliant Web server.*

Your work on the Lakewood Mountains Resort Web site has been a success. Using the tools provided by Microsoft FrontPage 2000, you've created an attractive and useful set of Web pages. There's just one thing left to do: publish your Web to a Web server.

In this lesson, you will learn how to check spelling on your Web pages prior to publishing them on the Internet or on a company intranet, how to publish your Web locally to make a backup copy of your Web files, how to publish your Web to a Web server that has the FrontPage Server Extensions and to a Web server that does not, how to update and maintain your Web on the Web server, how to rename your Web, and how to delete your Web from a Web server.

Import the Lesson 9 practice Web

In this exercise, you create a new Web based on the files in the Lesson09 folder in the Web Publishing SBS Practice folder. You will use this Web for all the exercises in Lesson 9.

1 On the File menu, point to New, and then click Web.

FrontPage displays the New dialog box.

If your hard disk drive has a drive letter other than C, substitute the appropriate drive letter in step 2.

2 Click the Import Web Wizard icon. In the Specify The Location Of The New Web text box, delete the default text and type **C:\My Webs\Lesson09**, and click OK.

FrontPage displays the first Import Web Wizard dialog box.

3 Click the From A Source Directory Of Files option, click the Include Subfolders check box, and click the Browse button.

4 Browse to the Lesson09 folder in the Web Publishing SBS Practice folder, and click OK.

5 Click Next twice, and then click Finish.

FrontPage creates a new Web based on the practice files and places it in the Lesson09 folder.

Checking the Spelling on Web Pages

Before you publish a Web—whether on the Internet or on a company intranet—you want to make it as close to perfect as you can. Careless errors make a bad impression that extends beyond the Web site to your company itself.

At Impact Public Relations, your marketing copywriters have a saying: "No wun spels perfecly all the thyme." No matter how carefully you type information on the Web pages for Lakewood Mountains Resort, at least a few spelling errors are inevitable. To catch and correct these errors, you can use FrontPage's spelling checking feature. The spelling checker compares the words on your Web pages to the entries in its own spelling list. If FrontPage doesn't find a word in its list, it flags the word as a possible misspelling.

By default, FrontPage's spelling checker checks words as you type them on a page and underlines any words it doesn't recognize. If you like, you can correct any suspect words as soon as you see the spelling checker underline them. Because proper names and many technical terms are not included in the spelling dictionary, they are often flagged by the spelling checker. Click the Ignore button to continue checking spelling without changing the flagged word.

Most users prefer to check spelling all at once, checking a full page of text or the entire Web. In this section, you'll learn how to check spelling on an individual Web page or on your entire Web.

> ## tip
> Running a spelling check is very helpful, but it's no substitute for proofreading Web pages with your own eyes. For example, in the marketing copywriters' adage, the word *time* is misspelled as *thyme*. FrontPage's spelling checker, however, wouldn't catch that error, because *thyme* is a real word—although the wrong word in this particular context.

Check spelling on a single Web page

If you are not working through this lesson sequentially, follow the steps in "Import the Lesson 9 Practice Web," earlier in this lesson.

In this exercise, you check and correct spelling on a single page of the Lakewood Mountains Resort Web.

1 In the Folder List, double-click the file History.htm.

FrontPage displays the History and Personnel page in Page view.

2 On the Tools menu, click Spelling.

FrontPage displays the Spelling dialog box. FrontPage has flagged the word *Bromo* because the word doesn't appear in the spelling checker's word list. In this case, you know that Bromo is a proper name and is spelled correctly.

You can also press the F7 function key to check spelling.

Spelling	? X
Not in Dictionary:	Bromo
Change To:	Broom
Suggestions:	Broom / Brome / Brooms

Ignore   Ignore All
Change   Change All
Add   Suggest

Cancel

3 Click the Ignore button.

FrontPage displays the next apparent misspelling. In this case, the word *hotel* has been misspelled as *hotl*.

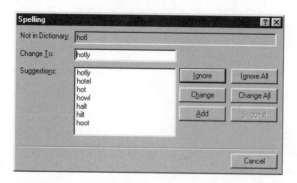

4 In the Suggestions list, click *hotel*, and then click the Change button.

FrontPage corrects the word on the Web page and displays the next apparent misspelling.

5 In the Suggestions list, click *problem*, and then click the Change button.

FrontPage corrects the word on the Web page and displays the next apparent misspelling. You know that *M.I.T.* is short for Massachusetts Institute of Technology, so the word is not misspelled.

6 Click the Ignore button.

FrontPage displays a message box stating that the spelling check is complete.

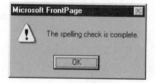

Save

7 On the toolbar, click the Save button.

FrontPage saves your changes.

8 On the File menu, click Close.

FrontPage closes the History and Personnel Web page.

tip

If you need to see a word in context to determine if it's misspelled, you can drag the Spelling dialog box to one side of the screen.

Check spelling on an entire Web

In this exercise, you check and correct spelling on the entire Lakewood Mountains Resort Web.

❶ On the Views bar, click the Navigation icon, and then on the Tools menu, click Spelling.

FrontPage displays the Spelling dialog box. The Entire Web option is selected.

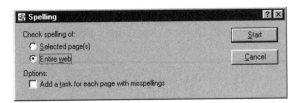

tip

If you want to have FrontPage locate spelling errors now, but you don't want to correct spelling until a later session, you can click the check box labeled Add A Task For Each Page With Misspellings, and then click the Start button. FrontPage will compile a list of pages with spelling errors and add them as tasks in Tasks view. When you decide to correct spelling, click the Tasks icon on the Views bar, and double-click pages that are flagged as having misspelled words.

❷ Click the Start button.

FrontPage displays a list of pages with apparent spelling errors. In each row, FrontPage lists the page, the number of apparent errors on that page, and the words that seem to be misspelled.

Publishing a Web

9

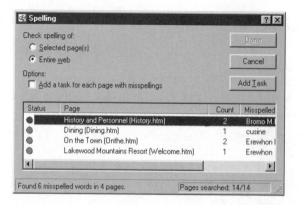

❸   In the Spelling dialog box, double-click the file Dining.htm.

FrontPage displays the Dining page in Page view and flags the misspelling.

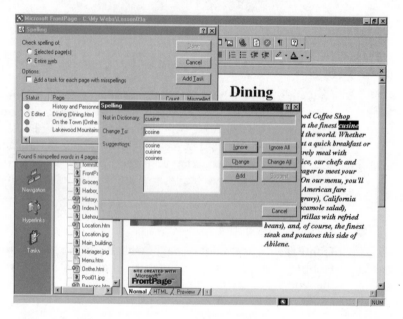

❹   In the Suggestions list, click *cuisine*, and then click the Change button.

FrontPage corrects the word and displays the Continue With Next Document? dialog box, as shown on the following page.

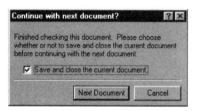

⑤ Click the Next Document button.

FrontPage saves your changes to the Dining page, closes the Dining page, and displays the next Web page that contains spelling errors.

⑥ Click the Cancel button three times to close the dialog boxes.

FrontPage ends the spelling check.

Publishing a Web

Once you've checked your Web for spelling errors, you're ready to publish it. Publishing your Web is the reason you've worked so hard to create a good looking Web in FrontPage. You should also publish a copy of your Web locally on your own hard disk drive. This local copy serves as a backup. If you make changes to your working copy of the Web (the one you will publish to a server) and then want to undo those changes, you can refer to this original copy of your Web (your locally published copy).

Before you can publish your Web, you should get the following information from your Internet service provider (ISP) or system administrator.

- The address of your Web server.
- The preferred home page name (index.htm or default.htm).
- The FTP server address if your Web server does not have the FrontPage Server Extensions).
- Folder information (if your Web server does not have the FrontPage Server Extensions).

Your Publishing Options

Many ISPs offer free Web hosting to their customers. To take advantage of this, you usually have to upload your Web to a subdirectory under the ISP's domain name. If your ISP's server name is isphost.com and your name is Tom Smith, for example, your Web address might be *www.isphost.com/ users/tsmith*. Depending on the purpose of the Web, this might be an acceptable option. However, this approach has several drawbacks. First, free Web space is often limited to 5 MB or less—not enough for a complex Web or a business Web site. Second, you have little control over the Web address you're assigned. For a commercial Web site, it's important that the address be easy to remember and type. To create a professional Web site, it is a good idea to register your own domain name, such as ActiveEd.com or HansonBrothers.net, using your company name or some variation, and set up a business Web site with a Web hosting company that can provide the space your site will need (typically 5 MB to 100 MB).

Before you can register a domain name, you must have the following information:

- Administrative contact (information for the person who will manage the registration paperwork).

- Technical contact (information for the person who will manage and update your Web site).

- Billing contact (information for the person who will handle payment for your domain name registration and the ultimate owner of the Web).

- Server names (the primary and secondary domain names of the server that will host your Web; your ISP can provide these to you).

- Net addresses (the IP addresses for your host server names; your ISP can provide these also).

Register your domain name

These steps are subject to change.

1. Start your browser and navigate to *www.internic.net*. Click in the Search text box.

2. Type your desired domain name in the text box and press Enter. Repeat the search, trying different variations of the name, until you receive a No Match Found message.

   You now have an unused domain name that you can register.

(continued)

continued

③ Make sure that your Web hosting service has mapped your domain name to their server names and net addresses.

④ Navigate to *www.internic.net* again, and click the Web Version Step-by-Step hyperlink under the Type column.

⑤ At the bottom of the page, click the Forms hyperlink. Enter the necessary information. Make sure the New Registration option is selected.

⑥ Click the Step 1: Organization Information Section button, enter the requested information, and click the Step 2: Technical Contact Information button.

⑦ Follow the steps to finish registering your domain name.

InterNIC will send e-mail confirmation. Copy this information and send it to *hostmaster@internic.net*. You will be mailed a printed invoice so that you can make payment.

Publish your Web locally

If you are not working through this lesson sequentially, follow the steps in "Import the Lesson 9 Practice Web," earlier in this lesson.

In this exercise, you publish a copy of your Web to your hard disk drive on your computer.

① On the File menu, click Publish Web.

FrontPage displays the Publish Web dialog box.

If your hard disk has a drive letter other than C, substitute the appropriate drive letter in step 2.

② In the Specify The Location To Publish Your Web To text box, type **C:\My Webs\Copy of Lesson09 Web**, and then click the Publish button.

FrontPage publishes a copy of your Web to your hard disk drive and displays a message box confirming that the Web site was published successfully.

3 Click the Done button.

FrontPage closes the message box.

Publish your Web to a Web server

In this exercise, you publish your Web to a Web server that has FrontPage Server Extensions—what is often referred to as a *FrontPage-compliant* Web server.

important

In order to complete the following exercise, you must have access to a Web server that has the FrontPage Server Extensions. You can find a list of Web hosting services that have the FrontPage Server Extensions at *www.microsoft.saltmine.com/frontpage/wpp/list/*.

1 If necessary, connect to the Internet or to the intranet to which you'll publish your Web.

2 On the File menu, click Publish Web.

FrontPage displays the Publish Web dialog box.

To find out the URL of your Web server and the folder to which your Web is published, check with your ISP, Web hosting service, or system administrator.

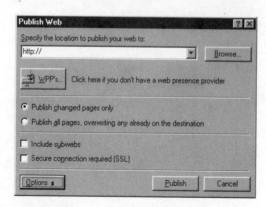

❸ In the Specify The Location To Publish Your Web To text box, type the URL of your Web server and the folder to which your Web should be published.

❹ Click the Publish button.

FrontPage connects to your Web server and for some servers, displays the Name And Password Required dialog box.

❺ If prompted, type your name in the Name text box, type your password in the Password text box, and click OK.

FrontPage publishes your Web to the selected folder of the Web server and displays a message box confirming that the Web site was published successfully.

❻ Click the Done button.

tip
On most Web servers, your user name and password are *case sensitive*, which means that the uppercase version of a letter is treated as a completely distinct letter from its lowercase counterpart. For example, if your password is *microsoft* and you type it *Microsoft*, the password will be rejected. Be sure to type your user name and password exactly as they were created for your account.

Publishing Your Web to Public Web Hosts

The number of ISPs and Web hosting services that support FrontPage is growing rapidly. (If you're not sure whether your ISP or Web hosting service has the FrontPage Server Extensions, its technical support staff can tell you.) However, some Web hosting services—especially free services—do not have the FrontPage Server Extensions.

There are two ways to publish your Web to these sites. First, you can use FTP (File Transfer Protocol), discussed later in this lesson. In many cases, however, the Web host has its own method that allows you to upload files to your folder on the Web server. GeoCities, as shown in the following figure, has a "file manager" that enables you to select files on your hard disk drive, one at a time, and upload them to your GeoCities Web folder.

You can also use the file manager to view and edit your Web page files on the server. Other public Web sites offer similar methods.

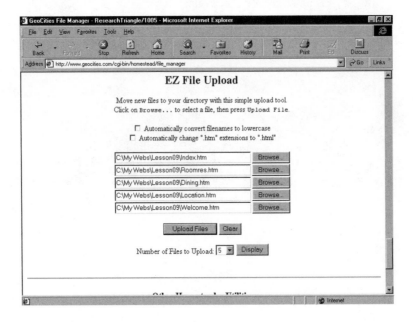

Updating and Maintaining a Web

Once you've published a Web, the job's not over. You'll continually update and improve your Web, both to enhance it with new ideas and to respond to requests from clients, such as the management of Lakewood Mountains Resort.

In this section, you will learn how to update some or all pages of your Web on a Web server, how to open a Web from the server in FrontPage, how to edit and delete your Web files on the server, how to rename your Web on the server, and how to delete your Web from the server.

Open your Web located on the Web server

To complete the following exercise, you must have published your Web to a Web server.

In this exercise, you use FrontPage to open your Web located on the remote Web server.

1 On the File menu, click Open Web.

FrontPage displays the Open Web dialog box.

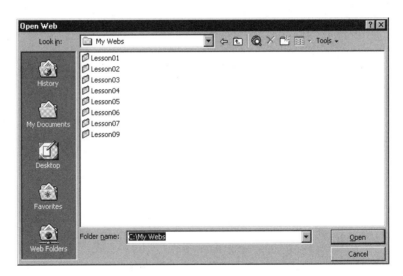

2 Click the Folder Name text box, type the URL of your Web site, and then click Open.

Your Web server may prompt you for a user name and password.

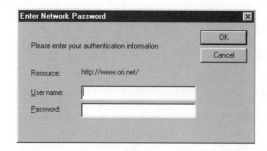

3 If prompted, type your user ID, and press Tab.

Your user or administrator ID is entered, and the insertion point moves to the Password text box.

4 If prompted, type your password, and then click OK.

FrontPage displays a list of your Web files on the Web server.

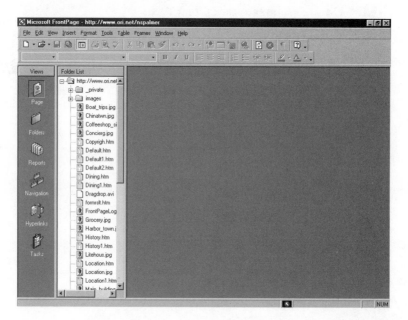

5 If necessary, click the file for the home page (index.htm or default.htm) and click the Open button.

FrontPage opens your home page in Page view from the Web server.

Publishing a Web

tip

When you open a file located on the Web server, FrontPage displays it in Page view, just the same as if you had opened a local copy of the file from your hard disk drive.

If you are connecting to your Web server with a dial-up connection, it might take a few minutes for your home page and Web information to download to your computer. While the download is in progress, FrontPage will display the message "Requesting data" in the status bar in the lower-left corner of your screen.

Maintain your Web

The Lakewood Mountains Resort manager has pointed out an error on the Web site that you need to correct. You've also found an unused video file that you want to delete to save space on the server.

In this exercise, you perform routine maintenance on your Web while it resides on the Web server.

1   In the Folder List, double-click the file History.htm.

FrontPage downloads the page from the Web server and displays it in Page view.

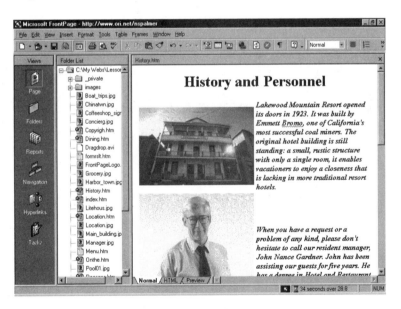

2   In the second line of body text, click between the *2* and the *3* in *1923*.

FrontPage positions the insertion point in the text.

Save

3 Press the Delete key once, and then type **4**.

FrontPage changes the date of the resort's founding to 1924.

4 On the toolbar, click the Save button.

FrontPage saves your change to the History.htm file on the Web server. Because you are updating a file on the remote Web server, it takes a little longer than it would if the file were on your hard disk drive.

5 In the Folder List, click the file Dragdrop.avi.

FrontPage selects the Dragdrop.avi file on the Web server.

6 Press the Delete key.

FrontPage displays the Confirm Delete dialog box.

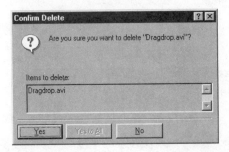

7 Click Yes.

FrontPage deletes the file from the Web server.

Update your Web on the Web server

In this exercise, you update your Web on a Web server that has the FrontPage Server Extensions. When you update a Web, you upload new Web pages or revised versions of existing Web pages.

1 On the File menu, click Publish Web.

FrontPage displays the Publish Web dialog box.

2 Click the Options button.

FrontPage displays the Options section of the dialog box. Notice that the Publish Changed Pages Only option is selected. With this option selected, FrontPage will upload pages to the server only if they've been changed since they were originally published on the server.

3 If you want to upload copies of all your Web page files, not just the ones that have changed, click the Publish All Pages option.

④ In the Specify The Location To Publish Your Web To text box, type the URL of your Web server and the folder to which your Web should be published.

⑤ Click the Publish button.

FrontPage connects to your Web server and, on some servers, displays the Name And Password Required dialog box.

If a dialog box asks whether or not to overwrite a file, click Yes.

⑥ If prompted, type your name in the Name text box, type your password in the Password text box, and click OK.

FrontPage updates your Web page files on the Web server and displays a message box confirming that the Web site was published successfully.

⑦ Click the Done button.

⑧ On the File menu, click Close Web.

FrontPage closes your Web.

Rename your Web

By default, your Web name is the same as the name of the folder in which your Web is kept—whether on your local hard disk drive or on the remote Web server. For example, if your Web is in a folder named *Lakewood*, FrontPage would title your Web simply *Lakewood*. In this exercise, you rename your Web.

important

The steps for renaming a Web are the same whether you're renaming a Web on your local hard disk drive or on the remote Web server. However, depending on your access permissions, you might not be able to rename your Web on the Web server. Check with your system administrator if you need help.

① On the Tools menu, click Web Settings.

FrontPage displays the Web Settings dialog box.

Publishing a Web

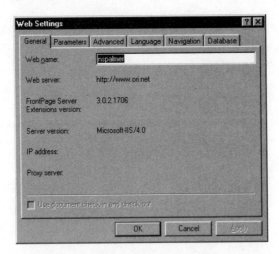

2 In the Web Name text box, delete the default name, type **Lakewood Mountains Resort** or another new name for the Web, and click OK.

FrontPage renames your Web.

Delete your Web files from the Web server

There are two ways in which you can delete your Web from a remote Web server. First, you can delete all the files in your Web but leave the Web folder intact. Second, you can delete the files and the Web folder. You can easily delete your Web files, but it's best to leave deleting your Web folder to your Web administrator.

In this exercise, you delete your Web files from the Web server.

To delete individual files from a Web server, simply select only the files you want to delete instead of selecting all the Web files.

1 Open your Web on the Web server using the steps described in the exercise "Open Your Web Located on the Web Server," earlier in this lesson.

FrontPage displays your Web server files in the Folder List.

2 On the Views bar, click the Folders icon.

FrontPage displays the Web files in Folders view.

3 On the Edit menu, click Select All.

FrontPage selects all the files in the Web folder.

4 Press the Delete key.

FrontPage displays a dialog box asking you to confirm the deletion.

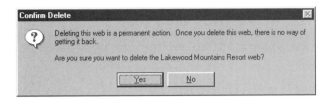

5 Click Yes.

FrontPage deletes the files from the Web server.

 Using FTP to Upload a Web

If your Web server does not have the FrontPage Server Extensions, FrontPage uses FTP (File Transfer Protocol) to upload your files to a server. The details of using FTP will vary depending on the Web host, but in general, you follow the same steps as if you were publishing to a Web server that has the FrontPage Server Extensions. When FrontPage connects to the Web server, it recognizes that the server does not have the FrontPage Server Extensions. After getting your user ID and password for the Web server, FrontPage prompts you to type an FTP address to which it can upload files.

Normally, you just enter the name of the Web site's FTP server, and the server automatically routes the files into your private Web folder. Though the files are uploaded to the FTP server, they will be accessible only to you.

important

The following exercise assumes you are using Internet Explorer 5 or later. If you are using an earlier version of Internet Explorer (or another Web browser that does not support FTP), you should obtain an FTP utility program. Many such programs are available on the Web from sources such as *www.download.com*. This exercise also assumes that you are uploading to a non–FrontPage-compliant Web server operated by a Web host that allows FTP uploads.

Use FTP to upload your Web files

If you are not working through this lesson sequentially, follow the steps in "Import the Lesson 9 Practice Web," earlier in this lesson.

In this exercise, you use FTP to publish your Web to a non–FrontPage-compliant Web server.

1 On the File menu, click Publish Web.

2 In the Specify The Location To Publish Your Web To text box, type the FTP address of your Web server, such as *ftp://ftp.mybigcompany.com.*

3 Click the Publish button.

FrontPage connects to the Web site's FTP server and displays a progress bar. When the connection is established, FrontPage may display the Name And Password Required dialog box.

4 If prompted, in the Name text box, type your user name, and in the Password text box, type your password. Click OK.

FrontPage uploads your files to the Web host's FTP server.

You must begin the address with ftp:// so that FrontPage knows you want to connect to an FTP server over a network, and not simply publish your Web files locally with "ftp" as part of the Web name.

important

Your user name and password for the FTP server might not be the same as your user name and password for the Web server. Check with your Web server's system administrator if you need help.

Finish the lesson

1 On the File menu, click Close Web.

2 For each page, if FrontPage prompts you to save changes, click Yes.

FrontPage saves your changes and closes the Lesson09 Web.

Lesson 9 Quick Reference

To	Do this
Check spelling on a Web page	In the Folder List, double-click the page you want to check, and on the Tools menu, click Spelling.
Check spelling on an entire Web	Click the Navigation icon on the Views bar. On the Tools menu, click Spelling, and click Start. Double-click pages in the page list to correct spelling.
Publish a Web locally	On the File menu, click Publish Web. In the Specify The Location To Publish Your Web To text box, type a folder name on your hard disk drive, and then click the Publish button.
Publish a Web to a FrontPage-compliant Web server	If necessary, connect to the Internet or company intranet. On the File menu, click Publish Web. In the Specify The Location To Publish Your Web To text box, type the URL of your Web server and your Web folder on the server, and click the Publish button. Type your user name and password, and then click OK.
Open a Web on a Web server	If necessary, connect to the Internet or company network. On the File menu, click Open, type the URL of your Web site, type a user name and password, and click OK.
Edit a page on a Web server	In FrontPage, open the Web on the Web server. In the Folder List, double-click the page you want to edit. In Page view, make the desired changes.
Delete a file from a Web on a Web server	In FrontPage, open the Web on the Web server. In the Folder List, click the file to delete, press the Delete key, and then click Yes.
Update a Web on a Web server	If necessary, connect to the Internet or company network. On the File menu, click Publish Web. Click Options and choose the desired update option. In the Specify The Location To Publish Your Web To text box, type the URL of the Web server and the Web folder on the server, and click the Publish button. Type your user name and password, and then click OK.
Rename a Web	On the Tools menu, click Web Settings. In the Web Name text box, delete the default text, type the new name, and click OK.

9

Publishing a Web

Lesson 9 Quick Reference

To	Do this
Publish a Web via FTP	In FrontPage, open a local copy of the Web and connect to the Internet or company intranet. On the File menu, click Publish Web. In the Specify The Location To Publish Your Web To text box, type **ftp://** and the URL of your FTP server, and click the Publish button. If necessary, type your user name and password, and click OK.

10

Managing and Enhancing a Web

**ESTIMATED
TIME
30 min.**

In this lesson you will learn how to:

✔ *View reports on the status of a Web.*

✔ *Change Reports view options.*

✔ *Create and assign tasks.*

✔ *Create a table of contents.*

✔ *Animate text with dynamic HTML.*

✔ *Create page transition special effects.*

✔ *Create a search page.*

You've created and published a Web for Lakewood Mountains Resort and have received praise for your fine work with Microsoft FrontPage 2000. Now you can use FrontPage to manage and enhance the Lakewood Web.

In this lesson, you will learn how to view reports on various aspects of a FrontPage-based Web, how to change Reports view options, how to create and assign tasks for updating or enhancing the Web, how to create a table of contents for a Web site, how to animate Web page text with dynamic HTML, how to create page transition special effects, and how to create a search page.

Import the Lesson 10 practice Web

In this exercise, you create a new Web based on the files in the Lesson10 folder in the Web Publishing SBS Practice folder. You will use this Web for all the exercises in Lesson 10.

❶ On the File menu, point to New, and then click Web.

FrontPage displays the New dialog box.

If your hard disk drive has a drive letter other than C, substitute the appropriate drive letter in step 2.

❷ Click the Import Web Wizard icon. In the Specify The Location Of The New Web text box, type **C:\My Webs\Lesson10**, and click OK.

FrontPage displays the first Import Web Wizard dialog box.

❸ Click the From A Source Directory Of Files option, click the Include Subfolders check box, and click the Browse button.

❹ Browse to the Lesson10 folder in the Web Publishing SBS Practice folder, and click OK.

❺ Click Next twice, and click Finish.

FrontPage creates a new Web based on the practice files and places it in the Lesson10 folder.

Getting Reports on Web Status

The first step in updating or enhancing a FrontPage-based Web is to find out what needs to be updated or enhanced. To do that, FrontPage provides a Reports view that lets you display information about different aspects of your Web such as which hyperlinks are broken, which pages load more slowly than others, and so on.

Use the Reports view

In this exercise, you use the Reports view to view reports on different aspects of the Lakewood Mountains Resort Web.

If you are not working through this lesson sequentially, follow the steps in "Import the Lesson 10 Practice Web," earlier in this lesson.

❶ On the Views bar, click the Reports icon.

FrontPage displays a Site Summary report, listing the categories of reports available, the number of files covered in each category, the total size of files in each category, and a description of each category.

tip

If a floating toolbar appears over the Reports window, close it by clicking the Close button at its top-right corner.

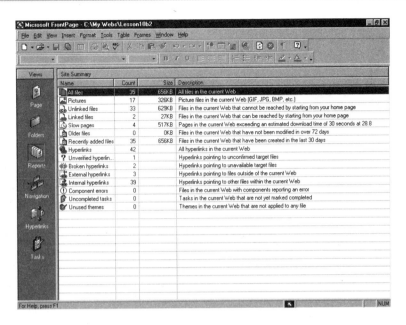

2 In the Site Summary report, double-click the line for Broken Hyperlinks.

FrontPage displays a list of possibly broken hyperlinks. In this case, three hyperlinks might be broken: two lead from the Lakewood front door page (Index.htm) to Web pages that have been renamed. The third hyperlink is not broken, but because it leads to a Web page on the Internet, FrontPage cannot verify that it is not broken.

If you prefer to skip the short-cut menu, you can simply double-click the broken hyperlink to open the Edit Hyperlink dialog box.

3 Right-click the Index1.htm line, and on the shortcut menu, click Edit Hyperlink.

FrontPage displays a smaller version of the Edit Hyperlink dialog box.

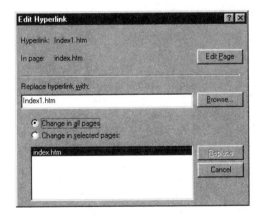

4 Click the Edit Page button.

FrontPage displays the page containing the broken hyperlink. Notice that the broken hyperlink (Use Frames) is already selected.

5 Right-click the broken hyperlink, and click Hyperlink Properties on the shortcut menu.

FrontPage displays the Edit Hyperlink dialog box.

6 Scroll down the file list, click Index01.htm, and click OK.

FrontPage repairs the broken hyperlink.

Save

7 On the toolbar, click the Save button. On the File menu, click Close, and click the Reports icon on the Views bar.

FrontPage displays the Broken Hyperlinks report. Two possibly broken hyperlinks remain.

8 On the View menu, point to Reports, and click Site Summary.

FrontPage redisplays the Site Summary report.

Change Reports view options

In this exercise, you change Reports view options by changing which files are considered "recent" and which pages are considered "slow to download." You also view the assumed speed of your Internet connection.

1 On the Tools menu, click Options.

FrontPage displays the Options dialog box.

2 Click the Reports View tab.

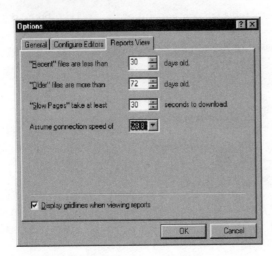

③ Click in the Recent Files Are Less Than text box, and type **20**.

In the Reports view, FrontPage will now list files added in the previous 19 days as Recently Added Files.

④ In the Slow Pages Take At Least text box, click the up arrow to increase the value to 40.

In the Reports view, FrontPage will now list files that take at least 40 seconds to download as slow pages.

⑤ Click the Assume Connection Speed Of drop-down arrow, and view the list options. Click the drop-down arrow again to close the list without changing the value.

⑥ Click OK.

FrontPage saves your changes.

Reports Created by FrontPage

Once you've created a Web in FrontPage, you can view reports on various aspects of your Web. The following table describes available reports.

Report	Lists
Site Summary	A summary of all available reports on the Web.
All Files	All files in the Web, with filename, title, location, size, file type, date last modified, and author.
Slow Pages	All files that take longer to load than an amount of time you specify.
Older Files	All files older than the number of days you specify.
Recently Added Files	All files added within the number of days you specify.
Recently Changed Files	All files changed within the number of days you specify.
Broken Hyperlinks	All broken or unverifiable hyperlinks.
Unlinked Files	All of the current Web's files that have no hyperlinks to or from them.

Managing a Web

10

(continued)

continued

Report	Lists
Component Errors	All FrontPage components that contain errors.
Review Status	Project status of individual pages in the Web.
Assigned To	The people to whom individual pages were assigned for updating.
Categories	Categories of Web pages if you have specified them for different types of pages in the Web.
Publish Status	Whether individual Web pages have been published to a Web server.
Uncompleted Tasks	Tasks created but not marked as completed.
Unused Themes	Themes used in the current Web but not applied to any file.

Managing FrontPage Tasks

Once you've used FrontPage's Reports view to identify the areas you'd like to update or enhance in your Web, you can use the Tasks list to track what's been done, by whom, and what still needs to be done.

To use the Tasks list, you simply click the Tasks icon on the Views bar. You can sort tasks in the Tasks list by status (Not Started or Completed), task name, the person to whom the task was assigned, priority, and date modified. You can create new tasks and edit previously created tasks. You can also create tasks from the Reports view.

Create and assign tasks

In this exercise, you create and assign tasks to members of your project team.

If you are not working through this lesson sequentially, follow the steps in "Import the Lesson 10 Practice Web," earlier in this lesson.

❶ On the Views bar, click the Tasks icon.

FrontPage displays the Tasks list. It's empty because you haven't yet created any tasks.

❷ On the File menu, point to New, and then click Task.

FrontPage displays the New Task dialog box. The Assigned To text box already has your name in it because you created the Web.

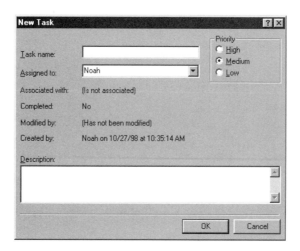

❸ Click in the Task Name text box, and type **Call Lakewood re: search page**.

❹ Click in the Assigned To text box, delete the default text, and type **Jim**.

You've assigned the task to Jim, a member of your project team.

❺ Click in the Description text box, type **Get verbal approval from resort manager to create a search page**, and then click OK.

FrontPage creates the new task and displays it in the Tasks list. The entry shows that the task has not yet been started and displays the rest of the task information in summary form.

❻ On the Views bar, click the Reports icon, and double-click the line for Broken Hyperlinks.

FrontPage displays a list of your Web's broken hyperlinks. If you have completed the exercise "Use the Reports View," earlier in this lesson, the Reports view will list only two possibly broken hyperlinks. If you have not completed the exercise, the Reports view will list three possibly broken hyperlinks.

❼ Right-click the line for the index03a.htm broken hyperlink, and on the shortcut menu, click Add Task.

FrontPage displays the New Task dialog box. The task name (Fix broken hyperlink) and description (Broken URL is index3a.htm) are already filled in for you.

10

Managing a Web

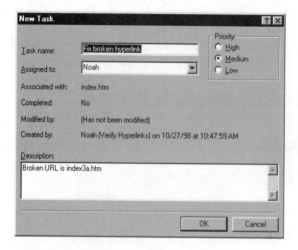

8   Click OK.

FrontPage creates a new task. In the Status column, the line for the broken hyperlink now says Added Task.

Perform a task

In this exercise, you perform a task and mark it as completed.

1   On the Views bar, click the Tasks icon.

FrontPage displays the Tasks list.

You can also right-click a task line and click Start Task on the shortcut menu.

2   Double-click the Fix Broken Hyperlink task.

FrontPage displays the Task Details dialog box.

3   Click the Start Task button.

FrontPage displays the page containing the broken hyperlink in Page view. Notice that the broken hyperlink (No Frames) is already selected.

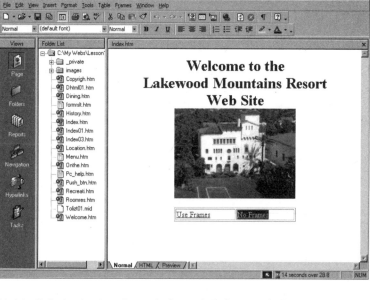

❹ Right-click the broken hyperlink, and click Hyperlink Properties on the shortcut menu.

FrontPage displays the Edit Hyperlink dialog box.

❺ Scroll down the file list, click Index03.htm, and then click OK.

FrontPage repairs the broken hyperlink.

Save

❻ On the toolbar, click the Save button.

FrontPage asks if you want to mark the task as completed.

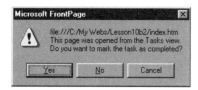

❼ Click Yes. On the File menu, click Close, and then click the Tasks icon on the Views bar.

FrontPage displays the Tasks list. The Fix Broken Hyperlink task is now marked Completed.

❽ Right-click the remaining task, *Call Lakewood,* and on the shortcut menu, click Mark As Completed.

FrontPage marks the task as completed.

Enhancing a Web

FrontPage provides scores of ways to enhance your Web—far more than can be covered here. However, three of the most popular ways to enhance a Web are to add a table of contents (which can be substituted for the links menu you created in Lesson 8), to animate text with dynamic HTML, and to create page transition special effects.

To create a table of contents, FrontPage uses its Table of Contents component. The advantage of using this component is that whenever you add a new page to your Web, the table of contents is updated automatically—unlike a standard hyperlinks menu, which you must update manually to add new hyperlinks or change old ones. The only disadvantage is that you have less control over what links are included in the table of contents than you do with a list of hyperlinks you create manually.

Text animation is another stunning set of effects that FrontPage makes as easy as clicking a few menu choices. You can animate Web page text so that it spirals into position, drops onto the page one word or one letter at a time, swoops in from the left or right, and appears with many other surprising effects.

Finally, you can create *page transitions* that control how one Web page disappears when another page loads. You can use circular or straight-line animations, make one page slide in from the left or right side over the previous page, and use other effects.

Create a table of contents

If you are not working through this lesson sequentially, follow the steps in "Import the Lesson 10 Practice Web," earlier in this lesson.

New

In this exercise, you create a table of contents and preview it in your Web browser.

1 On the Views bar, click the Page icon, and then click the New button on the toolbar.

FrontPage creates a new Web page and displays it in Page view.

2 On the Insert menu, point to Component, and then click Table Of Contents.

FrontPage displays the Table Of Contents Properties dialog box.

tip

Another way to create a table of contents is to use the Table Of Contents page template. Click the Page icon on the Views bar, point to New on the File menu, click Page, click the Table Of Contents template icon, and click OK. The result is the same as if you had inserted a Table of Contents component on a blank page.

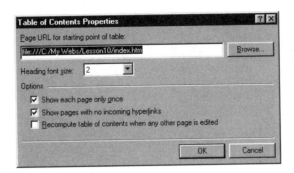

3 Click the Recompute Table Of Contents When Any Other Page Is Edited check box, and then click OK.

FrontPage inserts a Table of Contents component on the Web page.

4 Right-click a blank area of the Web page, and click Page Properties on the shortcut menu.

FrontPage displays the Page Properties dialog box.

5 In the Title text box, type **Table of Contents**, and then click OK.

The page's descriptive title will appear when a FrontPage user displays the Web in Folders view or when a dialog box displays a file list.

6 On the File menu, click Save As.

FrontPage displays the Save As dialog box.

7 In the File Name text box, type **Toc1.htm**, and then click the Save button.

FrontPage saves the Table of Contents page. Notice that Toc1.htm now appears in the Folder List.

*Preview
In Browser*

8 On the toolbar, click the Preview In Browser button.

FrontPage opens the page in your default Web browser, displaying the table of contents for the Web site. When a visitor clicks the links, he or she is taken to the corresponding pages in your Web site. Your Table of Contents page might differ from the one shown in the figure on the following page.

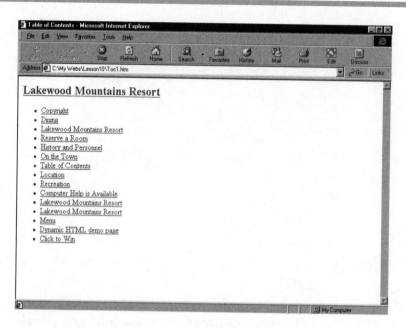

Close

9 Click the Close button at the top-right corner of your Web browser. Your Web browser closes and FrontPage reappears.

tip

If you've created a front door page that lets users select a frames or no-frames version of your Web, you can create a separate table of contents for each version. Right-click the Table of Contents component, and click Table Of Contents Properties on the shortcut menu. In the Table Of Contents Properties dialog box, click the Browse button, select the top page of the branch in the Web hierarchy, and click OK. The table of contents will include only pages below the selected page in the Web hierarchy—that is, pages on its particular branch of your Web.

Insert the table of contents in a contents frame

In this exercise, you insert the new table of contents into the contents frame of the home page, where it replaces the manually created hyperlinks menu.

1 In the Folder List, double-click the file Index01.htm.

FrontPage displays the frames home page in Page view.

2 Right-click a blank area of the menu (left) frame. On the shortcut menu, click Frame Properties.

FrontPage displays the Frame Properties dialog box.

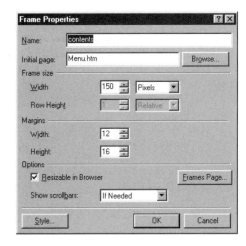

3 Click the Browse button.

FrontPage displays the Edit Hyperlink dialog box.

4 Scroll down the file list, click Toc1.htm, and click OK twice.

FrontPage inserts the table of contents page into the contents frame.

Save

5 On the toolbar, click the Save button, and then click the Preview In Browser button.

Your Web browser displays the frames home page with the table of contents page in the contents frame.

*Preview
In Browser*

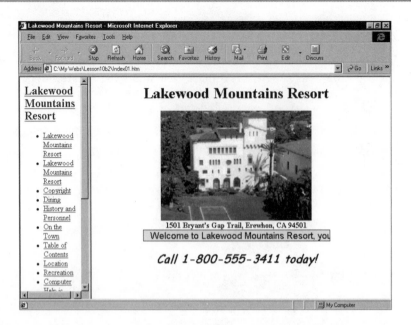

Close

6 Click the Close button at the top-right corner of your Web browser.

Your Web browser closes and FrontPage reappears.

Animate text with dynamic HTML

In this exercise, you animate text by using FrontPage's ready-to-use dynamic HTML features.

1 In the Folder List, double-click the file Dhtml01.htm.

FrontPage displays the Dhtml01.htm page in Page view.

2 Select the first line of text. On the Format menu, click Dynamic HTML Effects.

FrontPage displays the floating DHTML Effects toolbar.

3 Click the On drop-down arrow, and in the list, click Page Load.

The dynamic HTML effect will be activated when a user loads this page into a Web browser.

4 Click the Apply drop-down arrow, and in the list, click Drop In By Word.

When the page loads in a Web browser, the text will seem to drop from above onto the page.

⑤ Drag the DHTML Effects toolbar out of the way if necessary, and select the second line of text.

⑥ On the DHTML Effects toolbar, click the On drop-down arrow, and click Mouse Over. Click the Apply drop-down arrow and click Formatting.

⑦ Click the Choose Settings drop-down arrow, and click Choose Font.

FrontPage displays the Font dialog box.

⑧ In the Font list, click Arial. In the Size text box, type **18**. Click the Color drop-down arrow, click the Red color tile on the color palette, and click OK.

Close

⑨ Click the Close button at the top-right corner of the DHTML Effects toolbar. On the toolbar, click the Save button.

Save

FrontPage closes the DHTML Effects toolbar and saves the Web page with your changes.

Dynamic HTML will be displayed correctly only if your browser (such as Microsoft Internet Explorer 4.0, Netscape Navigator 4.0, or later versions) supports it.

Preview dynamic HTML effects

In this exercise, you preview the animated text effects you created with dynamic HTML.

① On the toolbar, click the Preview In Browser button.

FrontPage starts your Web browser and loads the dynamic HTML page. As the page loads, the top line of text drops into place.

② Move the mouse pointer over the second line of text.

The text font changes to Arial, the size increases to 18 points, and the text color changes to red.

Preview In Browser

③ Move the mouse pointer away from the text.

The text changes back to its original font, size, and color.

④ Click the Close button at the top-right corner of your Web browser window.

Your Web browser closes and FrontPage reappears.

Close

Create special transition effects

In this exercise, you create special transition effects for a Web page.

1 In the Folder List, double-click the file Index.htm.

FrontPage displays Index.htm in Page view.

2 On the Format menu, click Page Transition.

FrontPage displays the Page Transitions dialog box.

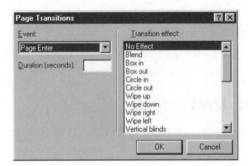

3 Click the Event drop-down arrow, and click Page Exit in the list.

The page transition effect will occur when a user exits from the selected Web page.

4 In the Duration (Seconds) text box, type **2**.

The page transition effect will last for two seconds.

5 In the Transition Effect list, click Vertical Blinds, and then click OK.

The Vertical Blinds transition effect is selected.

Save

*Preview
In Browser*

6 On the toolbar, click the Save button, and then click the Preview In Browser button.

7 If FrontPage displays a message box warning you that the page transition effect requires a Web browser that supports dynamic HTML, such as Internet Explorer 4.0 or higher, click OK.

FrontPage starts your Web browser and displays the selected Web page.

8 Click the Use Frames hyperlink.

As the new Web page loads, the old page disappears behind an effect that resembles opening vertical blinds on a window.

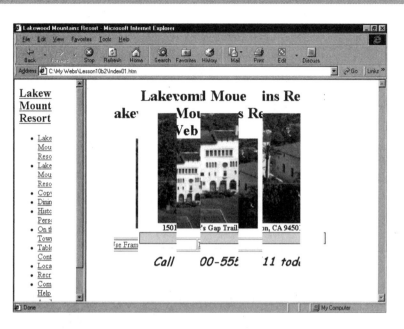

⑨ Click the Close button at the top-right corner of your Web browser window. Your Web browser closes, and FrontPage reappears.

Close

One Step Further **Using a Search Engine**

The Lakewood Web site contains quite a few pages. Even though you've provided descriptive hyperlinks from the home page to all the other pages, some Web site visitors might want to see a list of all the pages that deal with their favorite topics or activities. FrontPage makes it easy to provide this by creating a *search page*. In a search page, Web site visitors type in a word or phrase that is likely to occur on the pages they want to see, click a Submit button, and the FrontPage-compliant Web server returns a list of all pages on the Web site that contain that word or phrase.

Of course, there's a *search engine* that looks for the relevant pages on your Web site. However, FrontPage sets up the search engine behind the scenes: you don't even need to think about it. You only need to set up the search page.

Setting up the search page itself is easy. You simply click the Page icon on the Views bar, create a new page, and select the Search Page template in the New dialog box. FrontPage creates a search page with boilerplate text that you can modify for your own needs.

Create a search page

If you are not working through this lesson sequentially, follow the steps in "Import the Lesson 10 Practice Web," earlier in this lesson.

In this exercise, you create a search page for the Lakewood Mountains Resort Web site.

1 On the Views bar, click the Page icon.

FrontPage displays the Web in Page view.

2 On the File menu, point to New, and then click Page.

FrontPage displays the New dialog box.

3 Scroll down in the General pane, click the Search Page icon, and click OK.

FrontPage creates a new page using the Search Page template.

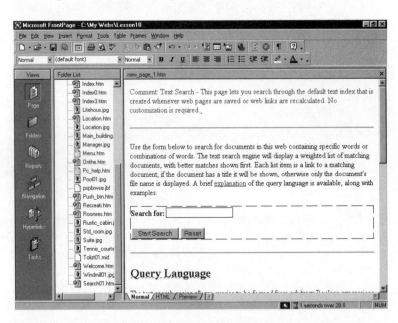

Center

Pressing Shift+Enter creates a "soft return," which allows you to retain the formatting attributes of the previous line without changing line spacing.

4 At the top of the page, delete the comment text, and select the Heading 1 style from the Style drop-down list on the toolbar.

5 Type **Lakewood Mountains Resort**, hold down the Shift key and press Enter, type **Search Page**, and click the Center button on the toolbar.

FrontPage creates a page heading and centers it on the page.

Center

6   Press Enter, and then click the Center button on the toolbar.

FrontPage inserts a new, left-aligned line under the heading.

7   Type **This page enables you to search for activities and services offered at Lakewood Mountains Resort**.

8   On the File menu, click Save As.

FrontPage displays the Save As dialog box.

9   In the File Name text box, type **Search01.htm**.

FrontPage enters Search01.htm as the filename for the new page.

10   Click the Change button. In the Set Page Title dialog box, type **Search this Web site** as the page title, and then click OK.

FrontPage changes the page title.

11   Click the Save button.

FrontPage saves your new search page.

Testing your search page

Because a search page is a type of form, it must be published to a FrontPage-compliant Web server in order to work. When you publish your Web—either to a separate Web server machine or on your own computer with the Microsoft Personal Web server installed—the search page will be displayed as a normal Web page form.

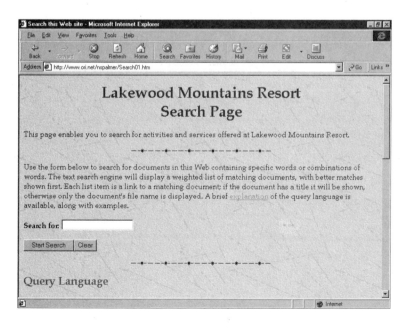

Users of the page on your Web site simply type their desired search word(s) in the Search For text box and click the Start Search button. The Web server returns a list of the pages on your Web that contain the search word(s).

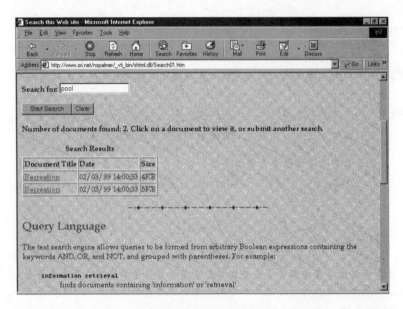

In the list, each list item is a hyperlink to the corresponding page. By clicking the hyperlink, users of your search page can display the desired page.

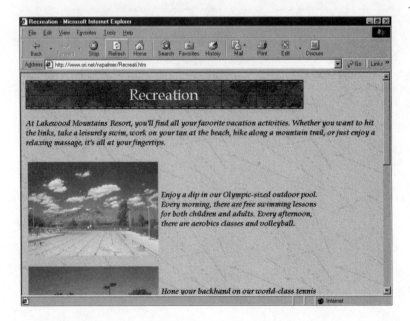

Finish the lesson

1 On the File menu, click Close Web.

2 For each page, if FrontPage prompts you to save changes, click Yes. FrontPage saves your changes and closes the Lesson10 Web.

Lesson 10 Quick Reference

To	Do this
Display a Site Summary report	Click the Reports icon on the Views bar.
Display an individual report	In the Reports view, double-click the line of the report you want to display.
Change Reports view options	On the Tools menu, click Options, click the Reports View tab, make the desired changes, and click OK.
Display the Tasks view	Click the Tasks icon on the Views bar.
Create a task	On the File menu, point to New, and then click Task. In the New Task dialog box, type a task name, description, priority, and the name of the person to whom the task is assigned. Click OK.
Complete a task	In the Tasks list, double-click the desired task, and click the Start Task button. Make the desired changes, click the Save button on the toolbar, and click Yes to mark the task as completed. *Or* right-click the task in the Tasks list, and click Mark As Completed on the shortcut menu.
Create a table of contents	In Page view, click the New button on the toolbar. On the Insert menu, point to Component, and click Table Of Contents. In the Table Of Contents Properties dialog box, make any desired changes, and then click OK. *Or* on the File menu, point to New, and then click Page. Click the Table Of Contents template icon, and click OK.
Animate text with dynamic HTML	In Page view, select the text you want to animate. On the Format menu, click Dynamic HTML Effects to display the DHTML Effects toolbar. On the toolbar, select the event to trigger the effect, the type of effect, and the settings. Click the Close button on the toolbar, save the Web page, and click the Preview In Browser button to view the animation.

Lesson 10 Quick Reference

To	Do this
Create page transition effects	Open the desired Web page in Page view. On the Format menu, click Page Transition. Select the event to trigger the effect, and specify the number of seconds the effect should last. In the Transition Effect list, click the desired effect, and click OK. On the toolbar, click the Save button, and click the Preview In Browser button to view the effect.
Create a Search page	Click the Page icon on the Views bar. On the File menu, point to New, and click Page. In the New dialog box, click the Search Page icon, and then click OK. Modify the search page as desired.

PART 2

Creating Web Page Elements with Microsoft PhotoDraw 2000

11

Creating Pictures with Microsoft PhotoDraw

In this lesson you will learn how to:

ESTIMATED TIME 45 min.

✔ *Navigate in the PhotoDraw work enviroment.*

✔ *Insert clip art and other images.*

✔ *Add and format text.*

✔ *Print from PhotoDraw.*

✔ *Customize the picture area.*

With Microsoft PhotoDraw 2000, you have the ability to create and modify graphic images for the World Wide Web and other publications. You can start with one of the many templates included with PhotoDraw, a clip art image from the Microsoft Clip Gallery, or you can create your own original image. Then you can change the image's colors, choose from a variety of effects for the image, and put all your changes together to produce an Internet-friendly image easily and quickly.

For example, let's say that you're in charge of producing the Web site for your company, Impact Public Relations, a small public relations firm. Because your graphic designer is using PhotoDraw to create Web images for the site, you know that you can easily change your mind about the text or color that will be used on an image. The graphic designer can make any changes without going to any extra trouble, and the project will remain on schedule.

The PhotoDraw Work Environment

When you work in PhotoDraw, you'll be combining different elements to create a finished picture. For example, if you're creating a banner to appear at the top of your Web page, you'll most likely want to design an image that contains different lines, text styles, colors, and a combination of various drawings or photos. In PhotoDraw, these different elements are called *objects,* and these objects are combined to create a picture, all of which is done within the PhotoDraw *workspace.*

Navigating in PhotoDraw

Creating a new picture in PhotoDraw can be fun and simple because of the program's many unique features designed to make your work easier. For example, PhotoDraw contains many palettes, which are predefined sets of colors, and menus that are designed to help you navigate in the workspace to create and modify your images.

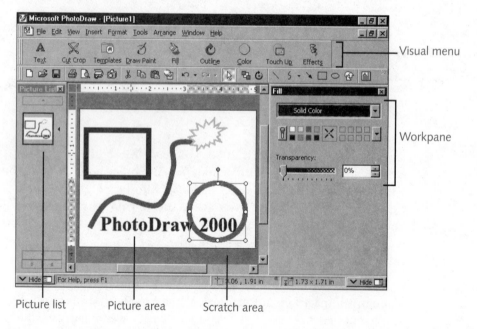

The elements of the PhotoDraw screen are as follows:

- The *Picture List,* located on the left side of the workspace, contains a thumbnail image of each picture that is open in PhotoDraw. This list makes it easy to view, edit, and arrange the individual images that comprise one picture in PhotoDraw.

- The white area in the center of the workspace is called the *picture area*. The picture area is where you create your images.

- The gray area around the picture area is called the *scratch area*. You can move elements back and forth from the scratch area to the picture area while you're creating your image. However, objects in the scratch area are not part of the finished picture and will not be printed.

- The *visual menu*, which contains the large buttons at the top of the workspace, provides quick access to many of the methods used to apply effects to any object.

- Each visual menu button has a related *workpane*. When you click a visual menu command, the corresponding workpane is automatically displayed on the right side of the workspace. Workpanes contain all of the options available for the particular visual menu selection.

Composing a Picture

When you create a picture in PhotoDraw, it is usually comprised of many different objects, like text and clip art or scanned images. All of the open pictures are listed in the Picture List at the left side of the workspace. You can see all of the objects in an open picture—even the objects in the scratch area—by clicking the arrow to the right of the picture in the Picture List.

The images in the object list are ordered from front to back. In other words, the image at the top of the object list is on top of the one below it. So if two images overlap, the topmost image would cover the image below it.

tip
You can rearrange the order in the object list by selecting an image in the list and dragging it up or down in the order.

File Formats for the Web

When you work with PhotoDraw, you might use any combination of elements—such as text, clip art, or photos—from a variety of sources. To create an ad for Impact Public Relations' Web site, for example, you might want to use a scanned version of the company's logo, an illustration created in another program, a few photographs, and you might want to include some of the clip art images that come with PhotoDraw.

In PhotoDraw you can *import*, or bring in, and work with a file created in just about any format, from any source. Some of the more common file formats include:

- Bitmap
- GIF (Graphic Interchange Format)
- JPG or JPEG (Joint Photographic Experts Group)
- Microsoft Image Composer
- Adobe PhotoShop
- TIFF (Tagged Image File Format)
- Windows metafile

Another file format to be aware of is the PhotoDraw (.mix) file format. To save your file as an .mix file, click Save As on the File menu, and select PhotoDraw (*.mix) from the Save As Type drop-down list in the Save As dialog box. It's a good idea to always save your pictures in the PhotoDraw format as well as in any other file format you want to use. When images are saved as JPG or GIF files for the Internet, for example, all of the objects in the picture are combined into one composite image, and therefore you can't edit them individually again. When you save an image as a PhotoDraw file, all of the object layers are preserved and will be fully editable the next time you open the picture in PhotoDraw.

Using Pictures and Clip Art

One of the easiest ways to learn how to use PhotoDraw's many features is to start applying them to an existing image. This enables you to begin using and mastering PhotoDraw's effects immediately, without having to spend time drawing or painting a picture first. Therefore, one of the first things you'll probably do in PhotoDraw is insert an image. This can be an image from the Clip Gallery, which is a large collection of free images that are included with Microsoft Office 2000, an image that has been previously scanned by you or by someone else, or an image that was created in another program and is on your hard disk drive or a floppy disk.

When you begin searching for an image to insert, you might find that certain images—clip art images in particular—have long, confusing file names that make it difficult to figure out what you're going to get when you insert them. PhotoDraw contains a very helpful feature called Visual Insert that eliminates that problem. When you select an image using Visual Insert, a small thumbnail representation of the image is displayed, allowing you to view the image before you insert it in your picture.

Insert a clip art image using Visual Insert

In this exercise, you create a banner to be used on a Web page, and you use a PhotoDraw clip art image as part of the banner.

1. Insert CD 3 of Microsoft Office 2000 Premium, which contains the Microsoft Clip Gallery, into your CD drive.

2. Click the Start button on the taskbar, point to Programs, and then click Microsoft PhotoDraw.

   The PhotoDraw application appears on your screen.

3. In the Microsoft PhotoDraw dialog box, click the Blank Picture option, and then click OK. If PhotoDraw is already open, on the File menu, click New.

   The New dialog box is displayed.

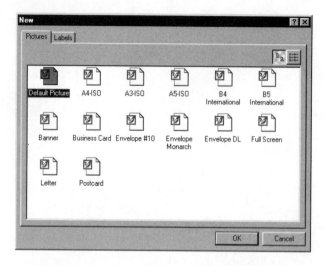

④ Click the Pictures tab of the New dialog box, and select the Banner template.

⑤ Click OK.

A new blank document is displayed in the rectangular shape of a Web banner.

⑥ On the Insert menu, click Visual Insert.

The Visual Insert dialog box appears.

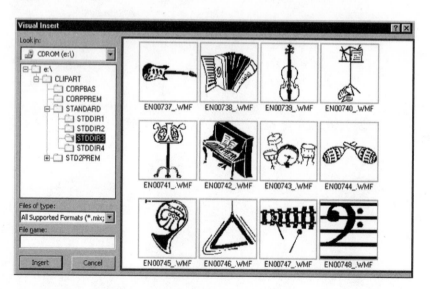

⑦ Select the drive letter that corresponds to your CD drive, and navigate to the PhotoDrw\Content\PDClips folder.

To use more than one image from a clip art gallery, hold down the Ctrl key while you select the images one at a time.

8 Select the Animals folder. The images in the gallery are displayed on the right side of the Visual Insert dialog box.

9 Select the picture of the peacock.

10 Click the Insert button.

The image is displayed in the PhotoDraw workspace, ready for you to add a little PhotoDraw magic.

You can also use Visual Insert to locate files on your hard disk drive or a floppy disk. With the Visual Insert dialog box open, select the appropriate location from the Look In drop-down list, and select the images of your choice.

Adding and Formatting Text

Adding text to an image in PhotoDraw can be a very effective way to convey your message to your audience. For instance, if you're creating buttons for navigating a Web site, you might want a button that says *Home Page*. In addition, if you're creating an image for a logo or Web ad banner, having text on your image becomes very important, as viewers will associate that image and its message with your company or organization. You might even want to create a text-only image to use as a heading in your Web site, for example. In PhotoDraw, all the text you type can easily be formatted to suit your needs.

11

Creating Pictures

Add text to a PhotoDraw image

In this exercise, you create text using the Text command on the Insert menu.

New

1 Click the New button on the Standard toolbar.

A new blank document is displayed.

2 On the Insert menu, click Text.

A text object is placed on the picture area with the words *Your text here* displayed. The Text workpane appears to the right of the PhotoDraw workspace.

You can also use the key-board shortcut Ctrl+T or select the Text button on the visual menu and choose Insert Text from the drop-down menu to open the Text workpane in PhotoDraw.

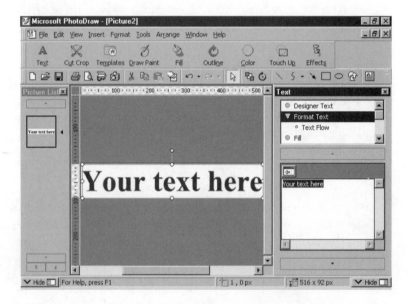

The text is too big for the banner; you'll adjust the size of the text in the next section.

3 In the Text workpane, the default text is selected. Type the text **My Cool**, press the Enter key, and then type **Graphic**.

The default text in the picture area is replaced with the words *My Cool Graphic*, set on two lines.

> **tip**
> By clicking and dragging the text object, it can be moved anywhere within the picture area or the scratch area.

Formatting the Text in a PhotoDraw Picture

After you've added text to a picture, you might want to change the text's appearance. This could include changing the font, size, and style. It's important to remember to choose a font style that fits into the look of your site. You should also make sure that the text is large enough, and you should choose a color that shows up against the background and is easily readable.

Format text

In this exercise, you format the text you added to the banner.

1 In the picture area, click to select the *My Cool Graphic* text object.

2 In the Text workpane, use the drop-down list to select the font Impact. All fonts installed on your computer will appear in the drop-down list.

3 Select 12.0 pt from the Size drop-down list.

The font size changes to 12.0 points.

4 Select the font style Italic from the Style drop-down list.

The text is formatted in the Italic font style.

11

Creating Pictures

5 Select Text Flow from the Text workpane to adjust the alignment of the text object within the picture area.

6 In the Align drop-down list, click Center.

The text is centered between the left and right margins.

7 In the Orientation area of the Text workpane, click the Vertical option button.

The text is rotated 90 degrees in the picture area.

Adding Special Effects to Text

Beyond font size and style, you can add many interesting effects to text using PhotoDraw. These effects include filling text with a texture, bending the text, outlining the text, and adding drop shadows to text, as well as applying lighting and 3-D effects. You can also use PhotoDraw to vary the transparency or opacity of text. When text is opaque, you cannot see through it, but if you use PhotoDraw's Transparency feature to make the text transparent, you can see any objects or images that are behind the text. The possibilities are limited only by your imagination.

Add a fill and drop shadow to a text object

In this exercise you add a textured fill to a text object and then add a drop shadow to complete the picture.

1 In the picture area, click to select the *My Cool Graphic* text object.

2 Select Fill from the Text workpane. If the Text workpane is not visible, double-click the text object.

3 From the drop-down menu on the Text workpane, select Texture.

A thumbnail list of available textures appears.

4 Select the texture of your choice by clicking the thumbnail.

The texture is automatically applied to the text object.

5 Click the Effects button on the visual menu, and then click Shadow.

The Shadow workpane appears.

6 In the Shadow workpane, select the Drop Right shadow.

A Drop Right shadow effect is automatically applied to the text object.

7 Make any adjustments to the shadow, including changing its color, transparency, and softness.

░ To change the color of the shadow, click the Color drop-down arrow and select a color on the palette.

░ To reduce the transparency of the shadow, move the Transparency slider to the left.

░ To decrease the softness of the shadow, move the Soften slider to the left.

You can create exciting, visually interesting images in minutes by selecting the Effects button on the visual menu, choosing one of the other effects, such as Fade Out, Distort, or 3-D, and making adjustments in the corresponding workpane.

tip

There are a large number of people using the Internet with their monitors set to only 256 colors. For this reason, you should consider choosing colors from PhotoDraw's *browser-safe* color palette if you're creating pictures for a Web page. By using a color from the Web palette, you can be sure that the color will be displayed correctly in most browsers used to view Internet content. If you choose a color that is not in the browser-safe palette, you run the risk that the color will appear slightly out of focus, or *dither,* as the user's monitor tries to display the color correctly. For more information on using PhotoDraw's browser-safe palette, see the section "Working with a Browser-Safe Color Palette" in Lesson 13.

Adjust the color and opacity of text

In the following exercise you'll change the color of the font using a browser-safe color palette, and you'll change the text object's opacity.

❶ In the picture area, click the *My Cool Graphic* text object.

❷ Click the Fill button on the visual menu, and select Solid Color from the menu.

The current active color is displayed to the left of the words *Solid Color* in the Text workpane, along with some suggested variations.

Click the arrow button to the right of the color variations.

A color pop-up menu appears.

❹ From the color pop-up menu, point to Active Palette.

A Web color palette appears.

⑤ Select a dark green color from the Web palette.

The text automatically changes to that color.

⑥ Slide the Transparency slider to adjust the opacity of the text. Moving the slider to the right lightens the text, making any darker elements under the text show through.

Eyedropper

tip

With Fill selected on the Text workpane, you can use the eyedropper button to select the color from any area of a picture currently in the picture area. The color that you choose becomes the active color and can be used to format text. This technique is useful when you want your text to match colors in a picture.

Printing a PhotoDraw Picture

When you create a picture in PhotoDraw, chances are you're eventually going to want to print it. Often the pictures you print will be fairly small, especially when you are creating pictures for the Internet. However, for the times when you need to print large pictures, PhotoDraw lets you print pictures as large as your printer and the paper you have chosen will allow.

Print a picture in PhotoDraw

In this exercise, you print a PhotoDraw picture to fit the size of your paper.

You can also use the keyboard shortcut Ctrl+P to open the Print dialog box.

① Open a picture in PhotoDraw, if necessary, and click Print on the File menu. The Print dialog box appears.

② Click the Size tab on the Print dialog box. The current width and height information of your picture is displayed, along with a thumbnail of the image.

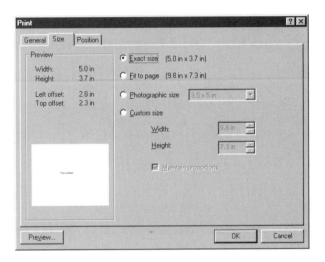

③ Select the Fit To Page option button.

The picture thumbnail is enlarged in the preview window, showing you how your image will look on the page when it's printed. The new printed size of the image is displayed, along with the exact size of the image as it appears in PhotoDraw.

④ Click OK.
The picture is printed.

One Step Further Customizing the Picture Area

The default color for the picture area is white. There may be times when you'll want to change this color to give your image the desired results. You may also want to change the unit of measure or the width and height of the picture area. You can make these changes easily in PhotoDraw.

11

Creating Pictures

Change the format of the picture area

In this exercise, you change the background color, width, height, and unit of measurement used in the picture area.

1 On the File menu, click Picture Setup.

The Picture Setup dialog box appears.

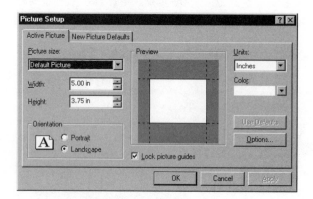

2 Select the yellow background color from the Color drop-down list.

The color of the background changes to yellow.

3 Select one of the preset picture sizes from the Picture Size drop-down list. To create a custom size, enter the appropriate size in the Width and Height text boxes.

The size of the picture area changes according to your specifications.

4 In the Units drop-down list, click Pixels.

The unit of measurement used in the picture area changes to pixels.

5 Click OK to close the Picture Setup dialog box.

tip

If you want certain options to be available for each new picture you create, select the New Picture Defaults tab on the Picture Setup dialog box and make the appropriate selections. Each subsequent picture will be created using these default values.

Finish the lesson

1   Close any open pictures by clicking the Close Window button in the upper right corner of the picture.

   If PhotoDraw prompts you to save any changes, click No.

2   On the File menu, click Exit to quit PhotoDraw.

Lesson 11 Quick Reference

To	Do this
Create a new blank picture from within PhotoDraw	Click New on the File menu, and then choose a blank document template in the New dialog box.
Insert clip art and other images	Click Visual Insert on the Insert menu, choose the location of the files you want to insert, and then use the thumbnail pictures to select the images you want to use.
Add text to a picture	Click the Text button on the visual menu, select Insert Text, and then type your text in the Text workpane.
Format text in a picture	Select the text object in the open picture, and then use the options in the Text workpane to format the font, size, and style.
Apply color to text in a picture	Select the text object in the open picture, and then select Solid Color from the Fill button on the visual menu. Click the arrow button to the right of the color variations on the Fill workpane, and then select the color of your choice.
Apply a texture to text in a picture	Select the text object in the open picture, and then select Texture from the Fill button on the visual menu. Select the texture of

Creating Pictures

11

Lesson 11 Quick Reference

To	Do this
	your choice from the Fill workpane.
Apply a drop shadow to text in a picture	Select the text object in the open picture, and then select Shadow from the Effects button on the visual menu. Adjust the shadow options in the Shadow workpane.
Change the color of a shadow	Select the text object in the open picture. On the visual menu, click the Effects button and select Shadow from the menu. Click the down arrow to the right of the Color option and select a color.
Change the transparency of a shadow	Select the text object in the open picture. On the visual menu, click the Effects button and select Shadow from the menu. Drag the Transparency slider to the left to decrease the transparency of the shadow or to the right to increase the transparency of the shadow.
Change the softness of a shadow	Select the text object in the open picture. On the visual menu, click the Effects button and select Shadow from the menu. Drag the Soften slider to the left to decrease the softness of the shadow or to the right to increase the softness of the shadow.
Manually adjust the dimensions of the picture area	Click Picture Setup on the File menu, and then make your adjustments to the width and height of the picture.
Print a picture to fit your printer paper	With a picture open in PhotoDraw, click Print on the File menu, and then select Fit To Page on the Size tab of the Print dialog box.

12

Creating and Manipulating Photos for the Web

ESTIMATED TIME 40 min.

In this lesson you will learn how to:

✔ *Touch up photos.*

✔ *Enhance the appearance of photos.*

✔ *Save photos for use on the Web.*

✔ *Colorize a black and white photo.*

Using photographs on a Web site is very popular these days. With more and more people accessing the Internet at faster speeds, photographs, once used selectively, can now be used on a more regular basis. It is still important, however, to create photographic images with the best quality, while maintaining the smallest file size you can get away with. The smaller the file size, the faster the photo will download in the user's browser, and the happier your site visitors will be.

You'll also find that many photographic effects are made easy in Microsoft PhotoDraw 2000. These effects can be applied to a photograph to fix a damaged or scratched area, for instance, or to fade out a portion of the photo.

PhotoDraw was designed to make the process of using photos on the Web easy for anyone. One nice feature that accomplishes this goal is called Save For Use In. It is a wizard that walks you step by step through the process of saving your images using the best possible settings for use on the Internet, in on-screen presentations, and in other Microsoft Office documents.

Improving Existing Photos

If you're lucky, the image you insert into PhotoDraw is already clean and clear. All you have to do is add the photo object to your picture and save it for use on the Web. Often, though, the existing image is too dark, too light, scratched or torn, or contains imperfections that make you think that the image is unusable. Included in PhotoDraw is a vast array of image manipulation techniques and effects that let you turn a once unusable photo—or just about any other image for that matter—into an image you'd be proud to use on any Web site.

Getting Photos onto Your Computer

Before you can insert a photo into PhotoDraw and take advantage of all of its great features, you must first have the photo saved in electronic form, ready for use on a computer.

There are a few different ways to get your photos onto your computer. One of the easiest and most popular ways to get an image into electronic form is to use a scanner. A scanner converts the continuous colors of your photograph into individual "digital" pixels that can be displayed by a computer monitor. If you don't have a scanner attached to your computer, don't worry; there are many places, such as your local copy center, that will scan your pictures for you. In addition, these days when you take your pictures to be developed, you usually have the option to get your pictures back on a floppy disk or a photo CD. Each of these methods creates an image that you can use on your computer. Another popular way to get photos onto your computer is to take the picture with a digital camera. A digital camera creates a pixel, or *digital*, version of your photo rather than a printed or continuous image.

If you have a scanner or a digital camera attached to your computer, you can bring images directly into PhotoDraw. By selecting Scan Picture or Digital Camera from the File menu, PhotoDraw launches the scanner software already on your computer. You can then scan a picture as usual and it will be placed into PhotoDraw, ready for use. If you have another TWAIN (Technology Without An Interesting Name) device attached to your computer, such as a video camera, select Other TWAIN Device from the File menu to launch the software associated with that device, and capture the image as usual.

Adjusting Brightness and Contrast Levels

If you're working with an image that is too dark or too light, you can adjust the brightness levels, fine-tuning the image until it meets your needs. If the shadow areas of your photograph are not distinctive enough or parts of the image are lost in the shadows, now is the time to adjust the contrast to improve these areas.

Adjust a photograph's brightness and contrast levels

In this exercise you will manipulate the brightness levels of a color photograph that is too dark.

1 Start PhotoDraw. In the Microsoft PhotoDraw Dialog box that appears, click the Blank Picture option, and then click OK.

The new dialog box is displayed.

2 Click the Pictures tab, if necessary, select the Default Picture icon, and click OK.

A new blank document appears.

3 On the Insert menu, click Visual Insert.

The Visual insert dialog box appears.

4 In the Look In drop-down list, select your hard disk drive. In the list of folders that appears, double-click the Web Publishing SBS Practice folder. Click the image darkphoto.jpg and click Insert.

The image is inserted into the workspace.

5 Select the photo object if it isn't already selected.

6 Click the Color button on the visual menu, and select Brightness And Contrast.

The Color workpane appears, with Brightness And Contrast selected in the Effect section.

Creating Photos

12

❼ On the Color workpane, drag the Brightness slider to the right to increase the brightness in the photograph.

tip

If you want to let PhotoDraw make the brightness and contrast settings for you, select the Automatic button. PhotoDraw adjusts the image using predefined settings that are designed to create the best possible results.

❽ Drag the Contrast slider to the right to add contrast to the image or to the left to decrease the contrast in the image.

Retouching a Damaged Photograph

There are many ways in PhotoDraw to fix a damaged photograph, and depending on the particular photo, you might need to use a combination of these tools. For example, you could use the Clone tool if you have a complicated background with a blemish and you want to use another area of the photograph's background to cover the blemish. You can use the Fix Red Eye tool to remove the red-eye effect caused by flash photography. PhotoDraw uses the surrounding pixel colors to fix scratches and other blemishes, so if you have a large area to fix, remove it a little at a time to get the best results.

Fix a scratch

In this exercise, you fix a scratch on an old photograph so that it looks as good as new.

New

❶ Click the New button on the Standard toolbar.

A new blank document appears.

❷ On the Insert menu, click Visual Insert.

The Visual Insert dialog box appears.

❸ Navigate to the Web Publishing SBS Practice folder on your hard disk drive, click the image scratchphoto.mix, and click Insert.

The image is inserted in the workspace.

❹ Select the photo object if it isn't already selected.

Pan and Zoom

❺ Click the Pan And Zoom button on the toolbar.

The Pan And Zoom dialog box is displayed.

❻ Drag the red box in the Pan And Zoom dialog box to bring the scratched area of the image into view.

PhotoDraw repositions the picture so that the portion contained in the red box is centered in the picture area.

7 Drag the slider bar on the Pan And Zoom dialog box to enlarge the image around the area that you want to retouch.

8 Close the Pan And Zoom dialog box by clicking the Close button in the upper right corner of the dialog box.

9 Click the Touch Up button on the visual menu, and select Remove Scratch.

The Touch Up workpane appears, along with a floating Scratch dialog box.

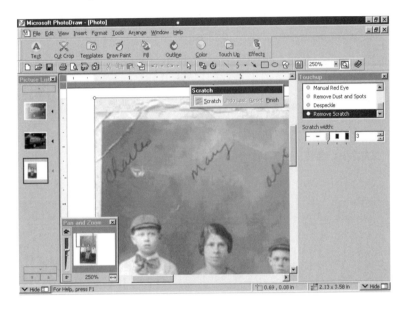

10 On the Touch Up workpane, select a width that closely matches the width of the scratch on the photograph.

11 On the photograph, click at the beginning of the scratch, and then click at the end of the scratch.

The scratch on the photograph is fixed automatically.

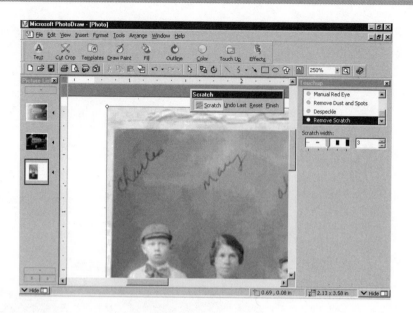

Using Other Touch Up Techniques

Besides fixing a scratch on an image, PhotoDraw gives you a few more techniques to help you retouch a damaged photograph. These other options, all available by selecting the Touch Up button on the visual menu, include the following:

- **Fix Red Eye**   Sometimes when you use a flash while taking pictures, the people in the pictures wind up with red eyes. This tool will remove the red eye from the photograph.

- **Remove Dust And Spots**   This tool will remove selected areas of spots and dirt on a photograph. Use this tool when you need to remove only one or two small spots on a photograph.

- **Despeckle**   You can remove a small flaw or blemish in a photograph with this tool. Use this tool when a photograph has many blemishes that you'd like to remove at once.

- **Clone**   You can use a particular area of a photograph and copy it to another area of the photograph to cover up an unwanted area of the original photo.

- **Smudge**   You can use this tool to smear an area of a photograph.

- **Erase**   You can erase or delete areas of a photograph with this tool.

Enhancing the Appearance of a Photograph

You can go beyond just touching up an existing image using the methods listed in the previous section; you can also use PhotoDraw's other features to help you enhance the appearance and color of a photograph. The color adjusting options, all available by selecting the Color button on the visual menu, include the following:

- **Tint**   Adds white or black to your image object. If you select the Automatic button, PhotoDraw makes the changes for you.

- **Hue and Saturation**   Changes the intensity of colors in your image object, or changes the color completely.

- **Colorize**   Adds color to a black and white image or changes the color in an image.

- **Color Balance**   Adjusts the Cyan/Red, Magenta/Green, and Yellow/ Blue color amounts in your image object.

- **Negative**   Changes a color in an image to its opposite color. This technique gives the image a negative film look.

- **Grayscale**   Takes all of the color information out of a photograph and replaces it with shades of gray.

tip

If you want to apply a color effect to only part of a photograph, select Correct By Painting from the Color workpane, choose a color, and paint the areas of the image that you want to colorize. To paint the areas of the image you want to change, simply click and drag across the image. The changes are applied when you release the mouse button.

Adding Special Effects

When you want to add a little something extra to an image, you'll find plenty of options by clicking the Effects button on the visual menu. You can easily make your image transparent, which is great for use as a background on a Web page. Or you can try one of the many Designer Effects included with PhotoDraw, which can make your image look like colorful tinfoil, a quilt, or plastic wrap. Most of the effects have a related workpane that lets you fine-tune the effect to suit your needs.

12

Creating Photos

tip

When you're working in PhotoDraw and experimenting with the different effects and options, it's always a good idea to work on an extra copy of the image. In other words, make a copy of the image *before* you bring it into PhotoDraw, just in case you want to start over. In Windows Explorer, right-click the image that you want to copy and click Copy on the shortcut menu that appears. Then right-click in the same location again, and click Paste on the shortcut menu. A copy of the image is created in the same location as the original with the words *Copy of* as the beginning of the file name.

Apply a fade-out effect to a photograph

In this exercise you add a fade-out effect to an image.

New

1 Click the New button on the Standard toolbar.

A new blank document appears.

2 On the Insert menu, click Visual Insert.

The Visual Insert dialog box appears.

3 Navigate to the Web Publishing SBS Practice folder on your hard disk drive, click the image colorpicture.jpg, and click Insert.

The image is inserted into the workspace.

4 Select the image if it isn't already selected.

5 Click the Effects button on the visual menu and select Fade Out.

The Transparency workpane appears, with Fade Out selected.

6 On the Transparency workpane, drag the Start and End sliders to define how transparent the start and end of the image will be. Dragging the sliders to the right will apply more transparency, while dragging the sliders to the left will apply less transparency.

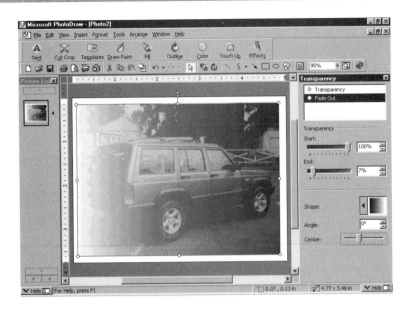

7 Click the Expand Gallery button next to Shape on the Transparency workpane, and choose the Linear With 180 Rotation shape for the fade-out effect.

8 Drag the Center slider to the left to make the fade-out start at the left of the image and fade out to the right of the image.

Saving Photos for Use on the Internet

PhotoDraw lets you save in just about any file format you choose. By clicking Save For Use In on the File menu, you can save for the Web, save as a thumbnail, or save for use in an Office document, an on-screen presentation, or in a publication.

To take the guesswork out of saving images for the Internet, PhotoDraw comes with an easy process, called a wizard, to make sure your photos are saved in the best possible format suited for Web site development. Typically, a photographic, or *raster*, image is saved using the JPG file format, and an illustrative, or *vector*, image is saved in the GIF file format.

Another option you'll have is to save your pictures as *thumbnails*, which are smaller (dimensionally) versions of the same larger image. This smaller picture, with its smaller file size, will be downloaded more quickly in the site visitors' browser. Often times thumbnails are used on a Web page that contains many photographs, and these smaller thumbnails are linked to the larger photograph. This gives site visitors the choice of whether or not they want to take the time to download and view the larger, slower picture.

12

Creating Photos

Save a photo for the Internet using the Save For Use In Wizard

In this exercise, you save an image for use on the Internet.

1 Click the New button on the Standard toolbar.

A new blank document appears.

2 On the Insert menu, click Visual Insert.

The Visual Insert dialog box appears.

3 Navigate to the Web Publishing SBS Practice folder on your hard disk drive, click the image scratchphoto.mix, and click Insert.

The image is inserted into the workspace.

4 On the File menu, click Save For Use In.

The Save For Use In Wizard dialog box appears.

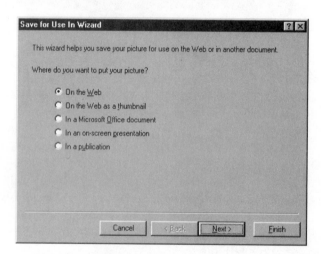

5 Select the On The Web option button, and then click Next.

The next dialog box in the wizard appears.

tip
If you want to save the picture as a thumbnail image, select the On The Web As A Thumbnail option button, and then click Next.

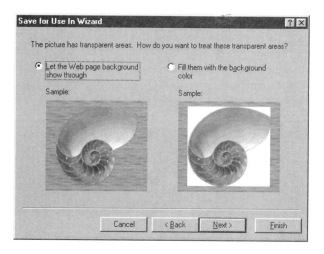

6 Select the Let The Web Page Background Show Through option button, and then click Next.

The next dialog box in the wizard appears.

tip

If you're using a solid color as a background on your Web page, select the Fill Them With The Background Color option button. In the next dialog box you'll have the chance to define the color you are using as a background on the Web page the image will appear on.

If you want to change your mind and use a background color instead of a tiled image, select the My Web Pages Background Is The Following Solid Color option button, and select the appropriate color.

7 In the next screen of the dialog box, the My Web Page's Background Is A Tiled Image option button should be selected automatically.

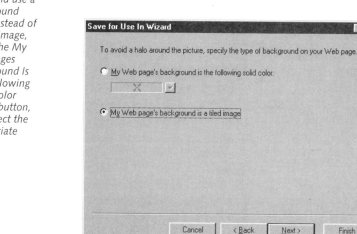

8   Click Next.

The next screen in the Save For Use In Wizard specifies how your picture is going to be saved. The information shown is based on the choices that you've made in the wizard, as well as the choices that PhotoDraw makes for you, such as using the Web color palette.

You'll find information on the picture's file type, color palette, compression, transparency, and background color.

tip

If any information is incorrect, or you want to change it, use the Back button to go back to the appropriate dialog box in the wizard.

9   Click the Save button.

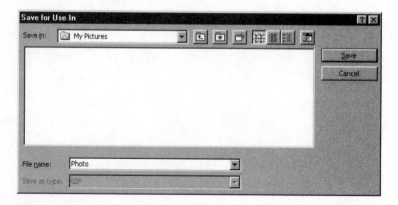

10 In the Save For Use In dialog box that appears, navigate to the Web Publishing SBS Practice folder on your hard disk drive. Type the file name **Internet** in the File Name box.

11 Click the Save button to finish the wizard.

The image is saved to the location you specified.

<table>
<tr><td>One
Step
Further</td><td></td></tr>
</table>

Colorizing a Black and White Photograph

If you're working with a black and white, or *grayscale*, photograph, and you want to add a little something extra, consider colorizing it. For example, if you have an old black and white family photo, you can give it that sepia-toned old-fashioned look using the Colorize feature in PhotoDraw.

When you colorize a black and white image, you replace the grayscale colors with a single color of your choice. It is the same idea as creating a duotone image for a printed publication. A duotone is created using two copies of the same image, each a different color, and then printing them one on top of another, slightly off center. A grayscale image is made up of pixels of black, white, and percentages of black. When you colorize your image, you are replacing the black and percentages of black with a color and percentages of that color.

Create a sepia-toned photograph

In this exercise, you colorize a grayscale photograph, using a light brown color to give it an old-fashioned appearance.

1 Click the New button on the Standard toolbar.

A new blank document appears.

2 On the Insert menu, click Visual Insert.

The Visual Insert dialog box appears.

3 Navigate to the Web Publishing SBS Practice folder on your hard disk drive, click the image B&Wphoto.jpg, and click Insert.

The image is inserted into the workspace.

4 Click the Color button on the visual menu and select Colorize.

The Color workpane appears.

5 On the Color workpane, click the drop-down arrow under Settings.

6 From the color drop-down list, point to the Active Palette, and choose a light brown color from the palette that appears.

The grayscale image is colorized using the light brown color.

12

Creating Photos

7 Adjust the density of the color by using the Amount slider.

Drag the slider to the right to add more color and to the left to use less color.

This technique can be used with any grayscale image and any color, and it applies the color to the entire image.

Finish the lesson

1 Close any open picutres by clicking the Close Window button in the upper right corner of the picture.

If PhotoDraw promps you to save changes, click No.

2 On the File menu, click Exit to quit PhotoDraw.

Lesson 12 Quick Reference

To	Do this
Adjust the brightness of an image	Select Brightness And Contrast from the Color button on the visual menu, and adjust the settings in the Color workpane.
Retouch a damaged photograph	Use Pan And Zoom from the View menu to enlarge the area that you want to retouch. Choose Remove Scratch from the Touch Up button on the visual menu. Click at the beginning of the scratch, and then click at the end of the scratch.
Add an effect to an image	Select the image object. Click the Effect button on the visual menu and choose the effect you want to use. Make your adjustments in the appropriate effects workpane.
Colorize a black and white photograph	Select the image object. Click the Color button on the visual menu, choose Colorize, and make your selections in the Color workpane.
Save a photo for use on the Internet	Make sure the image is contained in the picture area. Click Save For Use In on the File menu. Follow the directions in the Save For Use In Wizard.
Colorize a portion of a black and white photograph	Select the image object. Click the Color button on the visual menu and choose Colorize. In the Color workpane, select Correct By Painting, and draw on the photograph the areas that you want to be colorized.

13

Working with Picture Objects for the Web

ESTIMATED
TIME
45 min.

In this lesson you will learn how to:

✔ *Add and position picture objects.*

✔ *Size and crop picture objects.*

✔ *Draw and paint objects for the Web.*

✔ *Create 3-D picture objects.*

There are just about as many types of images you can add to your Web sites as there are people making those sites. In other words, if you wanted to, you could create, design, edit, and redesign images in Microsoft PhotoDraw 2000 and practically never do the same thing twice.

Of course, it is important to maintain a consistent look with your graphics, in style and in color. In your use of color, for instance, you should strive to develop a certain mood or feeling that best reflects the site you're creating graphics for. If you're creating a site for a law firm, for example, you might want to stick with blues and grays, which are nice professional colors. If you're creating a site for kids, you might want to use the primary colors—red, blue, and yellow—to appeal to the fun nature and playfulness of children.

Whatever your Web graphic challenge may be, PhotoDraw has the solution. From its ability to easily flip, flop, and resize images to its drawing and painting tools, it's all here—waiting for you and your imagination.

Adding and Positioning Picture Objects

Before you can create those wonderful Web graphics and take advantage of PhotoDraw's many options, you need to get a handle on the basics of adding and positioning picture objects in the PhotoDraw workspace. In PhotoDraw, you can add as many objects to a picture as you want, and each one can be moved or edited separately from the rest.

With PhotoDraw, you can choose from many alignment and positioning options such as rearranging the order of picture objects from back to front and top to bottom; aligning picture objects left, right, or centered relative to the other selected objects; or aligning the picture objects at the top, bottom, or middle of the workspace. You can also rotate and flip picture objects in any way you like. The possibilities are endless.

Work with a picture object

In this exercise, you add three picture objects, rotate one of them, and then align all three in the middle of the picture area.

❶   Start PhotoDraw, select the Blank Picture option from the Microsoft PhotoDraw dialog box, and click OK.

❷   In the New dialog box, click the Pictures tab, select the Default Picture option, and click OK.

PhotoDraw creates a new blank picture.

❸   On the Insert menu, click Visual Insert.

The Visual Insert dialog box is displayed.

❹   In the Look In drop-down list, select your hard disk drive. In the list of folders that appears, double-click the Web Publishing SBS Practice folder, and then click each of the following files while holding down the Ctrl key: rectangle.gif, circle.gif, and swirl.gif.

❺   Click the Insert button to insert all three images into your picture.

Your workspace should look similar to the one shown in the figure on the following page.

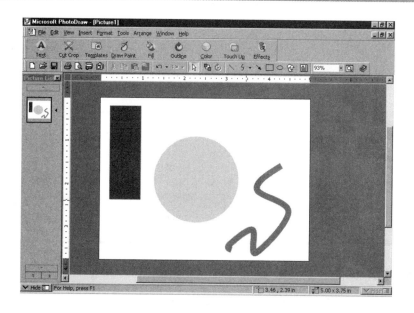

If your workspace is not exactly the same, don't worry. Just click each object and drag it around the workspace until your screen looks close to the screen above.

6 Select the blue rectangle, point to Rotate on the Arrange menu, and then click Rotate Right. The rectangle rotates to the right.

Your workspace should look similar to the following figure.

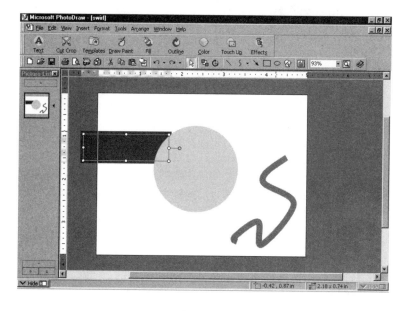

Working with Picture Objects   13

You can also choose Select All In Picture Area from the Edit menu to select all three picture objects at the same time.

7   To align all three picture objects in the middle of the picture area, select each of the three picture objects by holding down the Shift key and clicking each picture object, one at a time.

All three picture objects should be selected.

8   On the Arrange menu, point to Align and click Relative To Picture Area if it is not already turned on (pressed in).

9   On the Arrange menu, point to Align again and click Align Middle.

All three picture objects are now aligned in the middle of the picture area.

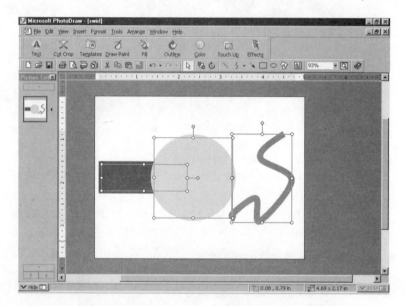

10   On the File menu, click Close, and click No in the resulting dialog box to close the picture without saving it.

tip

Selecting a picture object and clicking Arrange on the Arrange menu brings up the Arrange workpane. From the Arrange workpane, you can precisely adjust the size of the picture object, and you can position the picture object in a specific location relative to the top and left sides of the picture area. By selecting Rotate or Flip from the Arrange workpane, you can choose from a set of predefined flip and rotate options, each complete with a thumbnail representation so you can see what will happen even before you do it.

Sizing and Cropping Picture Objects

Many times when you insert an object into the workspace, it may not look the way you want it to. Maybe the picture object is too big or too small, or perhaps it contains more information than you need, and you want to delete, or *crop,* a portion of it.

When you use PhotoDraw's Crop, Erase, or Cut Out features to edit a picture object, you start by drawing a shape around the area of the image that you want to remove. When you click Finish, the area of the image that is outside of the shape is cut away and is no longer part of the image. When you use the Crop feature, the original image is altered. When you use the Erase feature, an area within the image is erased, or removed. When you use the Cut Out feature, PhotoDraw also creates a new picture containing just the cutout in the Picture List, leaving the original image intact. Each of these options opens its own workpane, which contains various shapes you can use, depending on the shape of the area you want to remove.

Use the Cut Out feature to create a special effect

In this exercise, you cut out the shape of a tree from within a circle.

New

1. Click the New buttton on the Standard toolbar.

   PhotoDraw creates a new blank picture.

2. Click Visual Insert on the Insert menu.

   The Visual Insert dialog box is displayed.

3. Navigate to the Web Publishing SBS Practice folder on your hard disk drive, click the image circle.gif, and click Insert.

   The image is inserted into the workspace.

4. On the Arrange menu, point to Align and click Align Middle.

   The circle should now be in the middle of the picture area. If it isn't in the middle of the picture area, point to Align on the Arrange menu and click Align Center.

5. Click the Cut Crop button on the visual menu and select Cut Out.

   The Cut Out workpane and a floating Cut Out toolbar appear.

6. Scroll down in the Cut Out workpane until you see the Pine Tree thumbnail.

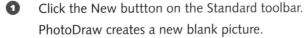

Working with Picture Objects   13

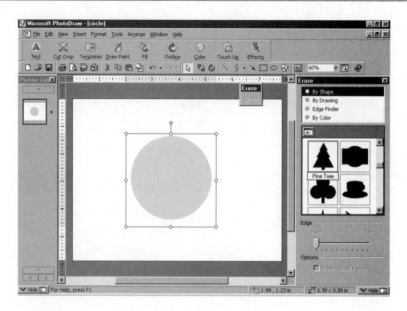

❼ Select the Pine Tree thumbnail.

An outline of the Pine Tree thumbnail is added to the workspace on top of the circle.

*Expand
Gallery*

tip

For each Cut Crop workpane that is opened, an Expand Gallery button appears at the top, above the thumbnails. Click the Expand Gallery button to get a larger view of the thumbnail options available.

❽ Resize the tree outline by dragging its resize handles—the circles in each corner of the selected cut out. The pine tree should be small enough to fit in the center of the circle.

❾ With the pine tree selected, point to Align on the Arrange menu and click Align Middle.

The pine tree is centered on the circle.

❿ Select the Cut Out Opposite Area check box in the Options area of the Cut Out workpane.

⓫ Click the Finish button on the floating menu to cut the pine tree shape out of the circle.

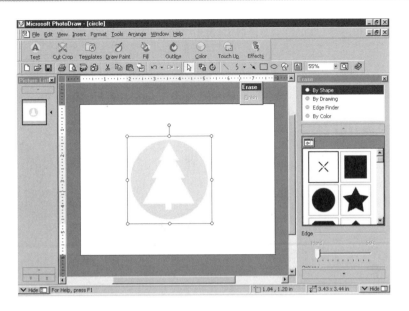

Drawing and Painting Objects for the Web

When you're ready to create original pictures with PhotoDraw, you'll be happy to know that you're armed with a nearly endless number of shapes, brushes, textures, and patterns from which to choose. Of course, each of the techniques can also be applied to an existing or scanned picture. For instance, you can insert a photograph of a person into the picture area and then add a colored callout, add some text, and create a unique blend of photography and illustration.

When you draw in PhotoDraw, you create solid lines and shapes, and when you paint in PhotoDraw, you create textured lines and shapes, similar to those you would create with a paintbrush. With either of these methods, you can add fill colors and effects such as fade-outs and shadows to your drawings. When you access one of PhotoDraw's drawing features, the AutoShapes dialog box appears from which you can choose predefined shapes, like stars, banners, arrows, and lines to create your pictures. These AutoShapes let you create otherwise complicated and time consuming shapes with ease. You can also draw and paint freely in PhotoDraw without using a predefined shape, and all of the colors and brush strokes can be applied to those images as well.

Working with Picture Objects 13

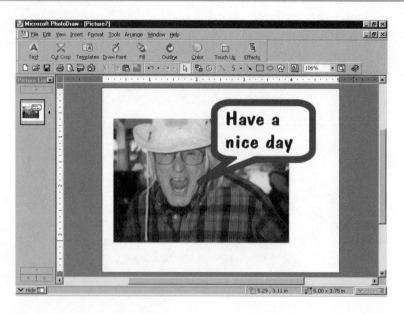

Draw in the picture area

If you wanted to create a star in a traditional illustration program, it would not only take some time, but it would also take plenty of finesse to get it just right. In this exercise you create a perfect star, change its color, and then change the solid outline of the star to a brush stroke special effect.

New

1 Click the New button on the toolbar.

A new blank picture appears.

2 Click the Draw Paint button on the visual menu, and select Draw.

The Outline workpane appears and the AutoShapes floating toolbar appears.

AutoShapes

3 Click the AutoShapes button on the AutoShapes floating toolbar, point to Stars And Banners, and select Explosion 2, which is second from the left in the top row.

4 In the picture area, click and drag to draw the star.

The Explosion 2 star appears in the picture area.

5 In the Width area of the Outline workpane, drag the slider until it reads 10.00 pt.

You can adjust the size of the star at any time by selecting the star and then dragging a handle on the outside of the selected object.

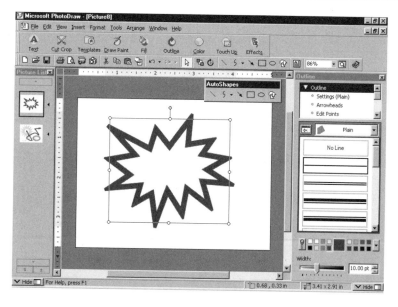

6 With the star selected, click the color drop-down arrow in the Outline workpane, and then point to Active Palette. Select a bright pink color from the Web palette pop-up menu.

The star automatically becomes bright pink.

7 Select Artistic Brushes from the Gallery Type drop-down list.
You may be prompted to insert an Office 2000 CD into your CD drive.

A scrolling list of brush strokes appears.

8 Select the brush stroke Crayon – Light.

The Crayon – Light brush stroke is automatically applied to the star.

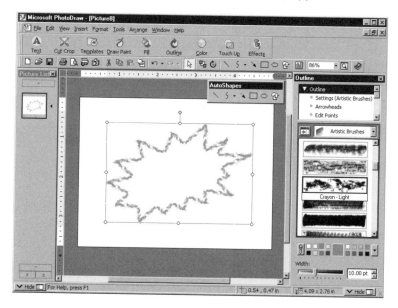

Working with Picture Objects 13

tip

If you want to create a solid shape, draw the shape in the picture area, and then select Fill from the Outline workpane and choose a fill color. Of course, the line and fill colors don't have to be the same.

Working with a Browser-Safe Color Palette

When you're creating graphics for use on the Internet, it's important to use a browser-safe color palette. A browser-safe color palette contains the 216 colors already determined to be displayed the best in the widest variety of situations. In other words, if you use these colors, your images will look the way you want them to when people visit your Web sites. You can use any color you want to, but you take the risk that the color may not appear correctly to all viewers. If a user's computer supports only the minimum 256 colors, any image that contains more colors will appear dithered or blurry.

To use a browser-safe color palette in PhotoDraw, select the color drop-down arrow from any workpane that contains color options, and then select More Colors from the resulting submenu. The More Colors dialog box then appears.

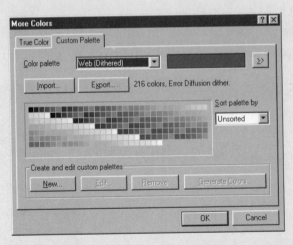

Using the More Colors dialog box, you can select a Web palette from the Color Palette drop-down list. The palette you choose then becomes the active palette, and from then on, you just need to select Active Palette from the color drop-down arrow to access these colors.

<table>
<tr><td>

**One
Step
Further**

</td><td>

Creating 3-D
Picture Objects

</td></tr>
</table>

In PhotoDraw, you can easily draw an image and choose from one of the many included 3-D effects to create pictures that will bring an extra dimension to any Web page. Once you've created a 3-D image, you can spin it around or change the direction of the light source on the image to vary the shadow effect—all with just a few clicks of the mouse.

Add and modify a 3-D picture object

In this exercise, you add 3-D effects to a simple circle and then modify these effects. You can, however, add 3-D effects to any drawn picture object in PhotoDraw.

New

Ellipse

To make a perfect circle, press and hold the Shift key while you drag.

① Click the New button on the toolbar.

A new blank document appears.

② Select Draw from the Draw Paint visual menu.

③ Click the Ellipse button on the AutoShapes toolbar, and then click and drag in the picture area to draw a circle.

④ On the visual menu, click the Effects button and select 3-D.

The 3-D workpane appears.

⑤ Select the Designer 3-D effect from the scrolling gallery on the 3-D workpane.

The effect is automatically applied to the circle.

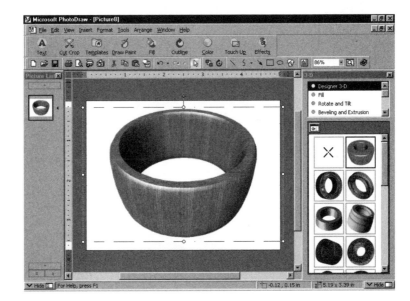

Working with Picture Objects **13**

Once you've added a 3-D effect to an image, you have more options available to you in the top portion of the 3-D workpane.

6 Choose Lighting from the 3-D workpane. You will probably have to scroll down a bit to see the Lighting option.

7 Select Lighting 27 from the scrolling gallery on the 3-D workpane.

The lighting effect is applied to the circle.

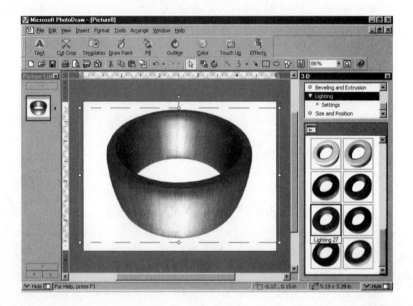

tip

When you're working with the various 3-D effects and their attributes, don't be afraid to experiment. It may take you a few tries to get exactly what you're looking for.

Finish the lesson

1 Close any open pictures by clicking the Close Window button in the upper right corner of the picture.

If PhotoDraw prompts you to save changes, click No.

2 On the File menu, click Exit to quit PhotoDraw.

Lesson 13 Quick Reference

To	Do this	Button
Add a picture object to the PhotoDraw workspace	With PhotoDraw open, click the Insert the button on the visual menu and select Visual Insert. Locate the image you want to insert, and then click the Insert button.	
Rotate a picture object	Select the object, point to Rotate on the Arrange menu, and then make your choice from the resulting submenu.	
Change the top-to-bottom order of a picture object	Select the picture object that you want to change. Point to Order on the Arrange menu, and make your choice from the resulting submenu.	
Align multiple picture objects in the same workspace	Select each picture object by holding down the Shift key and clicking each object. Point to Align on the Arrange menu, and make your choice from the resulting submenu.	
Crop or cut out a portion of a picture object	Select either Cut Out or Crop from the Cut Crop button on the visual menu. From the scrolling list, select the thumbnail shape that you want to use on the picture object. When you're done, select the Finish button on the accompanying floating toolbar.	
Erase a portion of a picture object	Select an image in the workspace, click the Cut Crop button on the visual menu, and select Erase. In the scrolling list, select the thumbnail shape that you want to remove from the selected image. When you're done, click the Finish button on the accompanying floating toolbar.	
Expand a thumbnail gallery	In any workpane that contains a scrolling thumbnail list, select the Expand Gallery button.	

Working with Picture Objects 13

Lesson 13 Quick Reference

To	Do this
Draw a shape	Click the Draw Paint button on the visual menu and select Draw. Click the AutoShapes button on the AutoShapes floating toolbar, and select the shape that you want to draw. Drag to draw the shape in the picture area.
Apply a brush stroke effect to a drawn picture object	Select the picture object, choose Artistic Brushes from the Gallery Type drop-down list, and make your choice from the scrolling thumbnail gallery.
Fill an enclosed shape	Select the enclosed shape in the picture area, choose Fill from the Outline workpane, and pick a fill color.
Select a browser-safe color palette	Click the drop-down arrow button in the color area of any workpane, and then select More Colors from the submenu. In the resulting More Colors dialog box, select the Web palette of your choice from the Color Palette drop-down list.
Apply a 3-D effect to a drawn picture object	Select the picture object, click the Effects button on the visual menu, select 3-D, and make your choice from the thumbnail picture gallery.

14

Using Templates to Create Web Graphics

In this lesson you will learn how to:

ESTIMATED TIME 30 min.

✔ *Use a PhotoDraw template to create a button.*

✔ *Use a PhotoDraw Designer Edge to stylize a photograph.*

Not everyone is a trained graphic designer, and not everyone has a creative background. If you're a person who does not have these skills, or if you just find yourself pressed for time to create a professionally designed Web button or banner, Microsoft PhotoDraw 2000 has the answer—templates. A template is a predesigned picture, usually with customizable text and graphics, which you can easily customize to create your own professional results without the degree in graphic design. Even a beginner can produce detailed business flyers, invitations, Web buttons, postcards, and much more using PhotoDraw's templates. And even if you are a professional graphic designer, you'll find the wide variety of template choices and the customization and ease of use to be invaluable resources.

When you use a template in PhotoDraw, you're presented with a series of workpanes, each with unique options that let you customize your image. When you've finished making changes to your image, all you have to do is click the Finish button, and your new creation is completed and displayed in the workspace.

At Impact Public Relations, you're in charge of putting together a new set of navigation buttons for a client's Web site. You decide that the best way to complete this task is to use a button template in PhotoDraw.

Using a PhotoDraw Template to Create a Button

Most of today's Web site creators use a picture image as a button on their Web pages. These buttons are usually hyperlinks that are used to navigate throughout a site. Your client wants to create a Web site with a Southwestern theme, so you'll want to take advantage of one of the Southwest button designs included with PhotoDraw to create the button you'll use to navigate to another destination in the Web site. Using this button template takes the guesswork out of designing and allows you to focus on creating an appropriate Web button for your client.

Create a button using a template

In this exercise you create a new Home Page button using a PhotoDraw button template.

If PhotoDraw is already open, click the Templates button on the visual menu, and choose Web Graphics from the submenu to open the Templates workpane.

1. Insert CD 4 of Office 2000 Premium. This is the CD that contains the PhotoDraw template content.

2. Start PhotoDraw, and click the Template option in the Microsoft PhotoDraw dialog box. Click OK.

   PhotoDraw starts with the Templates workpane open and thumbnail images representing the available templates visible in the picture area.

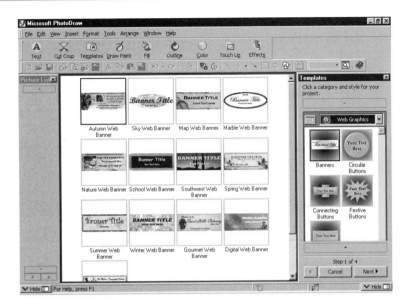

③ If it's not currently selected, select Web Graphics from the Templates workpane drop-down list.

The Web templates are now visible.

④ Choose Circular Buttons from the Templates workpane to display the button thumbnails.

tip

In the Templates workpane, you can click the Banners template to create a Web banner. Typically, Web banners are rectangular shaped ads that are found at the top or bottom of a Web page. Many Web sites charge companies a fee to include a banner ad on their site, which results in a steady stream of revenue for the site owner.

Notice that the button appears large in the workspace. To view the button at its actual size, click the Zoom drop-down arrow and select 100% from the drop-down list.

⑤ Select the Southwest Circle Button thumbnail, and click the Next button on the Templates workpane.

The button is displayed in the workspace with the words *Your Text Here* in the middle of the button.

⑥ To keep the Southwest background, select the Next button on the Template workpane.

The wizard advances to the next step, and the text area of the workpane is displayed.

14

Using Templates

Replace

tip

If you want to replace the background image on the button, click the Replace button in step 2 of 4 in the Templates workpane to replace the image with another picture open in PhotoDraw. If you want to replace the button background with a different image—one on your hard disk drive, for example—click the Browse button, locate the image you want, and then double-click it. The button background is replaced with the new image you select. Click the Next button on the Templates workpane when you're finished.

You can also format the text font, size and style in the text area of the Template workpane.

7 You want the word *Home* to appear on a separate line above the word *Page* on your finished button. In the text area of the Templates workpane, type the word **Home**.

The word *Home* replaces the default text.

8 Press the Enter key on your keyboard and type the word **Page**.

The words *Home Page* appear on the button.

9 Click the Next button on the Templates workpane, and then click the Finish button on the Templates workpane.

The finished button appears in the workspace, and the Templates workpane disappears.

Using a PhotoDraw Designer Edge to Stylize a Photograph

One Step Further

As you travel around the Internet, you'll see lots of photographs on Web pages. Most of the time these photographs are just rectangles—nothing fancy and not too interesting. With PhotoDraw's designer edges, you can eliminate those boring rectangles and add some spice to your photographs. You can think of a designer edge as a kind of template that automatically adds an effect to an image. But unlike other templates, a designer edge affects only the outline of the image. Of course, once you've applied a designer edge to an image, you can use any other PhotoDraw feature or effect to manipulate the image.

Add a designer edge to a photograph

In this exercise you add a stylized border to a rectangular photograph.

1 Insert CD 4 of Office 2000 Premium. This is the CD that contains the PhotoDraw templates and Designer Edge content.

New

2 Click the New button on the Standard toolbar.

A new blank document is displayed.

3 On the Insert menu, click Visual Insert.

The Visual Insert dialog box appears.

4 Navigate to the Web Publishing SBS Practice folder on your hard disk drive, click the image colorpicture.jpg, and click Insert.

The image is inserted into the workspace.

5 On the visual menu, click the Templates button, and then select Designer Edges from the menu. The Templates workpane opens with the Designer Edges thumbnails visible in the picture area.

14

Using Templates

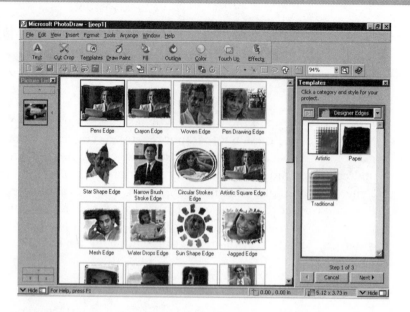

6 Select Artistic from the Templates workpane.

The Artistic edges thumbnails appear in the picture area.

7 Choose the Circular Strokes Edge thumbnail, and then click the Next button on the Templates workpane.

The thumbnail image appears in the picture area.

Replace

8 Click the Replace button on the Templates workpane, and then click the photograph you opened in step 2 in the Picture List. The designer edge is applied to the photograph.

If you want to adjust the area of the photograph that shows through the designer edge, choose the Picture Position button on the Templates workpane, and then drag the picture around the Picture Area until you have the image where you want it.

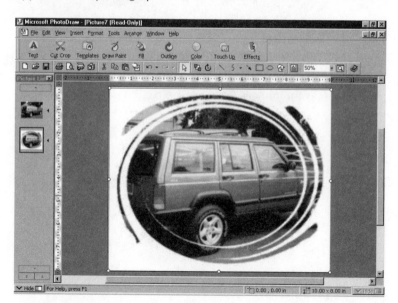

9 Click the Next button on the Templates workpane.

A reminder to save your picture when you're finished appears in the workpane.

10 Finally, choose the Finish button on the Templates workpane.

PhotoDraw creates a new picture in the Picture List with the designer edge added. The original picture remains in the Picture List untouched.

tip

With the original picture remaining untouched in the Picture List, you can try out many different edges on one photograph, or you can use the original photograph as a back-up copy for your records.

Finish the lesson

1 Close any open pictures by clicking the Close Window button in the upper right corner of the picture.

If PhotoDraw prompts you to save changes, click No.

2 On the File menu, click Exit to quit PhotoDraw.

Lesson 14 Quick Reference

To	Do this
Use a template to create a Web button	On the visual menu, click the Templates button, and select Web Graphics from the menu. Select the button style of your choice in the Templates workpane.
Create a custom background for a Web button	Select the button style of your choice in the Templates workpane, click Next to advance to the second page of the wizard, and then click the Replace button to select the image to use as the button background.
Format text on a Web button	Double-click the text object that you want to change. Make your changes in the Text workpane.

14

Using Templates

Lesson 14 Quick Reference

To	Do this
Add a designer edge to a photograph	Insert Office 2000 Premium CD 4 into your CD-ROM drive, and open the picture you want to change. Click the Templates button on the visual menu and select Designer Edges from the menu. Choose an edge style from the Templates workpane, and then click the thumbnail image that you want to use as your edge. Click the Replace button on the Templates workpane, and then click the picture you want to change in the Picture List.
Adjust the area of the photograph that shows through the designer edge	Once you've selected a designer edge for your button, click the Picture Position button in the Templates workpane, and then click the image in the workspace and drag it until you have it positioned the way you want it.

PART 3

Publishing on the Web with Microsoft Office 2000

15

Using Microsoft Office 2000 to Publish Documents on the Web

ESTIMATED TIME
55 min.

In this lesson you will learn how to:

✔ *Use Web themes in Office.*

✔ *Use the Web toolbar.*

✔ *Insert a hyperlink in an Office document.*

✔ *Save a file as a Web page.*

✔ *Publish a project for the Internet.*

✔ *Use and create Web folders.*

✔ *Access the Microsoft Web Update Web site.*

Microsoft Office 2000 is a complete suite of applications designed for the home office, small business, or home user. Each application in the suite is unique in its approach to a specific need of any user. The applications in Office 2000 Premium include:

▨ **FrontPage 2000** Create Web sites without knowing how to write HTML using FrontPage. For more information on using FrontPage to design and create a Web site, see Part 1 of this book.

▨ **Outlook 2000** Manage your e-mail, personal calendar, contacts list, and more with Outlook.

- **PhotoDraw 2000**   Create pictures, manipulate photographs, and design custom images with PhotoDraw.
- **Word 2000**   Create deep and feature-rich documents with Word.
- **Excel 2000**   With Excel, you can create spreadsheets and charts to keep track of all your business transactions.
- **PowerPoint 2000**   Create and display slide show presentations with PowerPoint.
- **Access 2000**   Build and manage a database using Access.
- **Publisher 2000**   Design and lay out desktop publishing projects with Publisher.

These Office 2000 applications are all designed to work together seamlessly, and they all have Internet features built into them. For example, you can create a presentation in PowerPoint and display it as a Web page, or you can use Access to build a database and connect it to the Web site you create using FrontPage.

When you're working in an office, sharing documents and collaborating with other people is a necessity. Microsoft Office 2000 applications make it easy for you to do this because they have a consistent interface and the ability to share documents with each other. In addition, when you're creating a Web site, you'll be glad to know that all of these applications migrate easily to the Internet. Many of the Office 2000 applications also share common features and dialog boxes, making it easy to switch between them and be able to complete a task without having to learn a new procedure.

Using Web Themes

A Web theme is a collection of graphical elements, such as bullets, backgrounds, fonts, and colors, which are all created to work together as a whole. These themes create a look for your Web pages, but unlike a template, they don't assist you in the actual creation of your Web pages. Themes are available in Word 2000, FrontPage 2000, and Publisher 2000.

Adding a Web Theme to a Finished Project

You can apply a theme to one page in a document or all of the pages in a document. For example, let's say you have just finished writing the annual report for Impact Public Relations in Word 2000, and you want to apply a theme to the entire report. The following exercise will explain how you can do this.

Apply a theme to an entire document

In this exercise, you apply a theme to all of the pages in a document at once.

1 From the Web Publishing SBS Practice folder on your hard disk drive, open the file AnnualReport.doc in Word.

2 On the Format menu, click Theme.

The Theme dialog box appears.

3 Click Artsy in the Choose A Theme scrolling list.

A preview of that theme appears in the dialog box.

4 Click OK to apply the theme.

The theme is applied to the entire document.

tip

If you want to see how the theme will look in a Web browser, before you publish the file to a Web server, click Web Page Preview on the File menu. The document is opened in your Web browser. This is nothing more than a preview, so close the Web browser after you finish viewing.

Creating a New Project Using a Web Theme

The process of adding a Web theme to Publisher projects is slightly different from the process of applying a theme to a Word document. If you want to add a Web theme to a new project in Word 2000, for instance, you use the Web Page Wizard. To access this wizard, on the File menu, click New. In the New dialog box, click the Web Pages tab, and then double-click the Web Page Wizard.

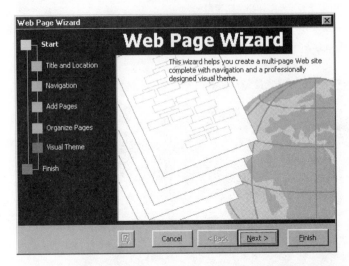

Follow the instructions in the wizard, choosing such things as page titles, navigation options, and Web themes. Click the Finish button when you're done to complete the Web site.

If you want to create a Web site using Publisher 2000, you'll need to use the Web Site Wizard and create the project from scratch. The Web Site Wizard guides you through the process of creating and designing an entire Web site, including choosing a theme. To access the Web Site Wizard in Publisher 2000, on the File menu, click New. In the Catalog dialog box, select Web Sites in the list of available wizards.

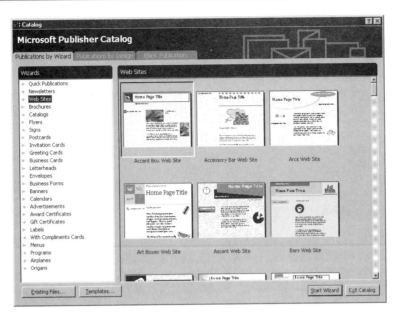

The list of Web sites includes a thumbnail showing the theme used in each site. For example, you could select the Bars Web Site for Impact Public Relations. Once you decide on a Web site, click the Start Wizard button to begin the Web site creation process.

As you go through the wizard, you can determine color schemes, backgrounds, and the types and numbers of pages you want to create, as well as the type of navigation (vertical or horizontal). You can even add sound or a form to the pages in your site. As you work through each page of the wizard, you're actually creating the pages in your Web site.

The Web Toolbar

Every application in Office 2000 is designed to work with the Internet. One of the features that help to make working on the Internet easier is the Web toolbar found in most Office 2000 programs.

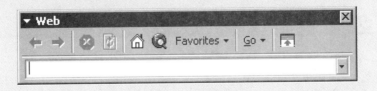

(Continued)

(Continued)

> The Web toolbar is a connection to your browser from within an application. In other words, if you have access to the Internet and you're using Microsoft Word 2000, you can use the Web toolbar to launch your browser and display a page by selecting a shortcut in your Favorites folder, or even type the URL you want to visit.

Inserting a Hyperlink in an Office 2000 Document

You can quickly insert a hyperlink into an Office application by using the keyboard shortcut Ctrl+K. Select some text before using this shortcut, or type the text in the dialog box when you add the hyperlink location.

If you're using an Office application to create an HTML page, eventually you're going to want to create a *hyperlink*. A hyperlink is a link, or connection, to a Web site, or a page within a Web site. This can be a link to an entirely new page anywhere on the Internet, or a link to an area within the same site. You can create a hyperlink from just about anything on a page, like text or a graphic element, for instance. When you're viewing a Web page, you can recognize a hyperlink by the hand pointer that appears when you move the mouse pointer over a hyperlink. Often a text hyperlink is underlined and in a different color than the rest of the text, but the only sure way to determine whether text is a hyperlink is to look for the hand pointer.

Before you create a hyperlink, choose the text or image you want to use as the hyperlink. To place a hyperlink in your Office 2000 application, on the Insert menu, click Hyperlink. The Insert Hyperlink dialog box appears.

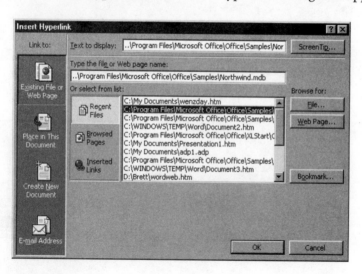

The Insert Hyperlink dialog box offers you many options. You can simply type the URL of the page you want to link to, or choose from recent files, browsed pages, or a link that is currently inserted on the page. You can also link to another place in the same document—not necessarily the current page. Another popular hyperlink is a link to an e-mail address. For instance, if you're creating a Contact Us page for the Impact Public Relations Web site, you might want to have an e-mail hyperlink. Visitors to the Contact Us page can just click the e-mail hyperlink and send an e-mail message to Impact Public Relations.

Saving Office Documents as Web Pages

You can save any Word 2000, Excel 2000, Publisher 2000, or PowerPoint 2000 document in the HTML file format by using the new and improved Save As dialog box.

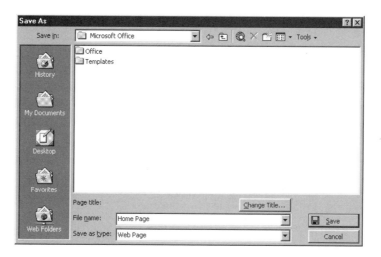

HTML, or Hypertext Markup Language, is the programming language used to create Web pages; a Web browser, such as Microsoft Internet Explorer 5, then reads and displays these pages. If you need to make changes, or *edit*, any Office file that has been converted into HTML, you can do that too. Simply open the Office HTML file in the application that you used to create it. For example, as a staff writer at Impact Public Relations, one of your jobs is to write the company press releases using Word 2000 and save them as HTML pages for use on the company Web site. When you need to make a change to a press release, all you have to do is open the file in Word 2000, and all of the rich editing features you're accustomed to using are available to you. Before these features were available, you had to write the press release in Word and hand it off to the

HTML programmer, who would convert it to HTML and post it to the Internet. Then when you needed to make a change, you had to rework the file in Word and start the entire process over again.

> **tip**
> The process for getting an Access 2000 database object on the Internet is slightly different from the process for other Office 2000 applications. This process is described in the section "Saving an Access Database Object as a Web Page," later in this lesson.

Save and edit a Word document as a Web page

In the following exercise, you save a Word document as an HTML file and then open the HTML file to be edited in Word.

Once a file is in HTML format, it can then be posted to a Web server connected to the Internet. When a document is posted to an Internet server, it's available to any Web browser that accesses that server.

❶ Make sure that the AnnualReport.doc file is open from the previous exercise. If it is not, open it from the Web Publishing SBS Practice folder on your hard disk drive.

❷ On the File menu, click Save As Web Page.

The Save As dialog box appears. Web Page is selected by default in the Save As Type box.

❸ Click the Save In drop-down arrow, and then browse to locate the Web Publishing SBS Practice folder on your hard disk drive. Click the folder.

The contents of the folder are displayed.

❹ Click the Save button.

The document is saved as an individual HTML page.

❺ Close the AnnualReport.htm file.

❻ On the File menu, click Open.

The Open dialog box appears.

❼ Click Web Pages in the Files Of Type drop-down list.

❽ Locate and select the AnnualReport.htm file in the Web Publishing SBS Practice folder, and click the Open button.

AnnualReport.htm opens in Word and is able to be edited.

important

In Publisher 2000, creating a Web site is slightly different. The first time you want to convert an existing publication to a Web format, click Create Web Site From Current Publication on the File menu. This will launch the Design Checker, which will scan your publication for potential problems before converting it to HTML format. Each subsequent time you want to save the file as a Web page, on the File menu, click Save As Web Page, and the Save As dialog box will save the entire publication in the HTML file format.

Saving an Access Database Object as a Web Page

Database objects in Access 2000 are not saved directly as HTML pages, as in other Office applications. Rather, they are saved in a format that you can use in an HTML document. This means that you can take any table, query, form, or report, and save it for use on a Web page. When you save database objects in Access, you won't be creating an HTML file; you'll be creating a file that you'll use to connect the object to an HTML page. Normally, this connection process could be time consuming and complicated. To help alleviate this problem, Access 2000 works with Word 2000 and Excel 2000 to publish your database object to the Web.

Save an Access database object as a Web page

In this exercise, you publish a table you created in Access to the Web.

1 From the Web Publishing SBS Practice folder on your hard disk drive, open the SampleIPR.mdb database, and double-click the IPR - Projects table in the database window.

The table opens in Access.

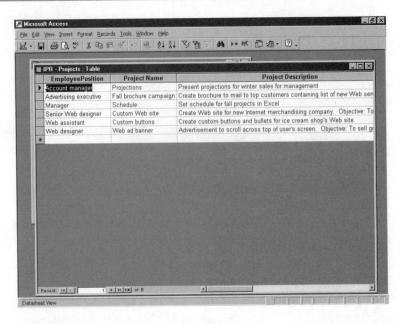

2 On the Tools menu, point to Office Links and click Publish It With MS Word.

The table is opened in Word, and the elements in the table are completely editable. You'll find that some of the information in the Access table is not needed on the Web page, and you can edit those entries in Word.

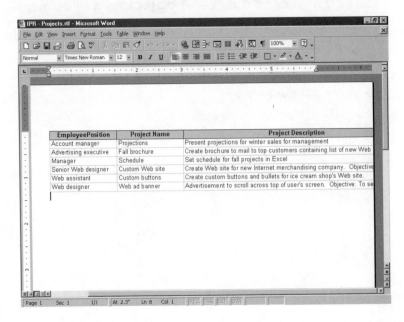

3 After you are finished editing the table in Word, on the File menu, click Web Page Preview.

The table is opened in your Web browser. Here you can get an idea of what the table will look like to visitors to your site.

If you want to bring the Access database object into Excel, where you can work with it just like any worksheet in Excel, open and select a table in Access, and on the Tools menu, point to Office Links and click Analyze It With MS Excel. The database object is opened in Excel and can then be edited and saved as a Web page.

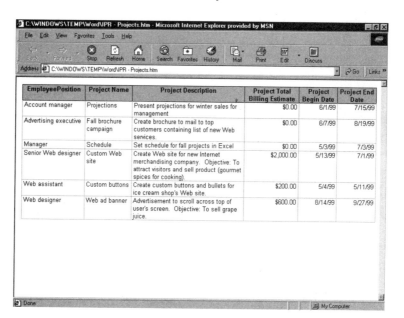

4 Close your browser. To save the file as a Web page from Word, on the File menu, click Save As Web Page.

The Save As dialog box appears.

5 Navigate to the Web Publishing SBS Practice folder on your hard disk drive, and then click Save.

The file is saved in HTML format and can be published to a Web server to be made available to users of the Internet.

Publishing a Project for the Internet

When you use Excel 2000, Publisher 2000, or PowerPoint 2000, you can save your entire project as HTML files—all at one time—right from the Save As dialog box. This publishing process can save the files to either your local hard drive or to an Internet server.

Using Office 2000 to Publish 15

Publish a presentation to your local hard disk drive

In the following exercise, you publish a PowerPoint 2000 presentation to your local hard drive.

1 Start PowerPoint 2000. In the PowerPoint dialog box that appears, click the Open An Existing Presentation option, and then click OK.

The Open dialog box is displayed.

2 Navigate to the Web Publishing SBS Practice folder on your hard disk drive, select the file CompanyMeeting.ppt, and click Open.

The presentation opens.

3 On the File menu, click Save As Web Page.

The Save As dialog box appears.

4 In the Save As dialog box, click the Publish button.

The Publish As Web Page dialog box appears.

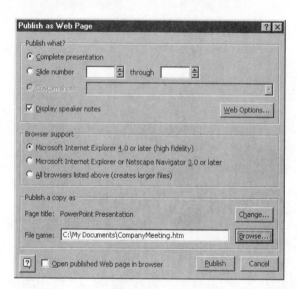

5 Select the following options in the Publish As Web Page dialog box.

  ▪ Click Complete Presentation to have all slides in the presentation published.

  ▪ In the Browser Support area, click Microsoft Internet Explorer 4.0 Or Later (High Fidelity). This insures that the presentation will perform as expected in all versions of Internet Explorer after version 4.0, but the presentation will be unavailable to other browsers.

If your hard disk has a drive letter other than C, substitute the appropriate drive letter instead.

  ▪ In the Publish A Copy As area, type **C:\Web Publishing SBS Practice\CompanyMeeting.htm** in the File Name text box.

❻ Click the Publish button to create and save the HTML files on your local hard disk.

When you click the Publish button from within Excel, you have the options of choosing which sheets to publish, adding interactivity—such as making calculations—to a spreadsheet or PivotTable, and selecting the location you want to publish to and the name you want to use for the file. When you've made your choices, click the Publish button and the HTML pages are created and saved.

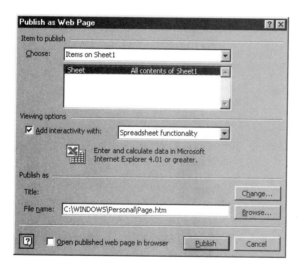

Web Folders

There are different ways to get your HTML files to a Web server so that they can be viewed on the Internet. You can, for example, use FTP (File Transfer Protocol) to upload the pages, or you can use a Web folder. A Web folder is used as a shortcut to a Web server. Files placed in a Web folder are in essence published to the Internet for viewing in a Web browser. Before you can create a Web folder, you must have a connection to the Internet, and your service provider must support the use of Web folders. It's important to check with your service provider prior to creating, or working with, a Web folder.

Creating a Web Folder

Before you create a Web folder, you need to have the Web address, or URL, of the Web server that you want publish to, and you must be connected to the Internet. For example, if you wanted to create a Web folder for Impact Public Relations, the Web address might be *www.impactpublicrelations!!10.com.*

Create a Web folder

In this exercise, you create a new Web folder.

important

To complete this exercise, you need to know the URL of your Web server.

❶   Double-click the My Computer icon on your computer's desktop. In the My Computer window, double-click the Web Folders icon, and then double-click the Add Web Folder icon that appears.

The Add Web Folder Wizard appears.

❷   In the text box, type the location of the server you want the Web folder to access. This is an absolute URL, such as *http:/www.impactpublicrelations!!10.com.*

tip

If you don't know the location of the server you want the Web folder to access, or if you just don't want to type it yourself, click the Browse button to use your Web browser to locate the URL. When you find the URL you want to use, it will be placed into the dialog box automatically.

❸ Click the Next button.

The next page of the wizard appears.

❹ Type a name for the Web folder, or use the URL as the name.

❺ Click the Finish button to create the Web folder.

The new Web folder can now be accessed and used to post HTML files to that server. Be aware, though, that any passwords needed to access the Web server will have to be entered before you can actually place any files into the Web folder.

Saving to a Web Folder

Saving a publication to a Web folder means that it is copied to a Web folder and is accessible from a browser connected to the Internet. To save a publication to a Web folder, you need to have a connection to the Internet and have a Web folder already created. While connected to the Internet, you can save files directly to a Web folder just as you would save a file to your hard disk drive, the difference being that instead of just creating a copy on your hard disk drive, the files are saved to the Internet server that was used to create the Web folder. For example, you can use the Save As Web Page feature in Microsoft Word 2000 to save an HTML page to a Web folder.

Save a publication to a Web folder

In this exercise, you save an HTML page created in Word 2000 to the Web folder that you created in the previous exercise.

important

To complete this exercise, you need access to a Web server and you need to have created a Web folder in the previous exercise.

Using Office 2000 to Publish 15

1. Start Word 2000. On the File menu, click Open.

   The Open dialog box appears.

2. Navigate to the Web Publishing SBS Practice folder on your hard disk drive, click the file WebPage.htm, and click Open.

   The file opens.

3. On the File menu, click Save As Web Page.

   The Save As dialog box appears.

4. In the Save As dialog box, click the Web Folders button on the left side of the window.

   All of the Web folders currently on your computer are listed.

If there is a password required to access the Web server you used to create the Web folder, you will be prompted to enter it before you can save any files to it.

5. Double-click the Web folder that you created in the previous exercise.

   Your screen should look similar to the following:

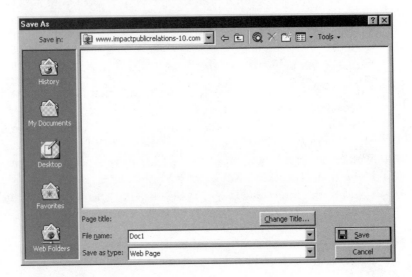

6. Click the Save button to copy the files to the Web folder.

   The page is saved to the Web folder.

Office on the Web Updates

When you're connected to the Internet and using an Office 2000 application, you can easily get the help you need. Beyond what the Help files included with the program offer, you can get answers to your questions, tips, and tricks, and even download some free tools.

(Continued)

(Continued)

To access the Office Update Web site, on the Help menu in any Office 2000 application, click Office On The Web. The Office application launches your Web browser and connects you to the Web site automatically.

Once you're at the Office Update Web site, you can find information on any application in Office 2000, regardless of which application you opened the site from. Remember, however, that you must be connected to the Internet when you want to access the Office Update Web site.

Finish the lesson

● Quit any open Office applications used in this lesson by clicking the Close button in the upper right corner.

If you are prompted to save any changes, click No.

Lesson 15 Quick Reference

To	Do this
Apply a Web theme	On the Format menu, click Theme. Choose a theme from the list, and then click OK.
Preview a file in a Web browser	On the File menu, click Web Page Preview.
Save a Word document as a Web page	Open the document in Word. On the File menu, click Save As Web Page. Choose a location for the file, and then click Save.
Edit an HTML page using its original application	Open the applicatin that created the original file. On the File menu, click Open. Click Web Pages in the Files Of Type drop-down list. Select the HTML file and click Open.
Save an Access database object as a Web page	Open the database object in Access. On the Tools menu, point to Office Links and click Publish It With MS Word. In Word, on the File menu, click Save As Web Page. Choose a location for the file, and then click Save.
Publish a PowerPoint presentation or Excel file to your hard disk drive	Open the presentation in its original application. On the File menu, click Save As Web Page. Click the Publish button. Select any publishing options, choose a file location, and then click Publish.

Using Office 2000 to Publish 15

Lesson 15 Quick Reference

To	Do this
Create a Web folder	Double-click the My Computer icon. Double-click the Web Folders icon, and then double-click the Add Web Folder icon. Type the server location and then click Next. Type a name for the Web folder, and then click Finish.
Save a publication to a Web folder	Open the publication. On the File menu, click Save As Web Page. Click the Web Folders button and then double-click a Web folder Click Save.

Upgrading from FrontPage 98

Microsoft FrontPage 2000 has many new features that make it easier for you to create Web pages and Web sites. Because you might need a little help making the transition from FrontPage 98 to FrontPage 2000, this appendix walks you through the most important issues that you face when you upgrade.

Replacing FrontPage 98 with FrontPage 2000

You don't need to uninstall FrontPage 98 before you install FrontPage 2000. In fact, it's much better if you *don't* uninstall FrontPage 98. When you install FrontPage 2000 on top of your old installation of FrontPage 98, the setup program will keep all of your settings and preferences from the previous version and use them in FrontPage 2000.

If you want to run FrontPage 2000 and keep your installation of FrontPage 98, you simply install FrontPage 2000 in a folder different from the one in which you have FrontPage 98.

Using FrontPage 98 Webs in FrontPage 2000

In the lessons of this book, you import Web files from the book's CD-ROM and create new FrontPage-based Webs with the imported files. To accomplish that, you use the Import Web Wizard. Note that if a set of Web files used a theme or had a Web page navigation hierarchy, those are not preserved when you import the files to create a Web.

When you create a Web in FrontPage (whether you use FrontPage 2000 or FrontPage 98), information about the Web theme, hierarchy, and other features is stored in the Microsoft Windows folder on your hard disk drive. You had to import Webs from the CD because the Web information wasn't on your hard disk drive. But when you install FrontPage 2000 on the same computer as your previous copy of FrontPage, the Web information is just where it ought to be. As a result, you can start using your existing Webs from FrontPage 98 as soon as you install FrontPage 2000.

Getting to Know FrontPage 2000's New Features

FrontPage 2000 has many new features that make it easier to design attractive, interactive Web sites. Navigation is easier, there are more ready-to-use components, and it is easy to integrate databases and spreadsheets into Web pages.

FrontPage 2000 also offers new themes, as well as the ability to modify existing themes or create your own. You can insert Microsoft Excel 2000 worksheets, PivotTables, and charts on Web pages, as well as a variety of new FrontPage components. It's easier to write and edit HTML and Web page script code.

Interface Changes

The FrontPage Editor and FrontPage Explorer are now integrated into a single program, as are many other features. The user interface changes are summarized in the table.

FrontPage 98	FrontPage 2000
FrontPage Editor and FrontPage Explorer	No longer separate programs. Integrated into a single FrontPage program.
All Files view	Integrated into the Folders view.
Hyperlink Status view	Integrated into the Reports view.
Themes view	Themes now accessed in a dialog box from the Format menu.

Ease of Use

FrontPage 2000 is designed to be even easier to use than FrontPage 98. Apart from the interface changes already discussed, FrontPage is now designed to look and work just like the other programs in Microsoft Office 2000—with the same themes, toolbars, menus, and shortcuts, as well as tools such as the Format Painter (familiar to users of Microsoft Word), HTML help, and background spelling checking. Some of the most important ease of use features are summarized in the table.

Ease of use feature	Explanation
Web themes	More themes (over 60) that are easier to apply, either to entire Webs or to individual pages.
Format Painter	FrontPage users can now copy the formatting from one block of text to another by positioning the mouse pointer on the text with the desired format, clicking the toolbar's Format Painter button, and selecting the text to be formatted.
Spelling checker	Spelling checking can now be done in the background as you type. If you prefer, it can still be done in a single operation as in FrontPage 98.
Personalized menus	Menu choices used most often are prominently placed on each menu, or menus can be expanded to display all menu choices. Menus also expand automatically as needed.
Personalized toolbars	Toolbars share screen space with each other based on how frequently they are used. When a toolbar is used often, it is "promoted" to occupy more screen space.
Customizable toolbars	Toolbars are easier to customize by dragging buttons.
HTML help	HTML help is now available while users work in FrontPage.
Answer Wizard	Users can ask questions in plain language and get the information they need.

Web Page Design

FrontPage includes many new features that make it easier to design attractive and functional Web pages. There are more themes than before, and it's easier to customize themes or create your own. With or without themes, it's now easier to customize color schemes of your Web pages. There's improved support for Cascading Style Sheets (CSS), and you can position items in exact locations on your Web pages. Finally, there are more ready-to-use FrontPage components that build features into your Web pages. The table summarizes some of the most important new features for Web page design.

Web page design feature	Explanation
Web themes	More themes (over 60) that are easier to apply, either to entire Webs or to individual Web pages.
Customized themes	Now easier to modify existing themes or create your own.
Color tools	Now easier to apply colors to graphics and text or use a color picker to select custom colors. Entire color schemes can be selected either by selecting a theme or by picking a custom color scheme from the color wheel.
Pixel precise positioning	Now you can place page elements in exact locations with relative or absolute positioning.
Cascading Style Sheets (CSS)	Improved support for Cascading Style Sheets, following the CSS2 standard.
More FrontPage components	New components include Category, Spreadsheet, PivotTable, and Chart.

Web Page Coding

If you're an advanced Web page designer, FrontPage now gives you more power and flexibility to write and customize your Web page code—whether it's HTML, DHTML, script code, XML, or ASP. Web page coding features are summarized in the table.

Web page coding feature	Explanation
HTML source code preservation	FrontPage 2000 does not modify the HTML code you write or insert, so you can write your own code or even import code from other Web tools. FrontPage even preserves tag and comment order, capitalization, and white space.
Quickly insert code in HTML view	Buttons and drop-down menus now make it easier to insert code directly on a Web page displayed in HTML view.
Personalized HTML formatting	You can now customize how you want your code indented, what colors tags should use, what to capitalize, and when optional tags are to be used. Your preferences are automatically applied to any new or imported HTML code.

Web page coding feature	Explanation
Reveal tags in WYSIWYG (What You See Is What You Get) view	With a page displayed in Normal view, you can select Reveal Tags to show which HTML tags are producing certain effects.
Edit code directly	With a page displayed in HTML view, it's now easier to edit HTML, DHTML, script code, XML, and ASP.
Microsoft Script Editor	You can now edit and debug scripts written in VBScript or JavaScript using the Microsoft Script Editor, which is a separate program on the Macro submenu of the Tools menu.

Web Publishing

FrontPage 2000 adds and improves several features that make it easier for you to publish and update your Webs on the Internet or on an intranet. You now have better control over publishing individual Web pages to update your Web site; you can create Webs in FrontPage without needing a Web server; and you can more easily publish your Webs to Web servers that don't have the FrontPage Server Extensions. The Web publishing improvements are summarized in the following table.

Web publishing feature	Explanation
Page-level control	You can now decide which pages to upload to the Web server by marking specific pages as "do not publish" or by choosing to publish only pages that have changed.
Create Webs anywhere	You can now create and test a Web on your computer without a Web server connection.
Publish Webs anywhere	You can more easily publish to non–FrontPage-compliant Web servers by using FrontPage's built-in FTP feature.
Progress Indicator	When you publish your Web, a progress indicator shows how much of the Web remains to be published.

APPENDIX

B

Features that Require the FrontPage Server Extensions

In an ideal situation, you develop a Web site in FrontPage and publish it to a Web server that has the FrontPage Server Extensions. However, if you don't have access to a FrontPage-compliant Web server, some features you create in FrontPage won't work.

Understanding FrontPage-Specific Features

There are two categories of features that require the FrontPage Server Extensions to work properly. The first category consists of *run-time components*. When Web pages are loaded into a browser, these components interact with the Web server. If the Web server isn't set up to work with FrontPage components, the components won't function properly.

Run-time component	Explanation
Confirmation field	Confirms the data a user enters in a form field.
Default form handler	Sends form data to a Web page file.
Hit Counter component	Counts and displays the number of times a page has been viewed by Web site visitors.
Registration component	Registers Web site visitors to create a members-only Web site.
Scheduled Include Page component	Inserts one Web page in another Web page at a specified time.
Scheduled Picture component	Inserts an image on a Web page at a specified time.
Search component	Inserts a search form on a Web page.

The second category consists of components that depend on extra Web information that is stored by FrontPage—in particular, information about the Web hierarchy that you can create in Navigation view. These components won't work because the server doesn't store and provide that information as needed.

Navigational component	Explanation
Navigation bar	Displays hyperlinks in shared borders.
Page Banner component	Displays the page title at the top of the page.
Table of Contents component	Creates and displays a Web site table of contents.

Using Workarounds for FrontPage Components

Navigational components are the easiest components to replace with Web page workarounds.

Navigational component	Replace with
Navigation bars	Manually created hyperlinks.
Page Banner component	Text page heading (use Heading 1 style).
Table of Contents component	A page of hyperlinks in a menu frame.

Run-time components can often be replaced by components designed for the specific non-FrontPage Web server to which you're publishing your Web. For example, the popular GeoCities Web site has its own hit counter, guest book, and other components that you can download. You can then use FrontPage to incorporate these components into your Web pages and upload them (manually, of course) to the Web site.

C

If You're New to Windows

If you are new to Microsoft Windows, this appendix will show you the basics you need to get started. You'll get an overview of Windows features, and you'll learn how to use online Help to answer your questions and find out more about using the Windows operating systems.

If You're New to Windows

Windows is an easy-to-use computer environment that helps you handle the daily work that you perform with your computer. You can use Windows 95, Windows 98, or Windows NT to run Microsoft Office Premium—the explanations in this appendix are included for all of these operating systems.

The way you use Windows 95, Windows 98, Windows NT, and programs designed for these operating systems is similar. The programs look much alike, and you use similar menus to tell them what to do. In this section, you'll learn how to operate the basic program.

Start Windows

Starting Windows is as easy as turning on your computer.

1. If your computer isn't on, turn it on now.
2. If you are using Windows NT, press Ctrl+Alt+Del to display a dialog box asking for your user name and password. If you are using Windows 95 or Windows 98, you will see this dialog box if your computer is connected to a network.
3. Type your user name and password in the appropriate boxes, and click OK.

    If you don't know your user name or password, contact your system administrator for assistance.

Close

❹ If you see the Welcome dialog box, click the Close button.

Your screen should look similar to the following illustration.

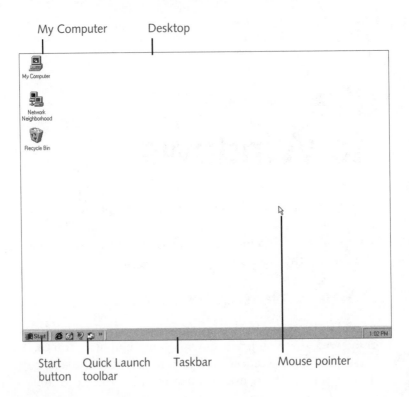

Using the Mouse

Although you can use the keyboard for most actions, many actions are easier to do using a *mouse*. The mouse controls a pointer on the screen, as shown in the above illustration. You move the pointer by sliding the mouse over a flat surface in the direction you want the pointer to move. If you run out of room to move the mouse, lift it up and then put it down in another location.

important

In this book, we assume that your mouse is set up so that the left button is the primary button and the right button is the secondary button. If your mouse is configured the opposite way, for left-handed use, use the right button when we tell you to use the left, and vice versa.

You'll use five basic mouse actions throughout this book.

When you are directed to	Do this
Point to an item	Move the mouse to place the pointer over the item.
Click an item	Point to the item on your screen, and quickly press and release the left mouse button.
Right-click an item	Point to the item on your screen, and then quickly press and release the right mouse button. Clicking the right mouse button often displays a shortcut menu with a list of command choices that apply to that item.
Double-click an item	Point to the item, and then quickly press and release the left mouse button twice.
Drag an item	Point to an item, and then hold down the left mouse button as you move the pointer. Once the item is moved to the appropriate location, release the left mouse button.

Using Window Controls

All programs designed for Windows have common elements that you use to scroll, size, move, and close a window.

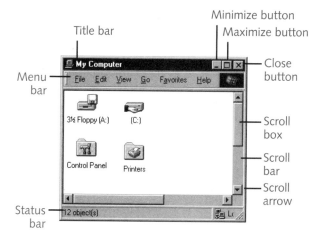

To	Do this	Button
Move, or *scroll*, vertically or horizontally through the contents of a window that extends beyond the screen	Click a scroll bar or scroll arrow, or drag the scroll box. The previous illustration identifies these screen elements.	
Enlarge a window to fill the screen	Click the Maximize button, or double-click the window title bar.	⬜
Restore a window to its previous size	Click the Restore button, or double-click the window title bar. When a window is maximized, the Maximize button changes to the Restore button.	🗗
Reduce a window to a button on the Windows taskbar	Click the Minimize button. To display a minimized window, click its button on the Windows taskbar.	—
Move a window	Drag the window title bar.	
Close a window	Click the Close button.	✖

Using Menus

Just like a restaurant menu, a program menu provides a list of options from which you can choose. On program menus, these options are called *commands*. To select a menu or a menu command, click the item you want.

tip

You can also use the keyboard to make menu selections. Press the Alt key to activate the menu bar, press the key that corresponds to the highlighted or underlined letter of the menu name, and then press the key that corresponds to the highlighted or underlined letter of the command name.

In the following exercise, you'll open and make selections from a menu.

Open and make selections from a menu

1 On the desktop, double-click the My Computer icon.

The My Computer window opens.

You can also press Alt+E to open the Edit menu.

2 In the My Computer window, on the menu bar, click Edit.

The Edit menu appears. Some commands are disabled; this means they aren't available.

Your screen should look similar to the following illustration.

Command is not available

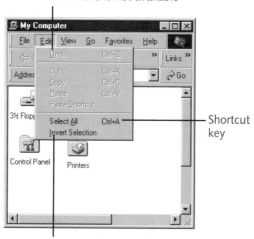

Shortcut
key

Command is available

❸ Click Edit again to close the menu.

❹ On the menu bar, click View to open the View menu.

❺ On the View menu, click Status Bar if there isn't a check mark beside it.
Then click View again.

Your screen should look similar to the following illustration.

*A check mark
means that
multiple items
within a group
can be simulta-
neously
selected. A
bullet means
that only one
item can be
selected.*

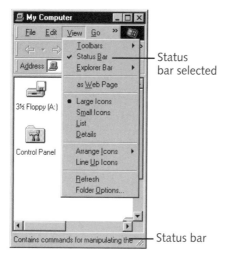

Status
bar selected

Status bar

❻ On the View menu, click Status Bar again.

The menu closes, and the status bar is no longer displayed.

Your screen should look similar to the following illustration.

Status bar
inactive

A right-point-ing arrow appearing after a command name means that additional commands are available.

7   On the View menu, click Status Bar again.

The status bar is displayed.

8   On the View menu, point to Arrange Icons.

A submenu listing additional menu choices appears.

9   Click By Drive Letter.

The icons representing the drives on your computer are arranged alphabetically by drive letter.

10   In the upper-right corner of the My Computer window, click the Close button to close the window.

Close

tip

If you do a lot of typing, you might want to learn the key combinations for commands you use frequently. Pressing the key combination is a quick way to activate a command. If a key combination is available for a command, it is listed to the right of the command name on the menu. For example, on the Edit menu, Ctrl+C is listed as the key combination for the Copy command.

Using Dialog Boxes

When you choose a command name that is followed by an ellipsis (...), a dialog box appears so that you can provide more information about how the command should be carried out. Dialog boxes have standard features, as shown in the following illustration.

You can also use the keyboard to select the item by holding down Alt as you press the underlined letter.

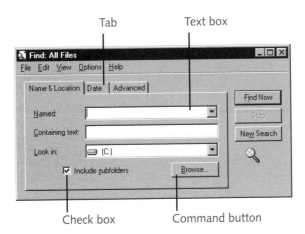

Tab   Text box

Check box   Command button

To enter text in a text box, click inside the box and begin typing. Or you can press the Tab key to move around the dialog box.

Display the Taskbar Properties dialog box

Some dialog boxes provide several categories of options displayed on separate tabs. In this exercise, you customize the list of programs that appears on your Start menu.

❶ On the Windows taskbar, click the Start button.

The Start menu appears.

❷ On the Start menu, point to Settings. In Windows 95 and NT, click Taskbar. In Windows 98, click Taskbar & Start Menu.

The Taskbar Properties dialog box appears.

Click the top of an obscured tab to make it visible.

❸ In the Taskbar Properties dialog box, click the Start Menu Programs tab to make it active.

❹ Click the Taskbar Options tab, and then select the Show Small Icons In Start Menu check box.

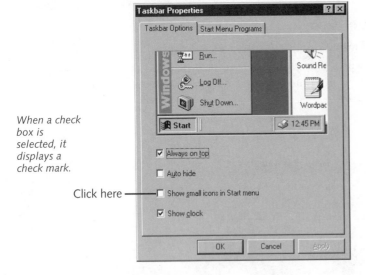

When a check box is selected, it displays a check mark.

Click here

5 Clear the check box, and then select it again; be sure to watch how the display in the dialog box changes.

Clearing a check box will turn off the option, and selecting a check box will turn on the option.

6 Click the Cancel button.

The dialog box closes without changing any settings.

Getting Help with Windows

When you're at work and you have a question, you might ask a coworker or consult a reference book. To find out more about functions and features in Windows, you can use the Help system. Using Windows Help is one of the quickest, most efficient ways to find your answer. You can access Windows Help from the Start menu. For Help specific to a program, such as FrontPage 2000, each Windows program also includes its own Help system.

After the Help window opens, you can choose one of three ways to best research your question. To find instructions about broad categories, you can look on the Contents tab. Or you can search the Help index to find information about specific topics. Finally, you can look on the last tab (in Windows 95 and Windows NT, the Find tab; in Windows 98, the Search tab) to search the Help files based on keywords that you provide. The Help topics are short and concise, so you can get the exact information you need quickly. There are also shortcut icons in many Help topics that you can use to directly go to or to perform the task you want or to list Related Topics.

In Windows 98, on the Help toolbar, click Web Help to automatically connect to Microsoft's Support Online Web site. Once connected, you can expand your search to include the Microsoft Knowledge Base, Troubleshooting Wizards, Newsgroups, and downloadable files. Just follow the directions on the screen.

Viewing Help Contents

The Contents tab is organized like a book's table of contents. As you choose top-level topics, called *chapters*, you see a list of more detailed subtopics from which to choose.

Find Help about general categories

Suppose you want to see what documents you've chosen to print. In this exercise, you look up Windows Help instructions for finding out this information.

Windows 95 and NT

1 On the Windows taskbar, click Start, and then click Help.

The Help Topics window appears.

2 If necessary, click the Contents tab to make it active.

3 Double-click How To.

The icon changes to an open book, and a set of subtopics appears.

4 Double-click Print.

More subtopics appear.

5 Double-click Viewing Documents Waiting To Be Printed.

A Help window appears.

6 In Windows 95, to see a definition of *print queue,* click the underlined words.

A pop-up window containing the definition of the term appears.

7 Click anywhere outside that window to close it.

8 In both Windows 95 and Windows NT, read the information about viewing documents in the print queue, and then close Help.

Windows 98

1 On the Windows taskbar, click Start, and then click Help.

The Windows Help window appears.

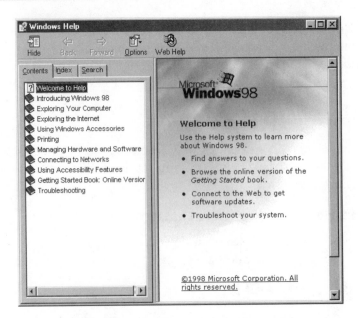

② If necessary, click the Contents tab to make it active.

③ Click Printing.

The icon changes to an open book, and a set of subtopics appears.

④ Click View A List Of Documents Waiting To Be Printed.

The topic appears in the right frame of the Windows Help window.

⑤ To see a definition of *print queue,* in the right frame, click the underlined words.

A pop-up window containing the definition of the term appears.

⑥ Click anywhere outside that window to close it.

⑦ Read the information about viewing documents in the print queue, and then close Windows Help.

Finding Help About Specific Topics

The two remaining tabs in the Windows Help window allow you to find specific Help topics. The Index tab is organized like a book's index. Keywords for topics are organized alphabetically. You can either type the keyword you want to find or scroll through the list of keywords. You can then select from one or more topic choices.

On the Find or Search tab, you can also enter a keyword. The main difference between these two tabs is that you get a list of all Help topics in which that keyword appears, not just the topics that begin with that word.

Find specific Help topics by using the Help index

In this exercise, you use the Help index to learn how to print help topics.

Windows 95

❶   On the Windows taskbar, click Start, and then click Help.
The Help Topics window appears.

❷   Click the Index tab to make it active.

❸   In the text box, type **printing**
A list of printing-related topics appears.

❹   In that list, click Help Information, Printing A Copy Of, and click Display.
The Windows Help window appears.

❺   Read the information, and then close Windows Help.

Windows NT

❶   On the Windows taskbar, click Start, and then click Help.
The Windows NT Help window appears.

❷   Click the Index tab to make it active.

❸   In the text box, type **printing**
A list of printing-related topics appears.

❹   In that list, click Help Topics, and then click Display.
The Windows NT Help window appears.

❺   Read the Help topic, and then close Windows Help.

Windows 98

❶   On the Windows taskbar, click Start, and then click Help.
The Windows Help window appears.

❷   Click the Index tab to make it active.

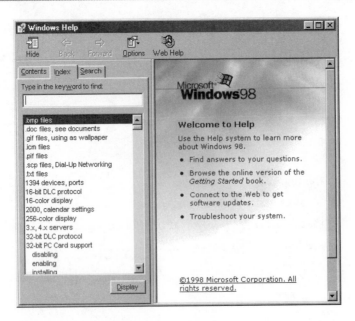

❸   In the Type In The Keywords To Find box, type **printing**

A list of printing-related topics appears.

❹   In that list, click Help Topics, and then click Display.

The topic is displayed in the frame on the right side of the Help window.

❺   Click the underlined word, *frame*.

A pop-up window containing an explanation of the term appears.

❻   Click anywhere outside that window to close it.

❼   Read the information about printing Help topics, and close Windows Help.

Find specific Help topics by using the Find or Search tab

In this exercise, you use the Find or Search tab to learn how to print a document.

Windows 95

❶   On the Windows taskbar, click Start, and then click Help.

The Help window appears.

❷   Click the Find tab to make it active.

❸   If you are using Find for the first time, the Find Setup Wizard dialog box appears. Click Next, and then click Finish to complete and close the wizard.

The wizard creates a search index for your Help files. This might take a few minutes.

4 In the text box, type **print**

All printing-related topics are displayed in the third list box.

5 In the Click A Topic Then Click Display list, scroll down, click Printing A Document, and then click Display.

The Windows Help window appears.

6 Read the information about printing a document, and close Windows Help.

Windows NT

1 On the Windows taskbar, click Start, and then click Help.

The Windows NT Help window appears.

2 Click the Find tab to make it active.

3 If the Find Setup Wizard appears, click Next, and then click Finish to complete and close the wizard.

The wizard creates a search index for your Help files. This might take a few minutes.

4 In the text box, type **printing**

All printing-related topics are displayed in the third list box.

5 In the Click A Topic Then Click Display list, scroll down, click To Print A Document, and then click Display.

The Windows NT Help window appears.

6 Read the information about printing a document, and then close Windows NT Help.

Windows 98

1 On the Windows taskbar, click Start, and then click Help.

The Windows Help window appears.

2 Click the Search tab to make it active.

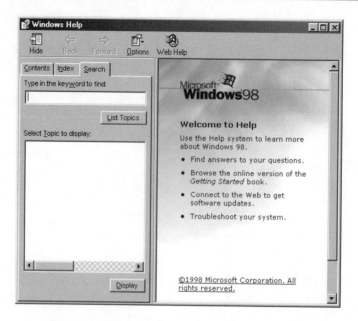

❸   In the Type In The Keyword To Find box, type **print** and click List Topics.

A list of print-related topics is displayed in the Select Topic To Display list box.

❹   In the Select Topic To Display list box, scroll down, click To Print A Document, and then click Display.

The topic is displayed in the right frame of the Windows Help window.

❺   Read the information about printing a document, and close Windows Help.

Find Help in a dialog box

Almost every dialog box includes a question mark–shaped Help button in the upper-right corner of its window. When you click this button and then click any dialog box item, a Help window appears that explains what the item is and how to use it. In this exercise, you'll get help in a dialog box.

❶   On the Windows taskbar, click Start, and then click Run.

The Run dialog box appears.

❷   Click the Help button.

The mouse pointer changes to an arrow with a question mark.

❸   Click the Open text box.

A pop-up window providing information about how to use the Open text box appears.

4   Click anywhere outside the Help window to close it.

The mouse pointer returns to its previous shape.

5   Close the Run dialog box.

> **tip**
> Windows NT and Windows 95 users can change the way the Help topics appear on the screen. In any Help topic window, click Options, point to Font, and then click a font size option to change the size of the text.

Quit Windows

Close

1   If you are finished using Windows, close any open windows by clicking the Close button in each window.

2   On the Windows taskbar, click Start, and then click Shut Down.

The Shut Down Windows window appears.

Windows 95

3   Be sure the Shut Down The Computer option is selected, and then click Yes.

A message indicates that it is now safe to turn off your computer.

Windows 98

3   Be sure the Shut Down option is selected, and then click OK.

A message indicates that it is now safe to turn off your computer.

> **important**
> To avoid loss of data or damage to your operating system, always quit Windows by using the Shut Down command on the Start menu before you turn off your computer.

Windows NT

3   Be sure the Shut Down The Computer option is selected, and then click Yes.

A message indicates that it is now safe to turn off your computer.

Index

SPECIAL CHARACTERS AND NUMBERS

3–D images, 263–64

A

absolute positioning, 127–28
Access 2000. *See* Microsoft Access 2000
adding Web pages, 37–41
Ad Manager, 79
All Files report, 203
Allow Multiple Selections, 148
alt.binaries.sounds.midi, 113
alternative text for images, 131
Americans with Disabilities Act, 164
anchors. *See* bookmarks
animated GIF files, 112
animated text, 219
applying inline style, 87
Arrange workpane, 256
Assigned To report, 204
Auto Thumbnail button, 110, 116, *116*

B

Back button, 55, *55*

backgrounds, 104–5
    command, 75
    copying, 105
    selecting, 75
    sounds, 120–21, 131
    themes, 74
backups, 183
banners, 79–82
    Ad Manager, 79
    creating, 227–29, 269
    inserting, 90
    properties, 82
    themes, 80
Berners-Lee, Tim, 4
blank pages, 47
BMP files, 110
bold text, 33
Bookmark command, 60
bookmarks, 59–64
    creating, 59–61, 68
    deleting, 64, 69
    dialog box, 60, *60*
    hyperlinks, 68
    testing, 62–64
borders
    shared, 170–74
    table cells, 102–3
Broken Hyperlinks report, 203
broken underlines, 61
browsers
    Back button, 55, *55*

ActiveEducation & Microsoft Press

Microsoft Web Publishing Step by Step has been created by the professional trainers and writers at ActiveEducation, Inc., to the exacting standards you've come to expect from Microsoft Press. Together, we are pleased to present this self-paced training guide, which you can use individually or as part of a class.

ActiveEducation creates top-quality information technology training content that teaches essential computer skills for today's workplace. ActiveEducation courses are designed to provide the most effective training available and to help people become more productive computer users. Each ActiveEducation course, including this Step by Step book, undergoes rigorous quality control, instructional design, and technical review procedures to ensure that the course is instructionally and technically superior in content and approach. ActiveEducation (*www.activeeducation.com*) courses are available in book form and on the Internet.

Microsoft Press is the book publishing division of Microsoft Corporation, the leading publisher of information about Microsoft products and services. Microsoft Press is dedicated to providing the highest quality computer books and multimedia training and reference tools that make using Microsoft software easier, more enjoyable, and more productive.

About the Author

Scott Palmer has worked in the computer industry for 18 years—almost since its inception. As a programmer, author, and teacher, he has written about computer technology for *The Wall Street Journal, USA Today, InfoWorld, PC World, PC Techniques, Government Computer News*, and many other publications. A former distinguished teacher at Indiana University, he has been teaching people to use computers since 1981. Currently he conducts computer training, programs, and consults. He is the author of 15 computer books.

MICROSOFT LICENSE AGREEMENT

Book Companion CD

IMPORTANT—READ CAREFULLY: This Microsoft End-User License Agreement ("EULA") is a legal agreement between you (either an individual or an entity) and Microsoft Corporation for the Microsoft product identified above, which includes computer software and may include associated media, printed materials, and "online" or electronic documentation ("SOFTWARE PRODUCT"). Any component included within the SOFTWARE PRODUCT that is accompanied by a separate End-User License Agreement shall be governed by such agreement and not the terms set forth below. By installing, copying, or otherwise using the SOFTWARE PRODUCT, you agree to be bound by the terms of this EULA. If you do not agree to the terms of this EULA, you are not authorized to install, copy, or otherwise use the SOFTWARE PRODUCT; you may, however, return the SOFTWARE PRODUCT, along with all printed materials and other items that form a part of the Microsoft product that includes the SOFTWARE PRODUCT, to the place you obtained them for a full refund.

SOFTWARE PRODUCT LICENSE

The SOFTWARE PRODUCT is protected by United States copyright laws and international copyright treaties, as well as other intellectual property laws and treaties. The SOFTWARE PRODUCT is licensed, not sold.

1. **GRANT OF LICENSE.** This EULA grants you the following rights:

   a. **Software Product.** You may install and use one copy of the SOFTWARE PRODUCT on a single computer. The primary user of the computer on which the SOFTWARE PRODUCT is installed may make a second copy for his or her exclusive use on a portable computer.

   b. **Storage/Network Use.** You may also store or install a copy of the SOFTWARE PRODUCT on a storage device, such as a network server, used only to install or run the SOFTWARE PRODUCT on your other computers over an internal network; however, you must acquire and dedicate a license for each separate computer on which the SOFTWARE PRODUCT is installed or run from the storage device. A license for the SOFTWARE PRODUCT may not be shared or used concurrently on different computers.

   c. **License Pak.** If you have acquired this EULA in a Microsoft License Pak, you may make the number of additional copies of the computer software portion of the SOFTWARE PRODUCT authorized on the printed copy of this EULA, and you may use each copy in the manner specified above. You are also entitled to make a corresponding number of secondary copies for portable computer use as specified above.

   d. **Sample Code.** Solely with respect to portions, if any, of the SOFTWARE PRODUCT that are identified within the SOFTWARE PRODUCT as sample code (the "SAMPLE CODE"):

      i. **Use and Modification.** Microsoft grants you the right to use and modify the source code version of the SAMPLE CODE, *provided* you comply with subsection (d)(iii) below. You may not distribute the SAMPLE CODE, or any modified version of the SAMPLE CODE, in source code form.

      ii. **Redistributable Files.** Provided you comply with subsection (d)(iii) below, Microsoft grants you a nonexclusive, royalty-free right to reproduce and distribute the object code version of the SAMPLE CODE and of any modified SAMPLE CODE, other than SAMPLE CODE, or any modified version thereof, designated as not redistributable in the Readme file that forms a part of the SOFTWARE PRODUCT (the "Non-Redistributable Sample Code"). All SAMPLE CODE other than the Non-Redistributable Sample Code is collectively referred to as the "REDISTRIBUTABLES."

      iii. **Redistribution Requirements.** If you redistribute the REDISTRIBUTABLES, you agree to: (i) distribute the REDISTRIBUTABLES in object code form only in conjunction with and as a part of your software application product; (ii) not use Microsoft's name, logo, or trademarks to market your software application product; (iii) include a valid copyright notice on your software application product; (iv) indemnify, hold harmless, and defend Microsoft from and against any claims or lawsuits, including attorney's fees, that arise or result from the use or distribution of your software application product; and (v) not permit further distribution of the REDISTRIBUTABLES by your end user. Contact Microsoft for the applicable royalties due and other licensing terms for all other uses and/or distribution of the REDISTRIBUTABLES.

2. **DESCRIPTION OF OTHER RIGHTS AND LIMITATIONS.**

   - **Limitations on Reverse Engineering, Decompilation, and Disassembly.** You may not reverse engineer, decompile, or disassemble the SOFTWARE PRODUCT, except and only to the extent that such activity is expressly permitted by applicable law notwithstanding this limitation.

   - **Separation of Components.** The SOFTWARE PRODUCT is licensed as a single product. Its component parts may not be separated for use on more than one computer.

   - **Rental.** You may not rent, lease, or lend the SOFTWARE PRODUCT.

   - **Support Services.** Microsoft may, but is not obligated to, provide you with support services related to the SOFTWARE PRODUCT ("Support Services"). Use of Support Services is governed by the Microsoft policies and programs described in the user manual, in "online" documentation, and/or in other Microsoft-provided materials. Any supplemental software code provided to you as part of the Support Services shall be considered part of the SOFTWARE PRODUCT and subject to the terms and conditions of this EULA. With respect to technical information you provide to Microsoft as part of the Support Services, Microsoft may use such information for its business purposes, including for product support and development. Microsoft will not utilize such technical information in a form that personally identifies you.

- **Software Transfer.** You may permanently transfer all of your rights under this EULA, provided you retain no copies, you transfer all of the SOFTWARE PRODUCT (including all component parts, the media and printed materials, any upgrades, this EULA, and, if applicable, the Certificate of Authenticity), **and** the recipient agrees to the terms of this EULA.

- **Termination.** Without prejudice to any other rights, Microsoft may terminate this EULA if you fail to comply with the terms and conditions of this EULA. In such event, you must destroy all copies of the SOFTWARE PRODUCT and all of its component parts.

3. **COPYRIGHT.** All title and copyrights in and to the SOFTWARE PRODUCT (including but not limited to any images, photographs, animations, video, audio, music, text, SAMPLE CODE, REDISTRIBUTABLES, and "applets" incorporated into the SOFTWARE PRODUCT) and any copies of the SOFTWARE PRODUCT are owned by Microsoft or its suppliers. The SOFTWARE PRODUCT is protected by copyright laws and international treaty provisions. Therefore, you must treat the SOFTWARE PRODUCT like any other copyrighted material **except** that you may install the SOFTWARE PRODUCT on a single computer provided you keep the original solely for backup or archival purposes. You may not copy the printed materials accompanying the SOFTWARE PRODUCT.

4. **U.S. GOVERNMENT RESTRICTED RIGHTS.** The SOFTWARE PRODUCT and documentation are provided with RESTRICTED RIGHTS. Use, duplication, or disclosure by the Government is subject to restrictions as set forth in subparagraph (c)(1)(ii) of the Rights in Technical Data and Computer Software clause at DFARS 252.227-7013 or subparagraphs (c)(1) and (2) of the Commercial Computer Software—Restricted Rights at 48 CFR 52.227-19, as applicable. Manufacturer is Microsoft Corporation/One Microsoft Way/Redmond, WA 98052-6399.

5. **EXPORT RESTRICTIONS.** You agree that you will not export or re-export the SOFTWARE PRODUCT, any part thereof, or any process or service that is the direct product of the SOFTWARE PRODUCT (the foregoing collectively referred to as the "Restricted Components"), to any country, person, entity, or end user subject to U.S. export restrictions. You specifically agree not to export or re-export any of the Restricted Components (i) to any country to which the U.S. has embargoed or restricted the export of goods or services, which currently include, but are not necessarily limited to, Cuba, Iran, Iraq, Libya, North Korea, Sudan, and Syria, or to any national of any such country, wherever located, who intends to transmit or transport the Restricted Components back to such country; (ii) to any end user who you know or have reason to know will utilize the Restricted Components in the design, development, or production of nuclear, chemical, or biological weapons; or (iii) to any end user who has been prohibited from participating in U.S. export transactions by any federal agency of the U.S. government. You warrant and represent that neither the BXA nor any other U.S. federal agency has suspended, revoked, or denied your export privileges.

DISCLAIMER OF WARRANTY

NO WARRANTIES OR CONDITIONS. MICROSOFT EXPRESSLY DISCLAIMS ANY WARRANTY OR CONDITION FOR THE SOFTWARE PRODUCT. THE SOFTWARE PRODUCT AND ANY RELATED DOCUMENTATION ARE PROVIDED "AS IS" WITHOUT WARRANTY OR CONDITION OF ANY KIND, EITHER EXPRESS OR IMPLIED, INCLUDING, WITHOUT LIMITATION, THE IMPLIED WARRANTIES OF MERCHANTABILITY, FITNESS FOR A PARTICULAR PURPOSE, OR NONINFRINGEMENT. THE ENTIRE RISK ARISING OUT OF USE OR PERFORMANCE OF THE SOFTWARE PRODUCT REMAINS WITH YOU.

LIMITATION OF LIABILITY. TO THE MAXIMUM EXTENT PERMITTED BY APPLICABLE LAW, IN NO EVENT SHALL MICROSOFT OR ITS SUPPLIERS BE LIABLE FOR ANY SPECIAL, INCIDENTAL, INDIRECT, OR CONSEQUENTIAL DAMAGES WHATSOEVER (INCLUDING, WITHOUT LIMITATION, DAMAGES FOR LOSS OF BUSINESS PROFITS, BUSINESS INTERRUPTION, LOSS OF BUSINESS INFORMATION, OR ANY OTHER PECUNIARY LOSS) ARISING OUT OF THE USE OF OR INABILITY TO USE THE SOFTWARE PRODUCT OR THE PROVISION OF OR FAILURE TO PROVIDE SUPPORT SERVICES, EVEN IF MICROSOFT HAS BEEN ADVISED OF THE POSSIBILITY OF SUCH DAMAGES. IN ANY CASE, MICROSOFT'S ENTIRE LIABILITY UNDER ANY PROVISION OF THIS EULA SHALL BE LIMITED TO THE GREATER OF THE AMOUNT ACTUALLY PAID BY YOU FOR THE SOFTWARE PRODUCT OR US$5.00; PROVIDED, HOWEVER, IF YOU HAVE ENTERED INTO A MICROSOFT SUPPORT SERVICES AGREEMENT, MICROSOFT'S ENTIRE LIABILITY REGARDING SUPPORT SERVICES SHALL BE GOVERNED BY THE TERMS OF THAT AGREEMENT. BECAUSE SOME STATES AND JURISDICTIONS DO NOT ALLOW THE EXCLUSION OR LIMITATION OF LIABILITY, THE ABOVE LIMITATION MAY NOT APPLY TO YOU.

MISCELLANEOUS

This EULA is governed by the laws of the State of Washington USA, except and only to the extent that applicable law mandates governing law of a different jurisdiction.

Should you have any questions concerning this EULA, or if you desire to contact Microsoft for any reason, please contact the Microsoft subsidiary serving your country, or write: Microsoft Sales Information Center/One Microsoft Way/Redmond, WA 98052-6399.

Microsoft®
Limited Warranty

Limited Express Warranty

Beperkte Garantie

Garantia Limitada

Garantie Limitée

Omezená záruka

Begrænset ansvar

Beschränkte Garantie

Garantía Limitada

Περιορισμένη Εγγύηση

Ograničena garancija

Garanzia Limitata

Korlátozott Garancia

Begrensede Garantien

Ograniczona Gwarancja

Omejena garancija

Garanţii Limitate

Obmedzená záruka

Rajoitettu takuu

Begränsad garanti

Ограниченная Гарантия

Sınırlı Garanti

Limited Warranties

Australia, New Zealand, Papua New Guinea — If you purchased your Microsoft Product in Australia, New Zealand, or Papua New Guinea, the limited express warranty that applies to you is on page **3**.

Benelux (Nederlands) — Indien u uw Microsoft-product hebt aangeschaft in de Benelux, vindt u de voor u toepasselijke beperkte garantie op pagina **3**.

Brasil — Caso você tenha adquirido o seu produto Microsoft no Brasil, a garantia limitada aplicável a você encontra-se na página **4**.

Canada (English) — If you purchased your Microsoft Product in Canada the limited warranty that applies to you is on page **5**.

Canada (Français) — Si vous avez acheté votre produit Microsoft au Canada, la garantie limitée qui vous est applicable se trouve à la page **5**.

Česká republika — Pokud jste produkt společnosti Microsoft získali v České republice, vztahuje se na vás omezená záruka na straně **6**.

Danmark — Hvis De har købt Deres Microsoft-produkt i Danmark, vil De være omfattet af det begrænsede ansvar, der er anført på side **7**.

Deutschland, Österreich, Liechtenstein, Schweiz — Falls Sie Ihr Microsoft-Produkt in Deutschland, Österreich, Liechtenstein oder in der Schweiz erworben haben, befindet sich die für Sie geltende beschränkte Garantie auf Seite **8**.

England, Scotland, Wales, Republic of Ireland — If you purchased your Microsoft Product in England, Scotland, Wales, or the Republic of Ireland, the limited express warranty that applies to you is on page **8**.

España — Si usted ha adquirido su Producto Microsoft en España, la garantía limitada que le es aplicable se encuentra en la página **9**.

Ελλάδα — Εάν προμηθευτήκατε αυτό το προϊόν της Microsoft στην Ελλάδα, ισχύει για την περίπτωσή σας η περιορισμένη εγγύηση που υπάρχει στη σελίδα **10**.

France, Suisse, Bénélux — Si vous avez acheté votre produit Microsoft en France, en Suisse ou au Bénélux, la garantie limitée qui vous est applicable se trouve à la page **11**.

Hrvatska — Ako ste Vaš Microsoft proizvod kupili u Hrvatskoj, na Vas se primjenjuje ograničena garancija koja se nalazi na stranici **11**.

Italia — Qualora Voi acquistiate i Vostri Prodotti Microsoft in Italia, la garanzia limitata applicabile, si trova a pagina **12**.

Magyarország — Amennyiben Microsoft termékét Magyarországon vásárolta, az Önre vonatkozó korlátozott garanciát a **13**. oldalon találja

México, América Central, América del Sur (excepto Brasil) — Si usted compró su Producto Microsoft en México, América Central o América del Sur (excepto Brasil) la sección correspondiente a la garantía limitada que le es aplicable se encuentra en la página **14**.

Norge — Hvis De har kjøpt Deres Microsoft-produkt i Norge, er den begrensede garantien som gjelder for Dem på side **14**.

Polska — Jeśli produkt firmy Microsoft został zakupiony w Polsce, obowiązuje Ograniczona Gwarancja znajdująca się na stronie **156**.

Portugal — Se adquiriu o seu Produto Microsoft em Portugal, a garantia limitada que se aplica a si está na página **16**.

România — Dacă aţi cumpărat produsul dumneavoastră Microsoft în România, **17**.

Slovenija — Če ste Microsoftov izdelek dobili v Sloveniji, za vas velja omejena garancija na strani **17**.

Slovenská republika — Ak ste nadobudli produkt spoločnosti Microsoft v Slovenskej republike, obmedzenú záruku, ktorá sa na vás vzťahuje, nájdete na strane **18**.

Suomi — Jos olette hankkinut Microsoft-tuotteenne Suomesta, Teitä koskevat takuuehdot ovat sivulla **19**.

Sverige — Om Ni har förvärvat Er Microsoft-produkt i Sverige, gäller den begränsade garanti som finns på sid **19**.

Территория бывшего СССР — если продукция корпорации Microsoft приобретена на территории бывшего СССР **20**.

Türkiye — Microsoft Ürününüzü Türkiye'de aldýýsanýz, size uygulanacak sınırlı garantiyi **21**. sayfada bulabilirsiniz.

Any Other Country — If you purchased your Microsoft Product in a country not listed above, the limited warranty that applies to you is on page **21**.

If you acquired your Microsoft Product in Australia, New Zealand, or Papua New Guinea, the following limited express warranty applies to you:

CONSUMER RIGHTS. Consumers may have the benefit of certain rights or remedies pursuant to the Trade Practices Act and similar state and territory laws in Australia or the Consumer Guarantees Act in New Zealand, in respect of which liability may not be excluded.   The warranties and rights set out below are provided by Microsoft and are in addition to those you may have under the above Acts against importers or resellers of the SOFTWARE PRODUCT.

LIMITED EXPRESS WARRANTY. Microsoft warrants that:

(a) the SOFTWARE PRODUCT will perform substantially in accordance with the accompanying written materials for a period of 90 days from the date of receipt; and

(b) any support services provided by Microsoft shall be substantially as described in applicable written materials provided to you by Microsoft, and Microsoft support engineers will make commercially reasonable efforts to solve any problem issues.

CUSTOMER REMEDIES. To the maximum extent permitted under applicable law, Microsoft's and its suppliers' entire liability and your exclusive remedy under this warranty is, at Microsoft's option, either (a) return of the price paid, if any; or (b) repair or replacement of the SOFTWARE PRODUCT which does not meet this warranty and which is returned to Microsoft with a copy of your receipt. This warranty is void if failure of the SOFTWARE PRODUCT has resulted from accident, abuse or misapplication. Any replacement SOFTWARE PRODUCT will be warranted for the remainder of the original warranty period or 30 days, whichever is longer. Outside the United States neither these remedies nor any product support services offered by Microsoft are available without proof of purchase from an authorised international source.

LIMITATION OF LIABILITY. To the maximum extent permitted by applicable law, Microsoft and its suppliers disclaim all other warranties and conditions, either express or implied, including, but not limited to, implied warranties of merchantability, fitness for a particular purpose, title, and non-infringement, with regard to the SOFTWARE PRODUCT, and the provision of or failure to provide support services. Consumers may nevertheless have the benefit of certain rights or remedies pursuant to the Trade Practices Act and similar state and territory laws in Australia or the Consumer Guarantees Act in New Zealand, in respect of which liability may not be excluded. Insofar as such liability may not be excluded, then to the maximum extent permitted by law, such liability is limited, at Microsoft's exclusive option, to (i) in the case of the SOFTWARE PRODUCT: (a) replacement of the SOFTWARE PRODUCT; or (b) correction of defects in the SOFTWARE PRODUCT; or (c) the cost of having defects in the SOFTWARE PRODUCT repaired; or (ii) in the case of support services: (a) resupply of the services or (b) payment of the cost of having the services supplied again.

EXCLUSION OF LIABILITY/DAMAGES. The following is without prejudice to any rights you may have at law which cannot legally be excluded or restricted. You acknowledge that no promise, representation, warranty or undertaking has been made or given by Microsoft (or its suppliers) or by any person or company on their behalf in relation to the profitability of or any other consequences or benefits to be obtained from the delivery or use of the SOFTWARE PRODUCT or written materials. You have relied upon your own skill and judgment in deciding to acquire the SOFTWARE PRODUCT, any accompanying hardware, manuals and written materials or support services. Except as and to the extent provided in this agreement, neither Microsoft nor its suppliers nor any related company will in any circumstances be liable for any other damages whatsoever (including, without limitation, damages for loss of business, business interruption, loss of business information or other indirect or consequential loss) arising out of the use, or inability to use, or supply, or non-supply, of the SOFTWARE PRODUCT or any written material) or any support services. Microsoft's total liability under any provision of this agreement is in any case limited to the amount actually paid by you for the SOFTWARE PRODUCT and/or any support services or US$5.00.

SUPPORT SERVICES AGREEMENT. If you have entered into a Microsoft support services agreement, Microsoft's entire liability regarding support services shall be governed by the terms of that agreement and not by the terms of this limited express warranty.

This agreement is governed by the laws of New South Wales, Australia or, where supplies are made in New Zealand, by the laws of New Zealand.

Indien u uw Microsoft-product in de Benelux hebt aangeschaft, geldt de volgende beperkte garantie voor u:

BEPERKTE GARANTIE. Microsoft garandeert dat (a) het SOFTWAREPRODUCT in hoofdzaak functioneert overeenkomstig de bijbehorende schriftelijke materialen gedurende een periode van negentig (90) dagen na de datum van ontvangst, en dat (b) alle vormen van Productondersteuning die door Microsoft worden geleverd in hoofdzaak zullen overeenkomen met de beschrijving ervan in de toepasselijke schriftelijke materialen die door Microsoft worden geleverd, en dat de technici van Microsoft Product Support Services zich binnen commercieel redelijke grenzen zullen inspannen om eventuele problemen op te lossen. Aangezien sommige staten en rechtssystemen beperking van de duur van een impliciete garantie niet toestaan, is de voorgaande beperking op u wellicht niet van toepassing. Voor zover is toegestaan op grond van toepasselijk recht zijn eventuele impliciete garanties met betrekking tot het SOFTWAREPRODUCT beperkt tot negentig (90) dagen.

VERHAALSMOGELIJKHEDEN VAN KLANTEN. De volledige aansprakelijkheid van Microsoft en haar leveranciers en uw enige tegemoetkoming krachtens deze Overeenkomst bestaat ter keuze van Microsoft in hetzij (a) restitutie van de eventuele licentievergoeding, of (b) reparatie of vervanging van het SOFTWAREPRODUCT dat niet voldoet aan voornoemde Beperkte Garantie en dat wordt geretourneerd naar Microsoft met een kopie van uw bewijs van aankoop. Deze Beperkte Garantie geldt niet indien het niet functioneren van het SOFTWAREPRODUCT het gevolg is van ongeval, misbruik of verkeerde toepassing. Voor een vervangend SOFTWAREPRODUCT zal een garantieperiode gelden gelijk aan de resterende tijd van de oorspronkelijke garantieperiode of, indien dat langer is, dertig (30) dagen. In landen buiten de Verenigde Staten zijn noch deze verhaalsmogelijkheden noch enige productondersteuning die wordt geboden door Microsoft, beschikbaar zonder het bewijs van licentieaankoop afkomstig van een geautoriseerde internationale bron.

GEEN ANDERE GARANTIES. VOOR ZOVER MAXIMAAL IS TOEGESTAAN OP GROND VAN TOEPASSELIJK RECHT WIJZEN MICROSOFT EN HAAR LEVERANCIERS ALLE GARANTIES VAN DE HAND EN ERKENNEN GEEN SPECIALE OMSTANDIGHEDEN, NOCH UITDRUKKELIJK NOCH IMPLICIET, DAARONDER MEDE BEGREPEN MAAR NIET BEPERKT TOT IMPLICIETE GARANTIES BETREFFENDE DE VERKOOPBAARHEID, DE GESCHIKTHEID VOOR EEN BEPAALD DOEL, HET EIGENDOMSRECHT OF HET NIET-INBREUKMAKEND KARAKTER VAN HET SOFTWAREPRODUCT EN HET VERSTREKKEN OF HET NIET VERSTREKKEN VAN PRODUCTONDERSTEUNING. DEZE BEPERKTE GARANTIE VERLEENT U SPECIFIEKE WETTELIJKE RECHTEN. HET IS MOGELIJK DAT U DAARNAAST NOG ANDERE RECHTEN

HEBT DIE VERSCHILLEN VAN STAAT/RECHTSGEBIED TOT STAAT/RECHTSGEBIED. INDIEN U DIT PRODUCT HEBT VERKREGEN IN BELGIË DOEN DE VOORGAANDE BEPALINGEN NIET AF AAN DE WETTELIJKE GARANTIES MET BETREKKING TOT VERBORGEN GEBREKEN WAAROP U MOGELIJK AANSPRAAK KUNT MAKEN OP GROND VAN ARTIKEL 1641 EV. VAN HET BURGERLIJK WETBOEK VAN BELGIË.

BEPERKTE AANSPRAKELIJKHEID. VOOR ZOVER IS TOEGESTAAN OP GROND VAN TOEPASSELIJK RECHT, WIJZEN MICROSOFT EN HAAR LEVERANCIERS ALLE AANSPRAKELIJKHEID VAN DE HAND VOOR BIJZONDERE, INCIDENTELE OF INDIRECTE SCHADE OF GEVOLGSCHADE (INCLUSIEF MAAR NIET BEPERKT TOT SCHADE ALS GEVOLG VAN WINSTDERVING, BEDRIJFSONDERBREKING, VERLIES VAN BEDRIJFSINFORMATIE OF ENIG ANDER GELDELIJK VERLIES) ALS GEVOLG VAN HET GEBRUIK OF DE VERHINDERING TOT GEBRUIK VAN HET SOFTWAREPRODUCT, OF ALS GEVOLG VAN HET VERSTREKKEN OF HET NIET VERSTREKKEN VAN PRODUCTONDERSTEUNING, ZELFS INDIEN MICROSOFT OP DE HOOGTE WAS GESTELD VAN DE MOGELIJKHEID VAN DIE SCHADE. IN IEDER GEVAL ZAL DE GEHELE AANSPRAKELIJKHEID VAN MICROSOFT OP GROND VAN ENIGE BEPALING VAN DEZE OVEREENKOMST BEPERKT WORDEN TOT HET WERKELIJKE BEDRAG DAT U HEBT BETAALD VOOR HET SOFTWAREPRODUCT OF 5,00 US $ IN LOKALE VALUTA, INDIEN DIT LAATSTE BEDRAG HOGER IS; ALS U ECHTER EEN OVEREENKOMST MET MICROSOFT BENT AANGEGAAN VOOR HET LEVEREN VAN PRODUCTONDERSTEUNING WORDT DE GEHELE AANSPRAKELIJKHEID VAN MICROSOFT BEHEERST DOOR DE BEPALINGEN IN DIE OVEREENKOMST. AANGEZIEN SOMMIGE STATEN EN RECHTSGEBIEDEN DE UITSLUITING OF BEPERKING VAN AANSPRAKELIJKHEID VOOR INCIDENTELE SCHADE OF GEVOLGSCHADE NIET TOESTAAN, IS HET MOGELIJK DAT BOVENSTAANDE BEPERKING NIET VOOR U GELDT.

DE BOVENSTAANDE BEPALINGEN MET BETREKKING TOT MICROSOFT'S BEPERKTE GARANTIES EN MICROSOFT'S BEPERKTE AANSPRAKELIJKHEID ZIJN VATBAAR VOOR SPLITSING. INDIEN OP GROND VAN TOEPASSELIJKE RECHT ENIGE BEPERKING OF UITSLUITING ONGELDIG WORDT GEACHT, ZULLEN DE OVERIGE BEPALINGEN VOLLEDIG VAN KRACHT BLIJVEN. INDIEN VAN ENIGE BEPERKING OF UITSLUITING WORDT VASTGESTELD DAT DEZE ONAANVAARDBAAR RUIM IS, ZAL DEZE BEPERKING OF UITSLUITING AFDWINGBAAR ZIJN VOOR ZOVER TOEGESTAAN OP GROND VAN TOEPASSELIJK RECHT.

Indien u dit product in Nederland hebt verkregen, wordt deze Overeenkomst beheerst door het recht van Nederland.

Indien u dit product in België hebt verkregen, wordt deze Overeenkomst beheerst door het recht van België.

Indien u dit product in Luxemburg hebt verkregen, wordt deze Overeenkomst beheerst door het recht van Luxemburg.

Indien u dit product buiten de hierboven genoemde landen hebt aangeschaft, kan lokaal recht van toepassing zijn.

Indien u vragen hebt met betrekking tot deze Overeenkomst of indien u om een andere reden contact wenst op te nemen met Microsoft, kunt u zich wenden tot de Microsoft-vestiging in uw land of schrijven naar: Microsoft Sales Information Center/One Microsoft Way/Redmond, WA 98052-6399, Verenigde Staten van Amerika.

Caso você tenha adquirido seu produto Microsoft no Brasil, a seguinte garantia limitada aplica-se a você:

GARANTIA LIMITADA — A Microsoft garante que (a) o SOFTWARE desempenhará suas funções substancialmente em conformidade com seu(s) manual(is), por um período de 90 (noventa) dias a contar da data da entrega; (b) qualquer Serviço de Suporte fornecido pela Microsoft será substancialmente, conforme descrito nos manuais aplicáveis, fornecido a você pela Microsoft, e os Engenheiros de Suporte da Microsoft farão os esforços comercialmente razoáveis para solucionar quaisquer problemas que ocorram. Alguns estados e jurisdições não permitem limitações à duração de garantia legal, hipótese na qual a limitação acima poderá não se aplicar a você. Sem prejuízo do disposto em lei aplicável, as garantias implícitas sobre o Software, se existentes, são limitadas a 90 (noventa) dias.

DIREITOS DO CLIENTE — A responsabilidade integral da Microsoft e de seus fornecedores, e o seu único direito será, a critério da Microsoft, (a) a devolução do preço pago, se existente, ou, alternativamente, (b) o conserto ou substituição do SOFTWARE, sujeito aos termos da Garantia Limitada, que seja devolvido à Microsoft com a cópia do recibo. Esta Garantia Limitada será nula e não gerará efeitos se o defeito do SOFTWARE resultar de acidente, utilização abusiva ou inadequada. Qualquer SOFTWARE substituído será garantido pelo prazo remanescente da garantia original ou por 30 (trinta) dias, no caso deste último prazo ser mais extenso. Fora dos Estados Unidos da América, nenhum destes direitos ou qualquer Serviço de Suporte ao produto oferecido pela Microsoft estará disponível sem a comprovação de compra de fonte internacional autorizada.

NENHUMA OUTRA GARANTIA — NA EXTENSÃO MÁXIMA PERMITIDA PELA LEI APLICÁVEL, A MICROSOFT E SEUS FORNECEDORES REJEITAM QUAISQUER GARANTIAS OU CONDIÇÕES, QUER SEJAM EXPRESSAS OU IMPLÍCITAS, INCLUINDO, MAS NÃO SE LIMITANDO A, GARANTIAS IMPLÍCITAS DE COMERCIALIZAÇÃO E ADEQUAÇÃO A UMA FINALIDADE ESPECÍFICA, TÍTULO E NÃO VIOLAÇÃO, COM RELAÇÃO AO SOFTWARE E À PRESTAÇÃO OU FALHA NA PRESTAÇÃO DE SERVIÇOS DE SUPORTE. ESTA GARANTIA LIMITADA LHE CONFERE DIREITOS ESPECÍFICOS. VOCÊ PODE GOZAR DE OUTROS DIREITOS, CONSIDERANDO QUE HÁ VARIAÇÃO DE ESTADO/JURISDIÇÃO PARA ESTADO/JURISDIÇÃO.

LIMITAÇÃO DE RESPONSABILIDADE — NA EXTENSÃO MÁXIMA PERMITIDA PELA LEI APLICÁVEL, EM NENHUMA HIPÓTESE A MICROSOFT OU SEUS FORNECEDORES SERÃO RESPONSÁVEIS POR QUAISQUER DANOS ESPECIAIS, INCIDENTAIS, INDIRETOS OU CONSEQÜENCIAIS (INCLUINDO, MAS NÃO SE LIMITANDO A, LUCROS CESSANTES, INTERRUPÇÕES COMERCIAIS, PERDA DE INFORMAÇÕES COMERCIAIS OU QUALQUER PERDA FINANCEIRA) DECORRENTES DO USO, OU DA INCAPACIDADE DE USAR O SOFTWARE OU DA PRESTAÇÃO OU FALHA NA PRESTAÇÃO DE SERVIÇOS DE SUPORTE, AINDA QUE A MICROSOFT TENHA SIDO ALERTADA QUANTO À POSSIBILIDADE DE TAIS DANOS. EM QUALQUER CASO, A RESPONSABILIDADE INTEGRAL DA MICROSOFT SOB ESTE CONTRATO LIMITAR-SE-Á AO VALOR EFETIVAMENTE PAGO PELO SOFTWARE OU US$5,00 (CINCO DÓLARES AMERICANOS), O QUE FOR MAIOR. CASO VOCÊ TENHA TOMADO PARTE EM UM CONTRATO DE SERVIÇOS DE SUPORTE DA MICROSOFT, A RESPONSABILIDADE INTEGRAL DA MICROSOFT

SERÁ REGIDA PELOS TERMOS DE TAL CONTRATO. CONSIDERANDO QUE ALGUNS ESTADOS/JURISDIÇÕES NÃO PERMITEM A EXCLUSÃO OU LIMITAÇÃO DE RESPONSABILIDADE, A LIMITAÇÃO ACIMA PODE NÃO SE APLICAR A VOCÊ.

Caso você tenha adquirido este produto nos Estados Unidos, este Contrato será regido pelas leis do Estado de Washington. Caso este produto tenha sido adquirido fora dos Estados Unidos, a legislação local poderá ser aplicada.

Se você tiver quaisquer dúvidas em relação a este Contrato de Licença ou desejar entrar em contato com a Microsoft por qualquer razão, entre em contato com a subsidiária da Microsoft no seu país ou escreva para: Microsoft Sales Information, One Microsoft Way, Redmond, Washington 98052-6399.

If you acquired your Microsoft Product in Canada, the following limited warranty applies to you:

LIMITED WARRANTY. Microsoft warrants that (a) the SOFTWARE PRODUCT will perform substantially in accordance with the accompanying written materials for a period of ninety (90) days from the date of receipt, and (b) any Support Services provided by Microsoft shall be substantially as described in applicable written materials provided to you by Microsoft, and Microsoft support engineers will make commercially reasonable efforts to solve any problem issues. Some states and jurisdictions do not allow limitations on duration of an implied warranty, so the above limitation may not apply to you. To the extent allowed by applicable law, implied warranties on the SOFTWARE PRODUCT, if any, are limited to ninety (90) days.

CUSTOMER REMEDIES. Microsoft's and its suppliers' entire liability and your exclusive remedy shall be, at Microsoft's option, either (a) return of the price paid, if any, or (b) repair or replacement of the SOFTWARE PRODUCT that does not meet Microsoft's Limited Warranty and which is returned to Microsoft with a copy of your receipt. This Limited Warranty is void if failure of the SOFTWARE PRODUCT has resulted from accident, abuse, or misapplication. Any replacement SOFTWARE PRODUCT will be warranted for the remainder of the original warranty period or thirty (30) days, whichever is longer. Outside the United States, neither these remedies nor any product support services offered by Microsoft are available without proof of purchase from an authorized international source.

NO OTHER WARRANTIES. TO THE MAXIMUM EXTENT PERMITTED BY APPLICABLE LAW, MICROSOFT AND ITS SUPPLIERS DISCLAIM ALL OTHER WARRANTIES AND CONDITIONS, EITHER EXPRESS OR IMPLIED, INCLUDING, BUT NOT LIMITED TO, IMPLIED WARRANTIES AND CONDITIONS OF MERCHANTABILITY, FITNESS FOR A PARTICULAR PURPOSE, TITLE, AND NON-INFRINGEMENT, WITH REGARD TO THE SOFTWARE PRODUCT, AND THE PROVISION OF OR FAILURE TO PROVIDE SUPPORT SERVICES. THIS LIMITED WARRANTY GIVES YOU SPECIFIC LEGAL RIGHTS. YOU MAY HAVE OTHERS, WHICH VARY FROM STATE/JURISDICTION TO STATE/JURISDICTION.

LIMITATION OF LIABILITY. TO THE MAXIMUM EXTENT PERMITTED BY APPLICABLE LAW, IN NO EVENT SHALL MICROSOFT OR ITS SUPPLIERS BE LIABLE FOR ANY SPECIAL, INCIDENTAL, INDIRECT, OR CONSEQUENTIAL DAMAGES WHATSOEVER (INCLUDING, WITHOUT LIMITATION, DAMAGES FOR LOSS OF BUSINESS PROFITS, BUSINESS INTERRUPTION, LOSS OF BUSINESS INFORMATION, OR ANY OTHER PECUNIARY LOSS) ARISING OUT OF THE USE OF OR INABILITY TO USE THE SOFTWARE PRODUCT OR THE PROVISION OF OR FAILURE TO PROVIDE SUPPORT SERVICES, EVEN IF MICROSOFT HAS BEEN ADVISED OF THE POSSIBILITY OF SUCH DAMAGES. IN ANY CASE, MICROSOFT'S ENTIRE LIABILITY UNDER ANY PROVISION OF THIS EULA SHALL BE LIMITED TO THE GREATER OF THE AMOUNT ACTUALLY PAID BY YOU FOR THE SOFTWARE PRODUCT OR AN AMOUNT EQUIVALENT TO U.S.$5.00 IN LOCAL CURRENCY; PROVIDED, HOWEVER, IF YOU HAVE ENTERED INTO A MICROSOFT SUPPORT SERVICES AGREEMENT, MICROSOFT'S ENTIRE LIABILITY REGARDING SUPPORT SERVICES SHALL BE GOVERNED BY THE TERMS OF THAT AGREEMENT. BECAUSE SOME STATES AND JURISDICTIONS DO NOT ALLOW THE EXCLUSION OR LIMITATION OF LIABILITY, THE ABOVE LIMITATION MAY NOT APPLY TO YOU.

If you acquired this product in the United States, this EULA is governed by the laws of the State of Washington.

If you acquired this product in Canada, this EULA is governed by the laws in force in the Province of Ontario, Canada. Each of the parties hereto irrevocably attorns to the jurisdiction of the courts of the Province of Ontario and further agrees to commence any litigation which may arise hereunder in the courts located in the Judicial District of York, Province of Ontario.

If this product was acquired outside the United States, then local law may apply.

Should you have any questions concerning this EULA, or if you desire to contact Microsoft for any reason, please contact the Microsoft subsidiary serving your country, or write: Microsoft Sales Information Center/One Microsoft Way/Redmond, WA 98052-6399.

Si vous avez acquis votre produit Microsoft au Canada, la garantie limitée suivante vous concerne :

GARANTIE LIMITÉE — Microsoft garantit que (a) la performance du LOGICIEL sera substantiellement en conformité avec la documentation qui accompagne le LOGICIEL, pour une période de quatre-vingt-dix (90) jours à compter de la date de réception ; et (b) tout support technique fourni par Microsoft sera substantiellement en conformité avec toute documentation afférente fournie par Microsoft et que les membres du support technique de Microsoft feront des efforts raisonnables pour résoudre toute difficulté technique découlant de l'utilisation du LOGICIEL. Certaines juridictions ne permettent pas de limiter dans le temps l'application de la présente garantie. Aussi, la limite stipulée ci-haut pourrait ne pas s'appliquer dans votre cas. Dans la mesure permise par la loi, toute garantie implicite portant sur le LOGICIEL, le cas échéant, est limitée à une période de quatre-vingt-dix (90) jours.

RECOURS DU CLIENT — La seule obligation de Microsoft et de ses fournisseurs et votre recours exclusif seront, au choix de Microsoft, soit (a) le remboursement du prix payé, si applicable, ou (b) la réparation ou le remplacement du LOGICIEL qui n'est pas conforme à la Garantie Limitée de Microsoft et qui est retourné à Microsoft avec une copie de votre reçu. Cette Garantie Limitée est nulle si le défaut du LOGICIEL est causé par un accident, un traitement abusif ou une mauvaise application. Tout LOGICIEL de remplacement sera garanti pour le reste de la période de garantie initiale ou pour trente (30) jours, selon la plus longue de ces périodes. À l'extérieur des États-Unis, aucun de ces recours non plus que le support technique offert par Microsoft ne sont disponibles sans une preuve d'achat provenant d'une source autorisée.

AUCUNE AUTRE GARANTIE — DANS LA MESURE PRÉVUE PAR LA LOI, MICROSOFT ET SES FOURNISSEURS EXCLUENT TOUTE AUTRE GARANTIE OU CONDITION, EXPRESSE OU IMPLICITE, Y COMPRIS MAIS NE SE LIMITANT PAS AUX GARANTIES OU CONDITIONS IMPLICITES DU CARACTÈRE ADÉQUAT POUR LA COMMERCIALISATION OU UN USAGE PARTICULIER EN CE QUI CONCERNE LE LOGICIEL OU CONCERNANT LE TITRE, L'ABSENCE DE CONTREFAÇON DUDIT LOGICIEL, ET TOUTE DOCUMENTATION ÉCRITE QUI L'ACCOMPAGNE, AINSI QUE POUR TOUTE DISPOSITION CONCERNANT LE SUPORT TECHNIQUE OU LA FAÇON DONT CELUI-CI A ÉTÉ RENDU. CETTE GARANTIE LIMITÉE VOUS ACCORDE DES DROITS JURIDIQUES SPÉCIFIQUES.

PAS DE RESPONSABILITÉ POUR LES DOMMAGES INDIRECTS — MICROSOFT OU SES FOURNISSEURS NE SERONT PAS RESPONSABLES EN AUCUNE CIRCONSTANCE POUR TOUT DOMMAGE SPÉCIAL, INCIDENT, INDIRECT, OU CONSÉQUENT QUEL QU'IL SOIT (Y COMPRIS, SANS LIMITATION, LES DOMMAGES ENTRAÎNÉS PAR LA PERTE DE BÉNÉFICES, L'INTERRUPTION DES ACTIVITÉS, LA PERTE D'INFORMATION OU TOUTE AUTRE PERTE PÉCUNIAIRE) DÉCOULANT DE L'UTILISATION OU DE L'IMPOSSIBILITÉ D'UTILISATION DE CE LOGICIEL AINSI QUE POUR TOUTE DISPOSITION CONCERNANT LE SUPPORT TECHNIQUE OU LA FAÇON DONT CELUI-CI A ÉTÉ RENDU ET CE, MÊME SI MICROSOFT A ÉTÉ AVISÉE DE LA POSSIBILITÉ DE TELS DOMMAGES. LA RESPONSABILITÉ DE MICROSOFT EN VERTU DE TOUTE DISPOSITION DE CETTE CONVENTION NE POURRA EN AUCUN TEMPS EXCÉDER LE PLUS ÉLEVÉ ENTRE I) LE MONTANT EFFECTIVEMENT PAYÉ PAR VOUS POUR LE LOGICIEL OU II) US$5.00. ADVENANT QUE VOUS AYEZ CONTRACTÉ PAR ENTENTE DISTINCTE AVEC MICROSOFT POUR UN SUPPORT TECHNIQUE ÉTENDU, VOUS SEREZ LIÉ PAR LES TERMES D' UNE TELLE ENTENTE.

La présente Convention est régie par les lois de la province d'Ontario, Canada. Chacune des parties à la présente reconnaît irrévocablement la compétence des tribunaux de la province d'Ontario et consent à instituer tout litige qui pourrait découler de la présente auprès des tribunaux situés dans le district judiciaire de York, province d'Ontario.

Au cas où vous auriez des questions concernant cette licence ou que vous désiriez vous mettre en rapport avec Microsoft pour quelque raison que ce soit, veuillez contacter la succursale Microsoft desservant votre pays, dont l'adresse est fournie dans ce produit, ou écrivez à : Microsoft Sales Information Center, One Microsoft Way, Redmond, Washington 98052-6399, États-Unis d'Amérique.

Pokud jste produkt spoleènosti Microsoft získali v Česká republice, vztahuje se na vás tato omezená záruka:

OMEZENÁ ZÁRUKA. Společnost Microsoft zaručuje, že (a) SOFTWARE bude pracovat v souladu s doprovodným písemným materiálem po dobu devadesáti (90) dnů ode dne převzetí a (b) veškeré Služby odborné pomoci poskytované společností Microsoft budou dostatečné podle příslušných písemných materiálů dodaných společností Microsoft a pracovníci Služeb odborné pomoci společnosti Microsoft vyvinou ekonomicky optimální úsilí směřující k řešení jakýchkoli problémů.

V některých zemích a právních řádech není povoleno dobu trvání záruky omezit, proto se výše uvedené omezení na vás nemusí vztahovat. V rozsahu povoleném rozhodným právem jsou předpokládané záruky na SOFTWARE, pokud nějaké existují, omezeny na devadesát (90) dní.

PRÁVA ZÁKAZNÍKA. Povinností společnosti Microsoft a jejích dodavatelů a vaším výlučným nárokem bude, na základě volby společnosti Microsoft, buď (a) vrátit zaplacenou částku, nebo (b) opravit nebo vyměnit SOFTWAROVÝ PRODUKT, který nesplňuje podmínky Omezené záruky společnosti Microsoft a který je vrácen společnosti Microsoft spolu s kopií účtu o zaplacení. Tato Omezená záruka pozbývá platnosti, pokud byla porucha SOFTWAROVÉHO PRODUKTU způsobena nehodou, špatným nebo nesprávným používáním. Jakýkoli vyměněný SOFTWAROVÝ PRODUKT bude mít záruční dobu do zbytku původní záruční doby nebo třicet (30) dnů podle toho, které z období je delší. Mimo území Spojených Států nejsou žádná z těchto práv ani služby odborné pomoci poskytované společností Microsoft k dispozici bez dokladu o koupi od autorizovaného mezinárodního prodejce.

ŽÁDNÉ DALŠÍ ZÁRUKY. V NEJVĚTŠÍM MOŽNÉM ROZSAHU POVOLENÉM ROZHODNÝM PRÁVEM NEUZNÁVÁ SPOLEČNOST MICROSOFT A JEJÍ DODAVATELÉ ŽÁDNÉ DALŠÍ ZÁRUKY A PODMÍNKY VÝSLOVNĚ UVEDENÉ NEBO PŘEDPOKLÁDANÉ VČETNĚ, ALE NIKOLI VÝHRADNĚ, PŘEDPOKLÁDANÝCH ZÁRUK VZTAHUJÍCÍCH SE K OBCHODOVATELNOSTI, VHODNOSTI PRO URČITÝ ÚČEL, VLASTNICKÝCH PRÁV A NEPORUŠENÍ SMLOUVY. TO SE TÝKÁ SOFTWARU A POSKYTNUTÍ NEBO NEPOSKYTNUTÍ SLUŽEB ODBORNÉ POMOCI. TATO OMEZENÁ ZÁRUKA VÁM DÁVÁ SPECIFICKÁ ZÁKONNÁ OPRÁVNĚNÍ. MŮŽETE MÍT DALŠÍ PRÁVA, KTERÁ SE LIŠÍ MEZI JEDNOTLIVÝMI ZEMĚMI NEBO PRÁVNÍMI ŘÁDY.

OMEZENÍ ODPOVĚDNOSTI. V NEJVĚTŠÍM MOŽNÉM ROZSAHU POVOLENÉM ROZHODNÝM PRÁVEM NENESE SPOLEČNOST MICROSOFT ANI JEJÍ DODAVATELÉ V ŽÁDNÉM PŘÍPADĚ ODPOVĚDNOST ZA ZVLÁŠTNÍ, NÁHODNÉ, NEPŘÍMÉ NEBO VEDLEJŠÍ ŠKODY, AŤ JSOU JAKÉKOLI (VČETNĚ A BEZ OMEZENÍ, ŠKODY ZE ZTRÁT ZISKU Z PODNIKÁNÍ, Z PŘERUŠENÍ PODNIKÁNÍ, ZE ZTRÁT PODNIKATELSKÝCH INFORMACÍ NEBO JAKÉKOLI DALŠÍ ZVLÁŠTNÍ ZTRÁTY) ZPŮSOBENÉ UŽÍVÁNÍM NEBO NEMOŽNOSTÍ UŽÍVAT TENTO SOFTWAROVÝ PRODUKT NEBO NA ZÁKLADĚ POSKYTNUTÍ NEBO NEPOSKYTNUTÍ SLUŽEB ODBORNÉ POMOCI, I KDYŽ BYLA SPOLEČNOST MICROSOFT

UPOZORNĚNA NA MOŽNOST VZNIKU TAKOVÝCH ŠKOD. V JAKÉMKOLI PŘÍPADĚ JSOU VEŠKERÉ ZÁRUKY SPOLEČNOSTI MICROSOFT OMEZENY NA ČÁSTKU SKUTEČNĚ ZA SOFTWAROVÝ PRODUKT ZAPLACENOU, NEBO NA ČÁSTKU V MÍSTNÍ MĚNĚ ODPOVÍDAJÍCÍ 5 USD, AVŠAK V PŘÍPADĚ, ŽE JSTE UZAVŘELI SMLOUVU O ODBORNÉ POMOCI SPOLEČNOSTI MICROSOFT, JSOU VEŠKERÉ ZÁRUKY SPOLEČNOSTI MICROSOFT TÝKAJÍCÍ SE ODBORNÉ POMOCI UPRAVENY PODMÍNKAMI PŘÍSLUŠNÉ SMLOUVY. PROTOŽE V NĚKTERÝCH ZEMÍCH A PRÁVNÍCH ŘÁDECH NENÍ DOVOLENO VYLOUČIT NEBO OMEZIT ODPOVĚDNOST, VÝŠE UVEDENÉ OMEZENÍ SE NA VÁS NEMUSÍ VZTAHOVAT.

Pokud jste tento produkt získali mimo území USA, může se tato smlouva řídit místními zákony.

Budete-li mít jakékoli dotazy týkající se této smlouvy EULA nebo budete-li se chtít z jakýchkoli důvodů spojit se společností Microsoft, kontaktujte zastoupení společnosti Microsoft ve své zemi, nebo pište na adresu: Microsoft Sales Information Center/One Microsoft Way/Redmond, WA 98052-6399, U.S.A.

Hvis De har erhvervet Deres Microsoft-produkt i Danmark, gælder følgende ansvarsbegrænsning for Dem:

BEGRÆNSET ANSVAR

BEGRÆNSET ANSVAR. Microsoft indestår for (a), at SOFTWAREPRODUKTET i alt væsentligt fungerer i overensstemmelse med de medfølgende skriftlige materialer i en periode af halvfems (90) dage fra modtagelsen, hvis De erhverver Softwareproduktet i forretningsøjemed eller et (1) år fra modtagelsen, hvis De er en forbruger, der køber Softwareproduktet i andet end forretningsøjemed, og (b) og at al Teknisk support leveret af Microsoft i al væsentlighed vil være i overensstemmelse med beskrivelsen i det skriftlige materiale, som er leveret til Dem af Microsoft. Microsoft Teknisk support vil foretage forretningsmæssigt rimelige skridt til at løse ethvert problem. I nogle stater og retskredse er det ikke tilladt at begrænse varigheden af et stiltiende ansvar, hvorfor ovennævnte begrænsning muligvis ikke gælder for Dem. I den maksimale udstrækning tilladt efter gældende ret er ethvert stiltiende eller forudsat ansvar vedrørende SOFTWAREPRODUKTET begrænset til halvfems (90) fra modtagelsen, hvis De erhverver Softwareproduktet i forretningsøjemed eller et (1) år fra modtagelsen, hvis De er en forbruger, der køber Softwareproduktet i andet end forretningsøjemed.

BRUGERENS MISLIGHOLDELSESBEFØJELSER

Microsofts og Microsofts leverandørers fulde ansvar og Deres eksklusive beføjelse er efter Microsofts valg enten a) refusion af den pris, der er betalt, eller b) reparation eller erstatning af det SOFTWAREPRODUKT, der ikke opfylder Microsofts ovenstående klausul om begrænset ansvar, og som returneres til Microsoft sammen med en kopi af kvitteringen. Dette begrænsede ansvar gælder ikke, såfremt fejlen i SOFTWAREPRODUKTET skyldes uheld, misbrug eller uretmæssig brug. Microsoft indestår for enhver erstatningssoftware i den resterende del af den oprindelige garantiperiode eller 30 dage, alt efter hvilken periode der er længst. Uden for USA er ingen af disse beføjelser og ingen teknisk support, som tilbydes af Microsoft, tilgængelig uden købsbevis fra en autoriseret international kilde.

INTET ANDET ANSVAR

I DET OMFANG GÆLDENDE LOVGIVNING GØR DET MULIGT, FRASKRIVER MICROSOFT OG MICROSOFTS LEVERANDØRER SIG ETHVERT ANDET ANSVAR OG ENHVER ANDEN BETINGELSE, DET VÆRE SIG UDTRYKKELIG ELLER STILTIENDE, HERUNDER, MEN IKKE BEGRÆNSET TIL, STILTIENDE ANSVAR FOR SALGBARHED, EGNETHED TIL SPECIELLE FORMÅL ELLER IKKE-OVERTRÆDELSE AF OPHAVSRETTIGHEDER, FOR SÅ VIDT ANGÅR SOFTWAREPRODUKTET, OG MED HENSYN TIL YDELSE, ELLER MANGLENDE YDELSE, AF TEKNISK SUPPORT. DETTE BEGRÆNSEDE ANSVAR GIVER DEM BESTEMTE JURIDISKE RETTIGHEDER. DE HAR MULIGVIS ANDRE RETTIGHEDER, AFHÆNGIGT AF LAND, STAT, REGION ELLER RETSKREDS.

BEGRÆNSNING AF ANSVAR

I DET OMFANG GÆLDENDE LOVGIVNING GØR DET MULIGT, KAN MICROSOFT ELLER MICROSOFTS LEVERANDØRER I INTET TILFÆLDE BLIVE HOLDT ANSVARLIG FOR NOGET SÆRSKILT, DOKUMENTERET TAB, NOGEN DIREKTE ELLER INDIREKTE SKADE ELLER NOGEN FØLGESKADE (HERUNDER, UDEN BEGRÆNSNING, PRODUKTANSVAR, SKADE I FORBINDELSE MED DRIFTSTAB, DRIFTSFORSTYRRELSER, TAB I FORBINDELSE MED MISTEDE FORRETNINGSOPLYSNINGER ELLER ANDRE ØKONOMISKE TAB) OPSTÅET VED BENYTTELSE AF ELLER UEGNETHED TIL AT BENYTTE SOFTWAREPRODUKTET ELLER YDELSE ELLER MANGLENDE YDELSE AF TEKNISK SUPPORT, SELVOM MICROSOFT ER BLEVET UNDERRETTET OM MULIGHEDEN FOR SÅDANNE SKADER. UNDER ALLE OMSTÆNDIGHEDER SKAL MICROSOFTS FULDE ANSVAR I HENHOLD TIL BESTEMMELSERNE I NÆRVÆRENDE SLUTBRUGERLICENSAFTALE VÆRE MAKSIMERET TIL DET BELØB, DE RENT FAKTISK HAR BETALT FOR SOFTWAREPRODUKTET, ELLER USD 5,00 I DEN LOKALE MØNTFOD AFHÆNGIG AF HVILKET BELØB, DER ER STØRST, DOG SÅLEDES AT MICROSOFTS FULDE ANSVAR I FORBINDELSE MED TEKNISK SUPPORT ER UNDERLAGT VILKÅRENE I AFTALEN OM TEKNISK SUPPORT, SÅFREMT DE HAR INDGÅET EN AFTALE MED MICROSOFT OM TEKNISK SUPPORT. DA NOGLE STATER OG/ELLER LANDE IKKE TILLADER UDELUKKELSE ELLER BEGRÆNSNING AF ANSVAR, ER DET MULIGT, AT OVENNÆVNTE BEGRÆNSNING IKKE GÆLDER FOR DEM.

Hvis De har erhvervet dette produkt i Danmark, er nærværende Slutbrugerlicensaftale underlagt lovgivningen i Danmark.

Hvis De har erhvervet dette produkt uden for Danmark, kan lokal ret finde anvendelse.

Hvis De har spørgsmål vedrørende nærværende Aftale, eller hvis De ønsker at kontakte Microsoft i anden forbindelse, bedes De skrive til Microsofts datterselskab i Deres land eller til Microsoft i USA på følgende adresse:

MICROSOFT SALES INFORMATION CENTER, ONE MICROSOFT WAY, REDMOND, WASHINGTON 98052-6399.

Falls Sie Ihr Microsoft-Produkt in Deutschland, Österreich, Liechtenstein oder der Schweiz erworben haben, gilt die nachfolgende beschränkte Garantie für Sie:

BESCHRÄNKTE GARANTIE. Microsoft garantiert (a) für einen Zeitraum von 90 Tagen ab Empfangsdatum, dass die SOFTWARE im wesentlichen gemäß den begleitenden gedruckten Materialien arbeitet, und, sofern dieses Produkt nicht in Deutschland erworben wurde, (b) dass jegliche Supportleistungen von Microsoft im wesentlichen den anwendbaren gedruckten Materialien entsprechen, die Ihnen von Microsoft zur Verfügung gestellt wurden, und die Microsoft-Servicetechniker alle vernünftigerweise notwendigen Anstrengungen unternehmen werden, um auftretende Probleme zu lösen. Falls Sie dieses Produkt in Deutschland erworben haben, unterliegt die Gewährleistung und Haftung von Microsoft im Zusammenhang mit Supportleistungen, soweit nicht ein zusätzlicher Vertrag über Supportleistungen abgeschlossen worden ist, den gesetzlichen Bestimmungen. **DA EINIGE STAATEN UND RECHTSORDNUNGEN ZEITLICHE BESCHRÄNKUNGEN DER GÜLTIGKEIT VON KONKLUDENTEN GEWÄHRLEISTUNGEN NICHT GESTATTEN, GILT DIE VORSTEHENDE BESCHRÄNKUNG FÜR SIE MÖGLICHERWEISE NICHT. SOWEIT ES DAS ANWENDBARE RECHT GESTATTET, SIND KONKLUDENTE GEWÄHRLEISTUNGEN BEZÜGLICH DES SOFTWAREPRODUKTS, SOFERN VORHANDEN, AUF NEUNZIG (90) TAGE BESCHRÄNKT.**

ANSPRÜCHE DES KUNDEN. Die gesamte Haftung von Microsoft und deren Lieferanten und Ihr alleiniger Anspruch besteht nach Wahl von Microsoft entweder (a) in der Rückerstattung des bezahlten Preises, soweit anwendbar, oder (b) in der Reparatur oder dem Ersatz des SOFTWAREPRODUKTS, das der beschränkten Garantie von Microsoft nicht entspricht, soweit es zusammen mit einer Kopie Ihrer Quittung an Microsoft zurückgegeben wird. Diese beschränkte Garantie gilt nicht, wenn der Fehler des SOFTWAREPRODUKTS auf einen Unfall, Missbrauch oder fehlerhafte Anwendung zurückzuführen ist. Für jedes Ersatz-SOFTWAREPRODUKT übernimmt Microsoft eine Garantie nur für den Rest der ursprünglichen Garantiefrist oder für 30 Tage, je nachdem, welcher Zeitraum länger ist. Sämtliche hierin bestimmten Rechte sowie jeglicher Produkt-Support durch Microsoft ist außerhalb der USA nur gegen Nachweis des Kaufes von einer autorisierten internationalen Geschäftsstelle erhältlich.

ANDERE GEWÄHRLEISTUNGSRECHTE UNBERÜHRT. Die obige Garantie wird von Microsoft als dem Hersteller des SOFTWAREPRODUKTS übernommen. Etwaige gesetzliche Gewährleistungs- oder Haftungsansprüche, welche Ihnen nach den Gesetzen Ihres Landes gegen den Händler zustehen, von dem Sie Ihr Exemplar des SOFTWAREPRODUKTS erhalten haben, werden hierdurch weder ersetzt noch beschränkt. Soweit anwendbar, gelten solche gesetzlichen Gewährleistungsrechte zusätzlich zu der hierin eingeräumten Garantie von Microsoft.

KEINE WEITEREN GEWÄHRLEISTUNGEN VON MICROSOFT. IM GRÖSSTMÖGLICHEN, DURCH DAS ANWENDBARE RECHT GESTATTETEN UMFANG LEHNEN MICROSOFT UND DEREN LIEFERANTEN ALLE SONSTIGEN GEWÄHRLEISTUNGEN UND BEDINGUNGEN IN BEZUG AUF DAS SOFTWAREPRODUKT UND DIE LEISTUNG BZW. NICHTLEISTUNG VON SUPPORTDIENSTEN AB, UNABHÄNGIG DAVON, OB SIE AUSDRÜCKLICH ODER KONKLUDENT GEWÄHRT WORDEN SIND, EINSCHLIESSLICH, ABER NICHT BESCHRÄNKT AUF, KONKLUDENTE GEWÄHRLEISTUNGEN DER HANDELSÜBLICHKEIT, EIGNUNG FÜR EINEN BESTIMMTEN ZWECK, EIGENTUM ODER NICHTVERLETZUNG VON SCHUTZRECHTEN DRITTER. DIESE BESCHRÄNKTE GARANTIE VERLEIHT IHNEN BESTIMMTE RECHTE. JE NACH STAAT ODER RECHTSORDNUNG KÖNNEN SIE MÖGLICHERWEISE WEITERE RECHTE HABEN.

HAFTUNGSBESCHRÄNKUNG. IM GRÖSSTMÖGLICHEN, DURCH DAS ANWENDBARE RECHT GESTATTETEN UMFANG LEHNEN MICROSOFT UND DEREN LIEFERANTEN JEDE HAFTUNG FÜR IRGENDWELCHE BESONDEREN, ZUFÄLLIGEN, INDIREKTEN ODER FOLGESCHÄDEN (EINSCHLIESSLICH, ABER NICHT BESCHRÄNKT AUF, SCHÄDEN AUS ENTGANGENEM GEWINN, GESCHÄFTSUNTERBRECHUNG, VERLUST VON GESCHÄFTSINFORMATIONEN ODER IRGENDWELCHEN ANDEREN VERMÖGENSSCHÄDEN) AB, DIE AUS DER VERWENDUNG ODER DER UNMÖGLICHKEIT DER VERWENDUNG DES SOFTWAREPRODUKTS ODER DURCH DIE LEISTUNG BZW. NICHTLEISTUNG VON SUPPORTLEISTUNGEN ENTSTEHEN; DIES GILT AUCH DANN, WENN MICROSOFT ZUVOR AUF DIE MÖGLICHKEIT SOLCHER SCHÄDEN HINGEWIESEN WORDEN IST. IN JEDEM FALL BESCHRÄNKT SICH DIE HAFTUNG VON MICROSOFT NACH DIESEM EULA AUF DEN BETRAG, DEN SIE FÜR DAS SOFTWAREPRODUKT BEZAHLT HABEN, ODER AUF DEN BETRAG, WELCHER IN ÖRTLICHER WÄHRUNG US$ 5,- ENTSPRICHT, WOBEI DER HÖHERE BETRAG MASSGEBEND IST. FALLS SIE MIT MICROSOFT EINEN VERTRAG ÜBER SUPPORTLEISTUNGEN ABGESCHLOSSEN HABEN, BESTIMMT SICH MICROSOFTS GESAMTE HAFTUNG IN BEZUG AUF SUPPORTLEISTUNGEN NACH DEN BESTIMMUNGEN DIESES VERTRAGES. DA EINIGE STAATEN ODER RECHTSORDNUNGEN HAFTUNGSBEGRENZUNGEN ODER HAFTUNGSAUSSCHLÜSSE NICHT GESTATTEN, GILT DIE VORSTEHENDE EINSCHRÄNKUNG FÜR SIE MÖGLICHER WEISE NICHT. IN DEUTSCHLAND GILT DIE OBEN GENANNTE HAFTUNGSBESCHRÄNKUNG NICHT FÜR ANSPRÜCHE NACH DEM PRODUKTHAFTUNGSGESETZ.

Wenn Sie dieses Produkt in Deutschland gekauft haben, unterliegt dieses EULA deutschem Recht.
Wenn Sie dieses Produkt in Österreich gekauft haben, unterliegt dieses EULA österreichischem Recht.
Wenn Sie dieses Produkt in Liechtenstein gekauft haben, unterliegt dieses EULA dem Recht des Fürstentums Liechtenstein.
Wenn Sie dieses Produkt in der Schweiz gekauft haben, unterliegt dieses EULA schweizer Recht.
Wenn Sie das Produkt außerhalb der oben angeführten Länder erworben haben, gilt möglicherweise das lokal anwendbare Recht.

Sollten Sie Fragen zu diesem Vertrag haben, oder möchten Sie sich mit Microsoft aus irgendwelchen Gründen in Verbindung setzen, wenden Sie sich an die für Ihr Land zuständige Microsoft-Niederlassung, oder schreiben Sie an: Microsoft Sales Information Center/One Microsoft Way/Redmond, WA 98052-6399, USA.

If you acquired your Microsoft Product in England, Scotland, Wales or the Republic of Ireland, the following limited express warranty applies to you:

LIMITED EXPRESS WARRANTY — Microsoft warrants that (a) the SOFTWARE PRODUCT will perform substantially in accordance with the accompanying written material(s) for a period of 90 days from the date of receipt; and (b) any Support Services provided by Microsoft shall be substantially as described in applicable written materials provided to you by Microsoft, and Microsoft support engineers will make commercially reasonable efforts to solve any problem issues.

CUSTOMER REMEDIES —Your remedy shall be, at Microsoft's option, either (a) return of the price paid or (b) repair or replacement of the SOFTWARE PRODUCT that does not meet Microsoft's Limited Express Warranty. If you are not dealing as a consumer in the UK or Ireland, this shall constitute your exclusive remedy and MICROSOFT's and its suppliers' entire liability. This Limited Express Warranty is void if failure of the SOFTWARE PRODUCT has resulted from accident, abuse, or misapplication. Any replacement SOFTWARE PRODUCT will be covered by the Limited Express Warranty for the remainder of the original warranty period or 30 days, whichever is longer. Outside the United States, neither these remedies nor any product support services offered by Microsoft are available without proof of purchase from an authorized international source.

TERMS THAT APPLY IF YOU ARE DEALING AS A CONSUMER IN THE UK OR IRELAND:

- **NO OTHER WARRANTIES FROM MICROSOFT.** **Microsoft does not make any other warranties or promises about the SOFTWARE PRODUCT**.

- **LIMITATION OF LIABILITY. Microsoft's and its suppliers' liability shall not in any event include losses related to your business, such as lost data, lost profits or business interruption. To the extent that you could have avoided damages by taking reasonable care, including by backing up your software and other files, Microsoft will not be liable for such damages.**

- **NOTE: As to any product that qualifies as "goods", your statutory rights are not affected.**

TERMS THAT APPLY IF YOU ARE NOT DEALING AS A CONSUMER IN THE UK OR IRELAND:

- **EXCLUSION OF IMPLIED TERMS**—TO THE MAXIMUM EXTENT PERMITTED BY APPLICABLE LAW, MICROSOFT DISCLAIMS ALL OTHER WARRANTIES, CONDITIONS OR OTHER TERMS, EITHER EXPRESS OR IMPLIED (WHETHER BY STATUTE, COMMON LAW, COLLATERALLY OR OTHERWISE), INCLUDING BUT NOT LIMITED TO IMPLIED WARRANTIES OF SATISFACTORY QUALITY AND FITNESS FOR PARTICULAR PURPOSE, WITH RESPECT TO THE SOFTWARE PRODUCT, AND THE ACCOMPANYING PRODUCT MANUAL(S) AND WRITTEN MATERIALS. Any implied warranties that are not deemed excluded are limited to 90 days or the shortest period permitted by applicable law, whichever is greater.

- **NO LIABILITY FOR CONSEQUENTIAL DAMAGES** — TO THE MAXIMUM EXTENT PERMITTED BY APPLICABLE LAW, MICROSOFT AND ITS SUPPLIERS SHALL NOT BE LIABLE FOR ANY OTHER DAMAGES WHATSOEVER (INCLUDING, WITHOUT LIMITATION, DAMAGES FOR LOSS OF BUSINESS PROFITS, BUSINESS INTERRUPTION, LOSS OF BUSINESS INFORMATION, OR OTHER PECUNIARY LOSS) ARISING OUT OF THE USE OF OR INABILITY TO USE THE SOFTWARE PRODUCT OR THE PROVISION OF OR FAILURE TO PROVIDE SUPPORT SERVICES (INCLUDING, WITHOUT LIMITATION, THROUGH NEGLIGENCE), EVEN IF MICROSOFT HAS BEEN ADVISED OF THE POSSIBILITY OF SUCH DAMAGES. IN ANY CASE, MICROSOFT'S ENTIRE LIABILITY UNDER ANY PROVISION OF THIS AGREEMENT SHALL BE LIMITED TO THE AMOUNT ACTUALLY PAID BY YOU FOR THE SOFTWARE AND/OR ANY SUPPORT SERVICES; PROVIDED, HOWEVER, IF YOU HAVE ENTERED INTO A MICROSOFT SUPPORT SERVICES AGREEMENT, MICROSOFT'S ENTIRE LIABILITY REGARDING SUPPORT SERVICES SHALL BE GOVERNED BY THE TERMS OF THAT AGREEMENT.**To the extent that you could have avoided damages by taking reasonable care, including by backing up your software and other files, Microsoft will not be liable for such damages.**

GENERAL TERMS. The SOFTWARE PRODUCT is designed and offered as general-purpose product, not for any user's particular purpose. You accept that no SOFTWARE PRODUCT is error-free. The above warranty and liability limitations do not apply in the case of direct personal injury or death caused by the negligence of Microsoft. This Agreement is governed by the laws of England if you acquired the Product in the United Kingdom. This Agreement is governed by the laws of the Republic of Ireland if you acquired this Product in the Republic of Ireland.

Should you have any questions concerning this Agreement, or if you desire to contact Microsoft for any reason, please use the address information enclosed in this product to contact the Microsoft subsidiary serving your country or write: Microsoft Sales Information Center, One Microsoft Way, Redmond, WA 98052-6399, USA.

Si usted ha adquirido su producto Microsoft en España, se aplicará la presente garantía limitada y limitación de responsabilidad:

I. GARANTÍA LIMITADA

GARANTÍA LIMITADA. Microsoft garantiza que (a) durante un período de ciento ochenta (180) días a contar desde la fecha de adquisición, el PRODUCTO SOFTWARE funcionará sustancialmente de acuerdo con lo especificado en los materiales impresos que lo acompañan, y que (b) cualquier Servicio Técnico proporcionado por Microsoft se llevará a cabo sustancialmente de acuerdo con lo especificado en los materiales impresos proporcionados por Microsoft y que los ingenieros de soporte de Microsoft harán los esfuerzos comercialmente razonables para resolver cualquier problema. Algunos estados y jurisdicciones no permiten limitaciones con respecto a la duración de una garantía implícita, de modo que la limitación anterior puede no serle aplicable. En la medida permitida por la ley aplicable, las garantías implícitas del PRODUCTO SOFTWARE, si existieran, se limitarán a ciento ochenta (180) días.

RECURSOS DEL CLIENTE. La responsabilidad total de Microsoft y de sus proveedores y el único recurso del cliente consistirá, a elección de Microsoft, ya sea en: (a) el reembolso del precio pagado, si corresponde o (b) la reparación o reemplazo del PRODUCTO SOFTWARE que no cumpla con la Garantía Limitada de Microsoft y que sea devuelto a Microsoft con copia de su recibo. Esta Garantía Limitada quedará sin efecto si los defectos del PRODUCTO SOFTWARE son consecuencia de accidente, abuso o uso indebido. Cualquier PRODUCTO SOFTWARE de reemplazo estará garantizado por el período de tiempo que reste hasta el vencimiento de la garantía original o un período de treinta (30) días, lo que resulte mayor. Ninguno de estos recursos o Servicios Técnicos ofrecidos por Microsoft se encontrará disponible fuera de los Estados Unidos de América, sin la constancia de compra emitida por una fuente internacional autorizada.

INEXISTENCIA DE OTRAS GARANTÍAS. HASTA LA MÁXIMA EXTENSIÓN PERMITIDA POR LA LEY APLICABLE MICROSOFT Y SUS PROVEEDORES NO RESPONDERÁN POR CUALQUIER OTRA GARANTÍA O CONDICIÓN, TANTO IMPLÍCITA COMO EXPLÍCITA, INCLUYENDO, SIN LIMITACIÓN, LAS GARANTÍAS DE TÍTULO Y NO INFRACCIÓN RESPECTO DEL PRODUCTO SOFTWARE. ESTA GARANTÍA LIMITADA LE OTORGA A USTED DERECHOS LEGALES ESPECÍFICOS. PODRÁ TENER OTROS DERECHOS QUE PODRÁN VARIAR DE UN ESTADO O JURISDICCIÓN A OTRO ESTADO O JURISDICCIÓN.

II. LIMITACIÓN DE RESPONSABILIDAD. HASTA LA MÁXIMA EXTENSIÓN PERMITIDA POR LA LEY APLICABLE, EN NINGÚN CASO, MICROSOFT NI SUS PROVEEDORES SERÁN RESPONSABLES POR NINGÚN DAÑO NI PERJUICIO (INCLUYENDO, SIN LIMITACIÓN, DAÑOS POR PÉRDIDA DE GANANCIAS O LUCRO CESANTE). QUE SE DERIVE DEL USO O IMPOSIBILIDAD DE USO DE ESTE PRODUCTO MICROSOFT, AUN CUANDO SE HUBIERA ADVERTIDO A MICROSOFT DE LA POSIBILIDAD DE DICHOS DAÑOS. EN CUALQUIER CASO, LA RESPONSABILIDAD TOTAL DE MICROSOFT CON RESPECTO A CUALQUIER CLÁUSULA DE ESTE CLUF SE LIMITARÁ A LA CANTIDAD QUE SEA MAYOR ENTRE EL PRECIO PAGADO POR EL PRODUCTO SOFTWARE O UNA CANTIDAD EQUIVALENTE A CINCO DÓLARES ESTADOUNIDENSES EN MONEDA LOCAL; CON LA CONDICIÓN, SIN EMBARGO, DE QUE SI SE HA COMPROMETIDO POR CONTRATO CON EL SERVICIO TÉCNICO MICROSOFT, LA TOTAL RESPONSABILIDAD DE MICROSOFT CON RESPECTO AL SERVICIO TÉCNICO ESTARÁ REGIDA POR LOS TÉRMINOS DE DICHO CONTRATO. DEBIDO A QUE ALGUNOS ESTADOS Y JURISDICCIONES NO PERMITEN LA EXCLUSIÓN O LIMITACIÓN DE RESPONSABILIDAD, LA LIMITACIÓN ANTERIOR PUEDE NO SERLE APLICABLE.

Si adquirió este producto en España, el presente CLUF se regirá por las leyes de España.

Si adquirió este producto fuera de España, será aplicable la legislación del lugar de adquisición.

Si tiene alguna duda con respecto a este CLUF o si desea ponerse en contacto con Microsoft por cualquier motivo, remítase a la subsidiaria Microsoft que atiende a su país o escriba en inglés a Microsoft Sales Information Center/One Microsoft Way/Redmond, WA 98052-6399/EE.UU.

Εάν προμηθευτήκατε αυτό το προϊόν της Microsoft στην Ελλάδα, ισχύει για την περίπτωσή σας η ακόλουθη περιορισμένη εγγύηση:

ΠΕΡΙΟΡΙΣΜΕΝΗ ΕΓΓΥΗΣΗ. Η Microsoft εγγυάται ότι (α) το ΠΡΟΪΟΝ ΛΟΓΙΣΜΙΚΟΥ θα λειτουργεί ουσιαστικά σύμφωνα με το έγγραφο υλικό που το συνοδεύει για περίοδο ενενήντα (90) ημερών από την ημερομηνία παραλαβής και ότι (β) οποιεσδήποτε Υπηρεσίες Υποστήριξης σας παρέχει θα είναι ουσιαστικά εκείνες που περιγράφονται στο αντίστοιχο έγγραφο υλικό που παρέχεται με το ΠΡΟΪΟΝ ΛΟΓΙΣΜΙΚΟΥ και ότι οι Μηχανικοί Υποστήριξης της Microsoft θα καταβάλουν προσπάθειες για να επιλύσουν κάθε πρόβλημα, εντός λογικών για τις εμπορικές συνολλαγές ορίων. Σε κάποιες πολιτείες και περιοχές δικαιοδοσίας, δεν επιτρέπονται περιορισμοί στη χρονική διάρκεια συναγόμενων εγγυήσεων, συνεπώς ο παραπάνω περιορισμός είναι δυνατό να μην ισχύει για εσάς. Στο μέγιστο βαθμό που αυτό επιτρέπεται από το εφαρμοστέο δίκαιο, η διάρκεια των συναγόμενων εγγυήσεων για το ΠΡΟΪΟΝ ΛΟΓΙΣΜΙΚΟΥ, αφόσον ισχύουν, περιορίζεται στις ενενήντα (90) ημέρες.

ΑΠΟΖΗΜΙΩΣΕΙΣ ΠΕΛΑΤΗ. Η όλη ευθύνη της Microsoft και των προμηθευτών της και η μόνη και αποκλειστική σας αποζημίωση θα είναι, κατ' επιλογή της Microsoft, είτε (α) η επιστροφή του καταβληθέντος τιμήματος, αφόσον υπήρξε τέτοιο τίμημα είτε (β) η επιδιόρθωση ή αντικατάσταση του ΠΡΟΪΟΝΤΟΣ ΛΟΓΙΣΜΙΚΟΥ που δεν ανταποκρίνεται στην Περιορισμένη Εγγύηση της Microsoft και το οποίο επιστρέφεται στη Microsoft με μία αντίγραφο της απόδειξής σας. Αυτή η Περιορισμένη Εγγύηση δεν ισχύει εάν η ανεπάρκεια του ΠΡΟΪΟΝΤΟΣ ΛΟΓΙΣΜΙΚΟΥ είναι είτε αποτέλεσμα ατυχήματος είτε αθέμιτης ή κακής χρήσης. Εκτός των Ηνωμένων Πολιτειών, αυτά τα δικαιώματα και οι υπηρεσίες υποστήριξης προϊόντων που παρέχει η Microsoft δεν σας διατίθενται, εάν δεν έχετε απόδειξη αγοράς από εξουσιοδοτημένο κέντρο διεθνών πωλήσεων.

ΟΥΔΕΜΙΑ ΑΛΛΗ ΕΓΓΥΗΣΗ. ΣΤΗ ΜΕΓΙΣΤΗ ΔΥΝΑΤΗ ΕΚΤΑΣΗ ΠΟΥ ΕΠΙΤΡΕΠΕΙ ΤΟ ΕΦΑΡΜΟΣΤΕΟ ΔΙΚΑΙΟ, Η MICROSOFT ΚΑΙ ΟΙ ΠΡΟΜΗΘΕΥΤΕΣ ΤΗΣ ΑΠΟΠΟΙΟΥΝΤΑΙ ΟΠΟΙΟΥΣΔΗΠΟΤΕ ΑΛΛΟΥΣ ΟΡΟΥΣ ΚΑΙ ΕΓΓΥΗΣΕΙΣ, ΡΗΤΕΣ Ή ΣΙΩΠΗΡΕΣ, ΠΕΡΙΛΑΜΒΑΝΟΜΕΝΩΝ, ΕΝΔΕΙΚΤΙΚΑ, ΤΩΝ ΣΙΩΠΗΡΩΝ ΕΓΓΥΗΣΕΩΝ ΕΜΠΟΡΕΥΣΙΜΟΤΗΤΑΣ, ΚΑΤΑΛΛΗΛΟΤΗΤΑΣ ΓΙΑ ΣΥΓΚΕΚΡΙΜΕΝΟ ΣΚΟΠΟ, ΤΙΤΛΟΥ ΚΑΙ ΜΗ ΠΡΟΣΒΟΛΗΣ ΔΙΚΑΙΩΜΑΤΩΝ ΤΡΙΤΩΝ, ΟΣΟΝ ΑΦΟΡΑ ΤΟ ΠΡΟΪΟΝ ΛΟΓΙΣΜΙΚΟΥ ΚΑΙ ΤΗΝ ΠΑΡΟΧΗ Ή ΤΗΝ ΑΔΥΝΑΜΙΑ ΠΑΡΟΧΗΣ ΥΠΗΡΕΣΙΩΝ ΥΠΟΣΤΗΡΙΞΗΣ. ΑΥΤΗ Η ΠΕΡΙΟΡΙΣΜΕΝΗ ΕΓΓΥΗΣΗ ΣΑΣ ΠΑΡΕΧΕΙ ΣΥΓΚΕΚΡΙΜΕΝΑ ΝΟΜΙΚΑ ΔΙΚΑΙΩΜΑΤΑ. ΕΝΔΕΧΕΤΑΙ ΤΑ ΔΙΚΑΙΩΜΑΤΑ ΣΑΣ ΝΑ ΔΙΑΦΕΡΟΥΝ ΑΝΑΛΟΓΑ ΜΕ ΤΗΝ ΠΟΛΙΤΕΙΑ ΚΑΙ ΠΕΡΙΟΧΗ ΔΙΚΑΙΟΔΟΣΙΑΣ ΣΤΗΝ ΟΠΟΙΑ ΒΡΙΣΚΕΣΤΕ.

ΠΕΡΙΟΡΙΣΜΟΣ ΤΗΣ ΕΥΘΥΝΗΣ. ΣΤΗ ΜΕΓΙΣΤΗ ΔΥΝΑΤΗ ΕΚΤΑΣΗ ΠΟΥ ΕΠΙΤΡΕΠΕΙ ΤΟ ΕΦΑΡΜΟΣΤΕΟ ΔΙΚΑΙΟ, Η MICROSOFT Ή ΟΙ ΠΡΟΜΗΘΕΥΤΕΣ ΤΗΣ ΔΕΝ ΦΕΡΟΥΝ ΣΕ ΚΑΜΙΑ ΠΕΡΙΠΤΩΣΗ ΟΥΔΕΜΙΑ ΕΥΘΥΝΗ ΓΙΑ ΕΙΔΙΚΕΣ, ΠΕΡΙΣΤΑΣΙΑΚΕΣ, ΕΜΜΕΣΕΣ Ή ΑΠΟΘΕΤΙΚΕΣ ΖΗΜΙΕΣ ΟΠΟΙΑΣΔΗΠΟΤΕ ΦΥΣΕΩΣ (ΠΕΡΙΛΑΜΒΑΝΟΜΕΝΩΝ, ΕΝΔΕΙΚΤΙΚΑ, ΖΗΜΙΩΝ ΑΠΟ ΑΠΩΛΕΙΑ ΕΠΙΧΕΙΡΗΜΑΤΙΚΩΝ ΚΕΡΔΩΝ, ΔΙΑΚΟΠΗ ΕΡΓΑΣΙΩΝ, ΑΠΩΛΕΙΑ ΕΠΙΧΕΙΡΗΜΑΤΙΚΩΝ ΠΛΗΡΟΦΟΡΙΩΝ Ή ΑΠΟ ΑΛΛΗ ΑΠΟΤΙΜΗΤΗ ΣΕ ΧΡΗΜΑ ΖΗΜΙΑ) ΠΟΥ ΠΡΟΚΥΠΤΟΥΝ ΑΠΟ ΤΗ ΧΡΗΣΗ Ή ΑΔΥΝΑΜΙΑ ΧΡΗΣΗΣ ΤΟΥ ΠΡΟΪΟΝΤΟΣ ΛΟΓΙΣΜΙΚΟΥ Ή ΑΠΟ ΤΗΝ ΠΑΡΟΧΗ Ή ΑΔΥΝΑΜΙΑ ΠΑΡΟΧΗΣ ΥΠΗΡΕΣΙΩΝ ΥΠΟΣΤΗΡΙΞΗΣ, ΑΚΟΜΗ ΚΑΙ ΑΝ Η MICROSOFT ΕΧΕΙ ΕΙΔΟΠΟΙΗΘΕΙ ΓΙΑ ΤΟ ΕΝΔΕΧΟΜΕΝΟ ΠΡΟΚΛΗΣΗΣ ΤΕΤΟΙΩΝ ΖΗΜΙΩΝ. ΣΕ ΚΑΘΕ ΠΕΡΙΠΤΩΣΗ, Η ΟΛΗ ΕΥΘΥΝΗ ΤΗΣ MICROSOFT, ΜΕ ΒΑΣΗ ΤΙΣ ΔΙΑΤΑΞΕΙΣ ΑΥΤΗΣ ΤΗΣ ΑΔΕΙΑΣ, ΔΕΝ ΜΠΟΡΕΙ ΝΑ ΥΠΕΡΒΕΙ ΤΟ ΠΟΣΟ ΠΟΥ ΚΑΤΕΒΑΛΑΤΕ ΓΙΑ ΤΟ ΠΡΟΪΟΝ ΛΟΓΙΣΜΙΚΟΥ Ή ΤΟ ΠΟΣΟ ΠΟΥ ΑΝΤΙΣΤΟΙΧΕΙ ΣΕ ΠΕΝΤΕ ΔΟΛΑΡΙΑ Η.Π.Α (5,00 US$) ΣΕ ΤΟΠΙΚΟ ΣΥΝΑΛΛΑΓΜΑ, ΟΠΟΙΟΔΗΠΟΤΕ ΕΙΝΑΙ ΜΕΓΑΛΥΤΕΡΟ. ΕΦΟΣΟΝ ΟΜΩΣ ΕΧΕΤΕ ΣΥΝΑΨΕΙ ΣΥΜΦΩΝΙΑ ΠΑΡΟΧΗΣ ΥΠΗΡΕΣΙΩΝ ΥΠΟΣΤΗΡΙΞΗΣ ΜΕ ΤΗ MICROSOFT, Η ΟΛΗ ΕΥΘΥΝΗ ΤΗΣ MICROSOFT, ΣΧΕΤΙΚΑ ΜΕ ΤΙΣ ΥΠΗΡΕΣΙΕΣ ΥΠΟΣΤΗΡΙΞΗΣ, ΘΑ ΔΙΕΠΕΤΑΙ ΑΠΟ ΤΟΥΣ ΟΡΟΥΣ ΕΚΕΙΝΗΣ ΤΗΣ ΣΥΜΦΩΝΙΑΣ. ΕΠΕΙΔΗ ΣΕ ΚΑΠΟΙΕΣ ΠΟΛΙΤΕΙΕΣ ΚΑΙ ΠΕΡΙΟΧΕΣ ΔΙΚΑΙΟΔΟΣΙΑΣ ΔΕΝ ΕΠΙΤΡΕΠΕΤΑΙ Ο ΑΠΟΚΛΕΙΣΜΟΣ Ή Ο ΠΕΡΙΟΡΙΣΜΟΣ ΤΗΣ ΕΥΘΥΝΗΣ, Ο ΠΑΡΑΠΑΝΩ ΠΕΡΙΟΡΙΣΜΟΣ ΕΙΝΑΙ ΔΥΝΑΤΟ ΝΑ ΜΗΝ ΙΣΧΥΕΙ ΓΙΑ ΕΣΑΣ.

Εάν αποκτήσατε αυτό το προϊόν στην Ελλάδα, η Άδεια διέπεται από το Ελληνικό δίκαιο.

Εάν αποκτήσατε αυτό το προϊόν εκτός της Ελλάδας ή των Η.Π.Α., ίσως να ισχύει το τοπικό δίκαιο.

Εάν έχετε οποιαδήποτε απορία σχετικά με την Άδεια αυτή ή επιθυμείτε να επικοινωνήσετε με τη Microsoft για οποιοδήποτε λόγο, επικοινωνήστε με τη Microsoft Hellas A.E., Λ. Κηφισίας 56, 151 25 Μαρούσι Αττικής ή γράψτε στη διεύθυνση: Microsoft Sales Information Center, One Microsoft Way, Redmond, WA 98052-6399, USA.

Si vous avez acheté votre produit Microsoft en France, en Suisse ou au Bénélux, la garantie limitée ci-après vous est applicable :

GARANTIE LIMITÉE.

GARANTIE LIMITÉE. Microsoft garantit (a) que le PRODUIT LOGICIEL permettra une utilisation conforme, pour l'essentiel, aux performances définies dans la documentation imprimée qui l'accompagne, pendant une période de quatre-vingt dix (90) jours suivant la date à laquelle vous l'aurez reçu, et (b) que les Services d'Assistance fournis par Microsoft seront conformes, pour l'essentiel, à la description qui en est faite dans les documents imprimés applicables qui vous sont remis par Microsoft, et que les ingénieurs de l'assistance Microsoft feront des efforts commercialement raisonnables pour résoudre tout problème soumis. Certains pays ou certaines juridictions n'autorisent pas les limitations de la durée des garanties implicites, de sorte que la limitation ci-dessus peut ne pas vous être applicable. Dans la mesure permise par la réglementation applicable, toute garantie implicite qui serait applicable au PRODUIT LOGICIEL sera limitée à quatre-vingt dix (90) jours.

RECOURS DU CLIENT. La seule responsabilité de Microsoft et de ses fournisseurs, et votre unique recours, seront, au choix de Microsoft, (a) soit le remboursement du prix payé, le cas échéant, (b) soit la réparation ou le remplacement du PRODUIT LOGICIEL qui n'est pas conforme à la Garantie Limitée de Microsoft et qui est retourné à Microsoft accompagné d'une copie de votre reçu. Cette Garantie Limitée sera inapplicable si le défaut du PRODUIT LOGICIEL résulte d'un accident, d'un usage ayant entraîné une détérioration ou d'une utilisation inappropriée. Tout PRODUIT LOGICIEL de remplacement sera garanti pendant le reste de la période de garantie initiale ou pendant 30 jours, si cette dernière période est plus longue. En dehors des États-Unis d'Amérique, vous ne pouvez bénéficier de ces recours ou des services d'assistance produit de Microsoft sans une preuve d'acquisition de licence provenant d'une source internationale autorisée.

EXCLUSION DE TOUTE AUTRE GARANTIE — DANS TOUTE LA MESURE PERMISE PAR LA RÉGLEMENTATION APPLICABLE, MICROSOFT ET SES FOURNISSEURS EXCLUENT TOUTE AUTRE GARANTIE, EXPRESSE OU IMPLICITE, CONCERNANT LE PRODUIT LOGICIEL ET LA FOURNITURE OU L'ABSENCE DE FOURNITURE DES SERVICES D'ASSISTANCE, NOTAMMENT TOUTE GARANTIE QUE LE PRODUIT LOGICIEL OU LES SERVICES D'ASSISTANCE PRÉSENTERAIENT CERTAINES QUALITÉS OU QU'ILS SERAIENT APTES À UNE UTILISATION SPÉCIFIQUE, AINSI QUE TOUTE GARANTIE DE PROPRIÉTÉ ET D'ABSENCE DE CONTREFAÇON. CETTE GARANTIE LIMITÉE VOUS ACCORDE DES DROITS SPÉCIFIQUES. VOUS POUVEZ ÊTRE TITULAIRE D'AUTRES DROITS, QUI VARIENT D'UN PAYS OU D'UNE JURIDICTION À L'AUTRE. SI VOUS AVEZ ACQUIS CE PRODUIT EN FRANCE OU EN BELGIQUE, LES DISPOSITIONS QUI PRÉCÈDENT NE FONT PAS OBSTACLE À L'APPLICATION DE LA GARANTIE LÉGALE CONTRE LES VICES CACHÉS DONT VOUS POURRIEZ BÉNÉFICIER LE CAS ÉCHÉANT EN APPLICATION DES ARTICLES 1641 ET SUIVANTS DU CODE CIVIL FRANÇAIS OU DU CODE CIVIL BELGE, SELON LE CAS.

LIMITATION DE RESPONSABILITÉ. DANS TOUTE LA MESURE PERMISE PAR LA RÉGLEMENTATION APPLICABLE, MICROSOFT ET SES FOURNISSEURS NE SERONT EN AUCUN CAS RESPONSABLES À RAISON D'UN PRÉJUDICE SPÉCIAL, INDIRECT OU ACCESSOIRE, DE QUELQUE NATURE QUE CE SOIT (NOTAMMENT LES PERTES DE BÉNÉFICES, INTERRUPTIONS D'ACTIVITÉ, PERTES D'INFORMATIONS COMMERCIALES OU AUTRES PERTES PÉCUNIAIRES), QUI RÉSULTERAIT DE L'UTILISATION OU DE L'IMPOSSIBILITÉ D'UTILISER LE PRODUIT LOGICIEL, DE LA FOURNITURE OU DE L'ABSENCE DE FOURNITURE DES SERVICES D'ASSISTANCE, ALORS MÊME QUE LA SOCIÉTÉ MICROSOFT AURAIT ÉTÉ PRÉVENUE DE L'ÉVENTUALITÉ DE TELS PRÉJUDICES. EN TOUTE HYPOTHÈSE, LA RESPONSABILITÉ TOTALE DE MICROSOFT AU TITRE DE CE CLUF SERA LIMITÉE À LA PLUS ÉLEVÉE DES SOMMES SUIVANTES : SOIT LE MONTANT EFFECTIVEMENT PAYÉ POUR LE PRODUIT LOGICIEL, SOIT UN MONTANT ÉQUIVALENT À CINQ (5) DOLLARS U.S. EN MONNAIE LOCALE. TOUTEFOIS, SI VOUS AVEZ CONCLU UN CONTRAT DE SERVICES D'ASSISTANCE MICROSOFT, LA RESPONSABILITÉ TOTALE DE MICROSOFT AU TITRE DE CES SERVICES D'ASSISTANCE SERA RÉGIE PAR LES TERMES DUDIT CONTRAT. CERTAINS PAYS OU CERTAINES JURIDICTIONS N'AUTORISENT PAS L'EXCLUSION OU LA LIMITATION DE RESPONSABILITÉ, DE SORTE QUE LA LIMITATION CI-DESSUS PEUT NE PAS VOUS ÊTRE APPLICABLE.

LES DISPOSITIONS CI-DESSUS, RELATIVES À LA LIMITATION OU À L'EXCLUSION DES GARANTIES ET DE LA RESPONSABILITÉ DE MICROSOFT, SONT INDÉPENDANTES LES UNES DES AUTRES. SI L'UNE QUELCONQUE DE CES LIMITATIONS OU EXCLUSIONS ÉTAIT JUGÉE NON VALABLE SELON LA RÉGLEMENTATION APPLICABLE, CETTE NON-VALIDITÉ N'AFFECTERAIT PAS LES AUTRES DISPOSITIONS. SI L'UNE QUELCONQUE DE CES LIMITATIONS OU EXCLUSIONS ÉTAIT CONSIDÉRÉE COMME AYANT UNE PORTÉE TROP LARGE, ELLE SERAIT NÉANMOINS OPPOSABLE DANS TOUTE LA MESURE PERMISE PAR LA RÉGLEMENTATION APPLICABLE.

Si vous avez acquis ce produit en France, le présent CLUF est régi par le droit français.

Si vous avez acquis ce produit en Belgique, le présent CLUF est régi par le droit belge.

Si vous avez acquis ce produit en Suisse, le présent CLUF est régi par le droit suisse.

Si vous avez acquis ce produit en dehors des pays mentionnés ci-dessus, le droit local pourra, le cas échéant, s'appliquer.

Pour toute question relative au présent CLUF, ou si vous désirez contacter Microsoft pour quelque raison que ce soit, veuillez vous adresser à la filiale Microsoft desservant votre pays, ou écrire à Microsoft Sales Information Center/One Microsoft Way/Redmond, WA 98052-6399, États-Unis d'Amérique.

Ako ste Vaš Microsoft proizvod kupili u Hrvatskoj, na Vas se odnosi slijedeća ograničena garancija:

OGRANIČENA GARANCIJA. Microsoft garantira: (a) da će SOFTWARSKI PROIZVOD raditi uglavnom sukladno s navedenim u priležećim pisanim materijalima, u razdoblju od devedeset (90) dana od dana primitka i (b) da će bilo koja usluga podrške koju pruža Microsoft uglavnom odgovarati onome što je navedeno u popratnim pisanim materijalima koje je izdao Microsoft i da će Microsoftovi inžinjeri za podršku uložiti trud koji se u trgovačkom smislu smatra razumnim kako bi razriješili bilo koji problem. Prava pojedinih država ne dopuštaju ograničenja trajanja prešutne garancije, te se stoga navedeno ograničenje možda ne odnosi na Vas. U mjeri u kojoj je to dopušteno mjerodavnim pravom, prešutne garancje na SOFTWARSKI PROIZVOD, ako takve postoje, ograničene su na razdoblje od devedeset (90) dana.

PRAVA KUPCA. Isključiva odgovornost Microsofta i njegovih dobavljača, kao i Vaše isključivo pravno sredstvo biti će, prema Microsoftovom nahođenju, (a) povrat uplaćenog iznosa, ako je takvog bilo ili (b) popravak odnosno zamjena SOFTWARSKOG PROIZVODA koji ne udovoljava Microsoftovoj ograničenoj garanciji ukoliko je isti vraćen Microsoftu zajedno s primjerkom Vašeg računa. Ova ograničena garancija ne važi u slučaju da je greška na SOFTWARSKOM PROIZVODU nastala kao posljedica nesreće, zloporabe ili nepravilne uporabe. Garancija za zamijenjeni SOFTWARSKI PROIZVOD važit će do isteka izvornog garantnog razdoblja ili u razdoblju od trideset (30) dana, koje god od navedenih razdoblja je duže. Izvan Sjedinjenih Država niti jedno od navedenih sredstava ili usluga podrške proizvoda koje pruža Microsoft, nisu dostupni bez dokaza o kupnji od ovlaštenog međunarodnog izvora.

ISKLJUČENJE BILO KAKVIH DRUGIH GARANCIJA. DO NAJVEĆE MOGUĆE MJERE DOPUŠTENE MJERODAVNIM PRAVOM, MICROSOFT I NJEGOVI DOBAVLJAČI ISKLJUČUJU, U ODNOSU NA SOFTWARSKI PROIZVOD KAO I U ODNOSU NA PRUŽANJE ILI NE-PRUŽANJE USLUGA PODRŠKE, BILO KAKVE DRUGE GARANCIJE ILI UVJETE, IZRIČITE ILI PREŠUTNE, UKLJUČUJUĆI ALI NE OGRANIČAVAJUĆI SE NA PREŠUTNE GARANCIJE TRGOVAČKE PODESNOSTI, POGODNOSTI ZA POJEDINU SVRHU I PRAVNIH MANA (VLASNIŠTVA I POVREDE PRAVA). OVA OGRANIČENA GARANCIJA DAJE VAM ODREĐENA PRAVA U SKLADU S PROPISIMA. VI MOŽETE IMATI I DODATNA PRAVA KOJA SE MOGU RAZLIKOVATI OD DRŽAVE DO DRŽAVE.

OGRANIČENJE ODGOVORNOSTI. DO NAJVEĆE MOGUĆE MJERE DOPUŠTENE MJERODAVNIM PRAVOM, MICROSOFT I NJEGOVI DOBAVLJAČI NEĆE SLUČAJU NI U KOJEM SLUČAJU BITI ODGOVORNI ZA BILO KAKVU POSEBNU, SLUČAJNU, NEIZRAVNU ILI POSLJEDIČNU ŠTETU (UKLJUČUJUĆI ALI NE OGRANIČAVAJUĆI SE NA ŠTETU ZBOG IZGUBLJENE DOBITI, PREKIDA POSLOVANJA, GUBITKA POSLOVNE INFORMACIJE ILI BILO KOJEG DRUGOG NOVČANOG GUBITKA) KOJA MOŽE NASTATI KAO POSLJEDICA UPORABE ILI NEMOGUĆNOSTI UPORABE SOFTWARSKOG PROIZVODA ILI PRUŽANJA ODNOSNO NE-PRUŽANJA PODRŠKE PROIZVODU, PA I U SLUČAJU DA JE MICROSOFT BIO OBAVIJEŠTEN O MOGUĆEM NASTANKU TAKVE ŠTETE. U SVAKOM SLUČAJU, UKUPNA MICROSOFTOVA ODGOVORNOST U SKLADU S BILO KOJOM ODREDBOM OVE EULA-E BITI ĆE OGRANIČENA NA VEĆI OD SLIJEDEĆIH IZNOSA: IZNOS KOJI STE VI PLATILI ZA SOFTWARSKI PROIZVOD ILI PROTUVRIJEDNOST IZNOSA OD USD 5,00 U MJESNOM SREDSTVU PLAĆANJA; UKOLIKO STE, MEĐUTIM, ZAKLJUČILI MICROSOFTOV UGOVOR O PRUŽANJU USLUGA PODRŠKE, MICROSOFTOVA CJELOKUPNA ODGOVORNOST GLEDE USLUGA PODRŠKE PROIZVODU BIT ĆE ODREĐENA TIM UGOVOROM. S OBZIROM DA PRAVA POJEDINIH DRŽAVA NE DOPUŠTAJU ISKLJUŠENJE ILI OGRANIČENJE ODGOVORNOSTI, MOGUĆE JE DA SE GORE ODREĐENO OGRANIČENJE NE ODNOSI NA VAS.

Ako ste ovaj proizvod kupili izvan Sjedinjenih Država, mjesno pravo može biti mjerodavno.

Ako imate kakvih pitanja u vezi s ovom EULA-om, ili ako želite stupiti u vezu s Microsoftom iz bilo kojeg razloga, molimo da se obratite Microsoftovom zavisnom društvu u Vašoj zemlji ili pišite na : Microsoft Sales Information Center/One Microsoft Way/Redmond, WA 98052-6399, SAD.

Ogni acquisto di prodotti Microsoft in Italia è sottoposto alle seguenti limitazioni di garanzia:

LIMITAZIONI DI GARANZIA. Microsoft garantisce che (a) il PRODOTTO SOFTWARE funzionerà in sostanziale conformità con il materiale scritto di accompagnamento per un periodo di novanta (90) giorni dalla data di ricevimento del PRODOTTO SOFTWARE; e (b) qualsiasi Servizio Supporto Tecnico fornito da Microsoft corrisponderà sostanzialmente a quanto descritto nel materiale scritto applicabile fornito da Microsoft all'utente e i responsabili del Servizio Supporto Tecnico Microsoft faranno tutto quanto in loro potere, entro limiti commercialmente ragionevoli, per risolvere gli eventuali problemi sorti. L'apposizione di limiti di durata alla garanzia implicita non è consentita in alcuni Stati o giurisdizioni; pertanto la limitazione di cui sopra potrebbe non essere applicabile. Nella misura massima consentita dalla legge in vigore, le eventuali garanzie implicite relative al PRODOTTO SOFTWARE sono limitate a un periodo di novanta (90) giorni.

TUTELA DEL CLIENTE. La responsabilità complessiva di Microsoft e dei suoi fornitori e i rimedi esclusivi dell'utente saranno, a discrezione di Microsoft, (a) la restituzione del prezzo pagato; ovvero (b) la riparazione o la sostituzione del PRODOTTO SOFTWARE che non rientra nella Garanzia di cui sopra, purché sia restituito a Microsoft con una copia della fattura di acquisto o ricevuta fiscale regolarmente emessa in Italia. La presente Garanzia viene meno qualora il vizio del PRODOTTO SOFTWARE derivi da incidente, uso inidoneo o erronea applicazione. Ogni PRODOTTO SOFTWARE sostitutivo sarà garantito per il rimanente periodo della garanzia originaria e in ogni caso per non meno di trenta (30) giorni. Fuori dal territorio degli Stati Uniti, l'utente non potrà beneficiare della tutela sopra descritta, né dei servizi di supporto al prodotto offerti da Microsoft senza la prova dell'avvenuto acquisto da una fonte autorizzata internazionale.

ESCLUSIONE DI ALTRE GARANZIE. NELLA MISURA MASSIMA CONSENTITA DALLA LEGGE IN VIGORE, MICROSOFT E I SUOI FORNITORI NON RICONOSCONO ALCUNA ALTRA GARANZIA, ESPRESSA O IMPLICITA, COMPRESE, TRA LE ALTRE, LA GARANZIA DI COMMERCIABILITÀ, DI IDONEITÀ PER UN FINE PARTICOLARE, DI TITOLARITA' E DI NON VIOLAZIONE DI DIRITTI ALTRUI, RELATIVAMENTE AL PRODOTTO SOFTWARE E ALLA FORNITURA O ALLA MANCATA FORNITURA DEL SERVIZIO DI SUPPORTO TECNICO. OLTRE AI PARTICOLARI DIRITTI LEGALI CONFERITI DALLA PRESENTE GARANZIA, L'UTENTE POTRÀ BENEFICIARE DI ALTRI DIRITTI CHE VARIANO DA PAESE A PAESE.

LIMITAZIONE DI RESPONSABILITÀ. NELLA MISURA MASSIMA CONSENTITA DALLA LEGGE IN VIGORE, IN NESSUN CASO MICROSOFT O I SUOI FORNITORI SARANNO RESPONSABILI PER GLI EVENTUALI DANNI SPECIALI,

ACCIDENTALI, DIRETTI O INDIRETTI (INCLUSI, SENZA LIMITAZIONI, IL DANNO PER PERDITA O MANCATO GUADAGNO, INTERRUZIONE DELL'ATTIVITÀ, PERDITA DI INFORMAZIONI O ALTRE PERDITE ECONOMICHE) DERIVANTI DALL'USO DEL PRODOTTO SOFTWARE MICROSOFT O DAL SUO MANCATO UTILIZZO OVVERO DALLA FORNITURA O DALLA MANCATA FORNITURA DEL SERVIZIO DI SUPPORTO TECNICO, ANCHE NEL CASO CHE MICROSOFT SIA STATA AVVERTITA DELLA POSSIBILITÀ DI TALI DANNI. IN OGNI CASO, LA RESPONSABILITÀ COMPLESSIVA DI MICROSOFT AI SENSI DEL PRESENTE CONTRATTO SARÀ LIMITATA ALL' IMPORTO MAGGIORE TRA QUELLO EFFETTIVAMENTE PAGATO PER IL PRODOTTO SOFTWARE E LA SOMMA EQUIVALENTE A CINQUE DOLLARI (US$ 5) NELLA VALUTA LOCALE; A CONDIZIONE, TUTTAVIA, CHE L'UTENTE ABBIA SOTTOSCRITTO UN CONTRATTO DI SUPPORTO TECNICO, LA RESPONSABILITÀ COMPLESSIVA DI MICROSOFT RELATIVAMENTE AI SERVIZI DI SUPPORTO TECNICO SARÀ DISCIPLINATA DAI TERMINI DI QUEL CONTRATTO. POICHÉ ALCUNI STATI O GIURISDIZIONI NON AMMETTONO L'ESCLUSIONE O LA LIMITAZIONE DI RESPONSABILITÀ, LA LIMITAZIONE DI CUI SOPRA POTREBBE NON ESSERE APPLICABILE.

Qualora questo prodotto sia stato acquistato in Italia, il presente contratto sara' disciplinato dalla legge Italiana.

Qualora questo prodotto sia stato acquistato fuori dall'Italia, il presente contratto potrebbe essere disciplinato dalla normativa del paese ove e' avvenuto l'acquisto.

Chiunque desideri porre domande in ordine a questo Contratto o contattare Microsoft per qualunque ragione, può rivolgersi alla filiale Microsoft responsabile per il proprio paese all'indirizzo accluso in questo prodotto oppure scrivere a: Microsoft Customer Sales and Service, One Microsoft Way, Redmond, Washington 98052-6399, U.S.A.

Amennyiben Microsoft termékét Magyarországon vásárolta, az alábbi korlátozott garancia vonatkozik Önre:

KORLÁTOZOTT GARANCIA. Microsoft garanciát vállal arra, hogy: (a) a SZOFTVER az átvételt követő kilencven (90) napon át alapvetően a mellékelt termékhasználati dokumentációban foglaltaknak megfelelően fog működni, valamint (b) minden Microsoft által nyújtott Terméktámogatás alapvetően megfelel a vonatkozó termékhasználati dokumentációban foglaltaknak, s a Microsoft szakemberei minden kereskedelmi szempontból ésszerű erőfeszítést megtesznek az esetlegesen felmerülő problémák megoldására. Néhány állam és jogszabály nem engedélyezi a jótállás időtartamának korlátozását, így előfordulhat, hogy a fent említett korlátozás Önre nem vonatkozik. A helyi törvényekben megengedett mértékig, a SZOFTVERRE vonatkozó jótállás időtartama kilencven (90) nap.

VÁSÁRLÓI JOGORVOSLATOK. Microsoft és szállítói maximális garanciavállalása és az Ön kizárólagos jogorvoslati lehetősége – Microsoft választásának megfelelően – az alábbiakra terjed ki: (a) a befizetett vételár visszatérítése, vagy (b) a Microsoft Korlátozott Garanciájában leírtaknak nem megfelelő SZOFTVER kicserélése vagy kijavítása, amelyet Ön a Microsoft részére a vásárlást bizonyító számlával együtt visszajuttat. Jelen Korlátozott Garancia érvényét veszíti, amennyiben a SZOFTVER hibája balesetből vagy nem a rendeltetésszerű, illetve nem az előírásoknak megfelelő használatból ered. A reklamációs csere során adott SZOFTVERRE vonatkozó garancia az eredeti garanciából fennmaradó időtartamra, illetve ha ez kevesebb, mint harminc (30) nap, akkor harminc (30) napra áll fenn.

TOVÁBBI GARANCIA KIZÁRÁSA. MICROSOFT ÉS SZÁLLÍTÓI A JOGALKALMAZÁSBAN MEGENGEDETT TELJES MÉRTÉKBEN ELZÁRKÓZIK MINDEN TOVÁBBI KIFEJEZETT VAGY HALLGATÓLAGOS GARANCIAVÁLLALÁSTÓL A SZOFTVER VONATKOZÁSÁBAN, NEM KIZÁRÓLAGOSAN BELEÉRTVE AZ ELADHATÓSÁGOT, A KÜLÖNLEGES CÉLRA ALKALMAZHATÓSÁGOT ÉS A NEM RENDELTETÉSSZERŰ HASZNÁLAT BÁRMILYEN KÖVETKEZMÉNYÉT. E KORLÁTOZOZOTT GARANCIA MEGHATÁROZOTT JOGOKAT BIZTOSÍT ÖNNEK. ÖN RENDELKEZHET TOVÁBBI JOGOKKAL IS, MELYEK ÁLLAMONKÉNT S A HELYI TÖRVÉNYEK SZERINT VÁLTOZHATNAK.

FELELŐSSÉG KORLÁTOZÁSA. A MICROSOFT ÉS SZÁLLÍTÓI AZ ÉRVÉNYES JOGSZABÁLYOK MEGENGEDTE LEGKISEBB MÉRTÉKBEN SEM VÁLLALNAK FELELŐSSÉGET SEMMIFÉLE EGYEDI, ELŐRE NEM LÁTHATÓ, KÖZVETETT VAGY KÖVETKEZMÉNYSZERŰ KÁRÉRT (ÍGY TÖBBEK KÖZÖTT AZ ÜZLETI HASZON ELMARADÁSÁBÓL, AZ ÜZLETI TEVÉKENYSÉG FÉLBESZAKADÁSÁBÓL, AZ ÜZLETI INFORMÁCIÓK ELVESZTÉSÉBŐL VAGY EGYÉB ANYAGI VESZTESÉGBŐL FAKADÓ KÁRÉRT SEM), AMELY A SZOFTVERTERMÉK HASZNÁLATÁBÓL VAGY NEM HASZNÁLHATÓSÁGÁBÓL, VAGY A TERMÉKTÁMOGATÁS BIZTOSÍTÁSÁBÓL, ILLETVE ANNAK ELMULASZTÁSÁBÓL ERED, MÉG ABBAN AZ ESETBEN SEM, HA A MICROSOFTOT TÁJÉKOZTATTÁK AZ ILYEN KÁROK BEKÖVETKEZTÉNEK LEHETŐSÉGÉRŐL. HACSAK AZ ALKALMAZANDÓ JOGSZABÁLYOK KÖTELEZŐ ÉRVÉNYŰ ELŐÍRÁSAI NEM HATÁROZNAK MEG NAGYOBB ÖSSZEGET, MICROSOFT TELJES FELELŐSSÉGE ÉS A JELEN EULA ALAPJÁN AZ ÖN KIZÁRÓLAGOS KÁRTALANÍTÁSA SEMMI ESETRE SEM HALADHATJA MEG AZ ÖN ÁLTAL A SZOFTVERTERMÉKÉRT VALÓSÁGOSAN KIFIZETETT ÖSSZEGET, VAGY ÖT USA DOLLÁRNAK (5,00 US$) MEGFELELŐ, AZ ADOTT ORSZÁG PÉNZNEMÉBEN KIFEJEZETT ÖSSZEGET. UGYANAKKOR HA ÖN A MICROSOFTTAL TERMÉKTÁMOGATÁSI MEGÁLLAPODÁST KÖTÖTT, A MICROSOFT TELJES FELELŐSSÉGVÁLLALÁSA ANNAK A MEGÁLLAPODÁSNAK ALAPJÁN TÖRTÉNIK. TEKINTVE, HOGY EGYES ORSZÁGOKBAN ÉS JOGRENDEKBEN AZ OKOZOTT, ILLETVE A VÉLETLENSZERŰ KÁRÉRT A FELELŐSSÉGET ELHÁRÍTANI, ILLETVE KORLÁTOZNI TILOS, LEHET, HOGY A FENTI KORLÁTOZÁS ÖNRE NEM VONATKOZIK.

Ha ezt a terméket Magyarországon szerezte be, a jelen EULÁ-ra a magyar jogszabályok az irányadóak.

Ha ezt a terméket nem Magyarországon szerezte be, a helyi jogszabályok válhatnak irányadóvá.

Amennyiben a jelen EULA szerződéssel kapcsolatban bármilyen kérdése lenne, vagy ha bármilyen más okból kapcsolatba kíván lépni a Microsofttal, kérjük keresse fel az adott országban illetékes Microsoft képviseletet, vagy írjon a következő címre:

MICROSOFT SALES INFORMATION CENTER/ONE MICROSOFT WAY/REDMOND, WA 98052-6399, U.S.A.

Si usted ha adquirido su producto Microsoft en México, América Central o América del Sur (excepto Brasil) se aplicará la presente garantía limitada:

GARANTÍA LIMITADA. Microsoft garantiza que (a) durante un período de noventa (90) días a contar desde la fecha de adquisición, el PRODUCTO SOFTWARE funcionará sustancialmente de acuerdo con lo especificado en los materiales impresos que lo acompañan, y que (b) cualquier Servicio Técnico proporcionado por Microsoft se llevará a cabo sustancialmente de acuerdo con lo especificado en los materiales impresos proporcionados por Microsoft y que los ingenieros de soporte de Microsoft harán los esfuerzos comercialmente razonables para resolver cualquier problema. Algunos estados y jurisdicciones no permiten limitaciones con respecto a la duración de una garantía implícita, de modo que la limitación anterior puede no serle aplicable. En la medida permitida por la ley aplicable, las garantías implícitas del PRODUCTO SOFTWARE, si existieran, se limitarán a noventa (90) días.

RECURSOS DEL CLIENTE. La responsabilidad total de Microsoft y de sus proveedores y el único recurso del cliente consistirá, a elección de Microsoft, ya sea en: (a) el reembolso del precio pagado, si corresponde o (b) la reparación o reemplazo del PRODUCTO SOFTWARE que no cumpla con la Garantía Limitada de Microsoft y que sea devuelto a Microsoft con copia de su recibo. Esta Garantía Limitada quedará sin efecto si los defectos del PRODUCTO SOFTWARE son consecuencia de accidente, abuso o uso indebido. Cualquier PRODUCTO SOFTWARE de reemplazo estará garantizado por el período de tiempo que reste hasta el vencimiento de la garantía original o un período de treinta (30) días, lo que resulte mayor. Ninguno de estos recursos o Servicios Técnicos ofrecidos por Microsoft se encontrará disponible fuera de los Estados Unidos de América, sin la constancia de compra emitida por una fuente internacional autorizada.

INEXISTENCIA DE OTRAS GARANTÍAS. HASTA LA MÁXIMA EXTENSIÓN PERMITIDA POR LA LEY APLICABLE MICROSOFT Y SUS PROVEEDORES RECHAZAN CUALQUIER OTRA GARANTÍA O CONDICIÓN, TANTO IMPLÍCITA COMO EXPLÍCITA, INCLUYENDO, SIN LIMITACIÓN, LAS GARANTÍAS IMPLÍCITAS DE COMERCIABILIDAD, ADECUACIÓN PARA UN FIN DETERMINADO, TÍTULO Y NO INFRACCIÓN RESPECTO DEL PRODUCTO SOFTWARE Y LA PRESTACIÓN O FALTA DE PRESTACIÓN DEL SERVICIO TÉCNICO. ESTA GARANTÍA LIMITADA LE OTORGA A USTED DERECHOS LEGALES ESPECÍFICOS. PODRÁ TENER OTROS DERECHOS QUE PODRÁN VARIAR DE UN ESTADO O JURISDICCIÓN A OTRO ESTADO O JURISDICCIÓN.

LIMITACIÓN DE RESPONSABILIDAD. HASTA LA MÁXIMA EXTENSIÓN PERMITIDA POR LA LEY APLICABLE, EN NINGÚN CASO, MICROSOFT NI SUS PROVEEDORES SERÁN RESPONSABLES POR NINGÚN DAÑO, ESPECIAL, INCIDENTAL, INDIRECTO O CONSECUENCIAL O CUALQUIERA QUE SEA (INCLUYENDO, SIN LIMITACIÓN, DAÑOS POR PÉRDIDA DE GANANCIAS, INTERRUPCIÓN EN LOS NEGOCIOS, PÉRDIDA DE INFORMACIÓN COMERCIAL O CUALQUIER OTRA PÉRDIDA PECUNIARIA) QUE SE DERIVE DEL USO O IMPOSIBILIDAD DE USO DE ESTE PRODUCTO MICROSOFT, AUN CUANDO SE HUBIERA ADVERTIDO A MICROSOFT DE LA POSIBILIDAD DE DICHOS DAÑOS. EN CUALQUIER CASO, LA RESPONSABILIDAD TOTAL DE MICROSOFT CON RESPECTO A CUALQUIER CLÁUSULA DE ESTE CLUF SE LIMITARÁ A LA CANTIDAD QUE SEA MAYOR ENTRE EL PRECIO PAGADO POR EL PRODUCTO SOFTWARE O UNA CANTIDAD EQUIVALENTE A CINCO DÓLARES ESTADOUNIDENSES EN MONEDA LOCAL; CON LA CONDICIÓN, SIN EMBARGO, DE QUE SI SE HA COMPROMETIDO POR CONTRATO CON EL SERVICIO TÉCNICO MICROSOFT, LA TOTAL RESPONSABILIDAD DE MICROSOFT CON RESPECTO AL SERVICIO TÉCNICO ESTARÁ REGIDA POR LOS TÉRMINOS DE DICHO CONTRATO. DEBIDO A QUE ALGUNOS ESTADOS Y JURISDICCIONES NO PERMITEN LA EXCLUSIÓN O LIMITACIÓN DE RESPONSABILIDAD, LA LIMITACIÓN ANTERIOR PUEDE NO SERLE APLICABLE.

Si adquirió este producto en los Estados Unidos de América, el presente CLUF se regirá por las leyes del Estado de Washington.

Si adquirió este producto fuera de los Estados Unidos de América, se podrá aplicar la legislación local.

Si tiene alguna duda con respecto a este CLUF o si desea ponerse en contacto con Microsoft por cualquier motivo, remítase a la subsidiaria Microsoft que atiende a su país o escriba en inglés a Microsoft Sales Information Center/One Microsoft Way/Redmond, WA 98052-6399/EE.UU.

Hvis De har kjøpt Deres Microsoft-produkt i Norge, gjelder følgende avtale om Begrensede Rettigheter for Dem:

BEGRENSEDE RETTIGHETER innebærer at a) PROGRAMVAREPRODUKTET i det vesentlige skal fungere i overensstemmelse med medfølgende brukerveiledning(er) for en periode på nitti (90) dager fra dato for mottagelsen, og at b) all kundestøtte som gis av Microsoft i det vesentlige skal svare til beskrivelsen i det relevante skriftlige materialet De har fått fra Microsoft. Microsofts kundestøtteteknikere vil gjøre det som med rimelighet kan forventes for å løse eventuelle problemer i forbindelse hermed. I den grad ikke annet følger av ufravikelig lovgivning, er Microsofts ansvar for PROGRAMVAREPRODUKTET som nevnt ovenfor, begrenset til nitti (90) dager.

KUNDENS RETTIGHETER Microsofts og dets leverandørers fulle ansvar og Deres eneste krav skal, etter Microsofts valg, være enten a) tilbakebetaling av kjøpesummen eller b) reparasjon eller omlevering av PROGRAMVAREPRODUKTET som ikke oppfyller ovennevnte Begrensede Rettigheter, og som er returnert til Microsoft sammen med en kopi av Deres faktura. De Begrensede Rettigheter gjelder ikke dersom mangler ved PROGRAMVAREPRODUKTET skyldes uhell, misbruk eller feilaktig anvendelse. For eventuelle omleverte

PROGRAMVAREPRODUKTER skal de Begrensede Rettigheter gjelde for den lengste periode av den gjenværende rettighetsperioden eller tredve (30) dager. Utenfor USA er verken disse rettighetene eller kundestøttetjenestene som tilbys av Microsoft tilgjengelige uten bevis på kjøp fra en godkjent kilde utenfor USA.

INTET ØVRIG ANSVAR I DEN GRAD IKKE ANNET FØLGER AV UFRAVIKELIG LOVGIVNING, FRASKRIVER MICROSOFT OG DETS LEVERANDØRER SEG ETHVERT ØVRIG ANSVAR, ENTEN DETTE ER DIREKTE ELLER STILLTIENDE, HERUNDER, MEN IKKE BEGRENSET TIL, STILLTIENDE ANSVAR ELLER GARANTIER OM SALGBARHET OG ANVENDELIGHET FOR SÆRSKILTE FORMÅL SAMT ANSVAR SOM FØLGE AV EVENTUELL KRENKELSE AV TREDJEPARTS RETTIGHETER, BÅDE NÅR DET GJELDER PROGRAMVAREPRODUKTET OG KUNDESTØTTEN ELLER MANGLENDE KUNDESTØTTE. DISSE BEGRENSEDE RETTIGHETER ER SÆRSKILT GITT DEM FRA MICROSOFT. ANDRE RETTIGHETER KAN FØLGE AV GJELDENDE LOVGIVNING.

ANSVARSBEGRENSNING I DEN GRAD IKKE ANNET FØLGER AV UFRAVIKELIG LOVGIVNING, SKAL MICROSOFT ELLER DETS LEVERANDØRER IKKE I NOE TILFELLE VÆRE ANSVARLIGE FOR NOEN FORM FOR SPESIELLE, TILFELDIGE ELLER INDIREKTE TAP ELLER FØLGESKADER (HERUNDER, MEN IKKE BEGRENSET TIL, PRODUKTANSVAR, TAP AV FORTJENESTE, DRIFTSAVBRUDD, TAP AV INFORMASJON I VIRKSOMHETEN ELLER ØVRIG ØKONOMISK TAP) SOM OPPSTÅR SOM FØLGE AV BRUKEN AV ELLER MANGLENDE EVNE TIL Å BRUKE PROGRAMVAREPRODUKTET ELLER SOM FØLGE AV KUNDESTØTTE ELLER MANGLENDE KUNDESTØTTE. DETTE GJELDER SELV OM MICROSOFT ER BLITT INFORMERT OM MULIGHETEN FOR SLIKE SKADER ELLER TAP. I ALLE TILFELLER SKAL MICROSOFTS FULLE ANSVAR ETTER DENNE AVTALEN BEGRENSES TIL DET BELØP DE FAKTISK HAR BETALT FOR PROGRAMVAREPRODUKTET. HVIS DE HAR INNGÅTT EN SÆRSKILT AVTALE OM KUNDESTØTTE FRA MICROSOFT, FÅR BESTEMMELSENE I DEN AVTALEN ANVENDELSE NÅR DET GJELDER MICROSOFTS ANSVAR I FORBINDELSE MED KUNDESTØTTEN. ETTERSOM ENKELTE JURISDIKSJONER IKKE TILLATER FRASKRIVELSE ELLER BEGRENSNING AV ANSVAR, KAN DET HENDE AT OVENNEVNTE BEGRENSNING IKKE GJELDER FOR DEM.

For denne avtalen gjelder norsk rett, og begge parter godtar Oslo byrett som verneting.

FORBRUKERKJØP – Denne avtalen gjelder med de begrensninger som følger av kjøpslovens ufravikelige bestemmelser om forbrukerkjøp, jf. lov av 13. mai 1988 nr. 27 om kjøp § 4.

Hvis De har spørsmål vedrørende denne Lisensavtalen, eller De ønsker å kontakte Microsoft av andre årsaker, kan De skrive til Microsofts representasjonskontor i Norge eller til Microsoft Sales Information Center, One Microsoft Way, Redmond, WA 98052-6399, USA.

Jeśli produkt firmy Microsoft został zakupiony w Polsce, obowiązuje Nabywcę niniejsza Ograniczona Gwarancja.

OGRANICZONA GWARANCJA. Firma Microsoft gwarantuje, że: (a) OPROGRAMOWANIE będzie funkcjonowało w istotnym zakresie w sposób zgodny z załączonymi materiałami drukowanymi przez okres dziewięćdziesięciu (90) dni od dnia odbioru, oraz (b) usługi Pomocy Technicznej świadczone przez firmę Microsoft są w istotnym zakresie zgodne z opisem zamieszczonym w odpowiednich materiałach drukowanych dostarczonych Licencjobiorcy przez firmę Microsoft, a pracownicy Pomocy Technicznej firmy Microsoft poczynią wszelkie, ekonomicznie uzasadnione wysiłki w celu rozwiązania ewentualnych problemów. Ponieważ zgodnie z ustawodawstwem niektórych państw, nie jest dopuszczalne takie całkowite wyłączenie lub ograniczenie odpowiedzialności, powyższe ograniczenia mogą nie dotyczyć Licencjobiorcy. Wszelkie uprawnienia z tytułu gwarancji na OPROGRAMOWANIE są ograniczone do dziewięćdziesięciu (90) dni. Jeżeli prawo właściwe przewiduje dłuższy minimalny okres gwarancji, wówczas znajdą zastosowanie te ostatnie przepisy.

UPRAWNIENIA LICENCJOBIORCY. Całkowita odpowiedzialność firmy Microsoft oraz jej dostawców i wyłączne uprawnienia Licencjobiorcy polegają na: (a) zwrocie uiszczonej kwoty, albo (b) naprawie lub wymianie OPROGRAMOWANIA, które nie odpowiada warunkom OGRANICZONEJ GWARANCJI FIRMY MICROSOFT i które zostało zwrócone firmie Microsoft wraz z kopią rachunku. Wybór sposobu zaspokojenia roszczenia klienta należy do firmy Microsoft. Niniejsza Ograniczona Gwarancja traci ważność, jeśli wadliwe działanie OPROGRAMOWANIA nastąpiło w wyniku wypadku lub jego nieprawidłowego wykorzystania. Wymienione na nowe OPROGRAMOWANIE będzie objęte gwarancją do końca okresu ważności pierwotnej gwarancji albo przez okres trzydziestu (30) dni od daty wymiany, przy czym obowiązuje ten spośród terminów, który upłynie później. Poza terytorium USA powyższe uprawnienia przysługują pod warunkiem przedstawienia dowodu nabycia od autoryzowanego dostawcy.

BRAK INNYCH GWARANCJI. WYŁĄCZENIE RĘKOJMI. W MAKSYMALNYM ZAKRESIE DOZWOLONYM PRZEZ PRAWO WŁAŚCIWE, FIRMA MICROSOFT ORAZ JEJ DOSTAWCY NIE UDZIELAJĄ JAKICHKOLWIEK INNYCH GWARANCJI I WYŁĄCZAJĄ WSZYSTKIE SWOJE POZOSTAŁE OBOWIĄZKI Z TYTUŁU GWARANCJI/RĘKOJMI, ZARÓWNO SFORMUŁOWANE WPROST, JAK I W SPOSÓB DOROZUMIANY. OBEJMUJE TO TAKŻE, CHOĆ NIE WYŁĄCZNIE, USTAWOWĄ ODPOWIEDZIALNOŚĆ Z TYTUŁU RĘKOJMI ZA WADY FIZYCZNE I PRAWNE. DOTYCZY TO TAKŻE ŚWIADCZENIA LUB NIEMOŻNOŚCI UDZIELENIA POMOCY TECHNICZNEJ. NINIEJSZA OGRANICZONA GWARANCJA PRZYZNAJE LICENCJOBIORCY OKREŚLONE UPRAWNIENIA. ZALEŻNIE OD WŁAŚCIWEGO PRAWA LICENCJOBIORCY MOGĄ PRZYSŁUGIWAĆ RÓWNIEŻ INNE UPRAWNIENIA.

OGRANICZENIE ODPOWIEDZIALNOŚCI ZA SZKODĘ. W MAKSYMALNYM ZAKRESIE DOZWOLONYM PRZEZ PRAWO WŁAŚCIWE, FIRMA MICROSOFT LUB JEJ DOSTAWCY NIE BĘDĄ PONOSIĆ ODPOWIEDZIALNOŚCI ZA JAKIEKOLWIEK SZKODY (OBEJMUJĄCE ZWŁASZCZA UTRACONE KORZYŚCI, SZKODY WYNIKAJĄCE Z ZAKŁÓCENIA DZIAŁALNOŚCI, UTRATY INFORMACJI GOSPODARCZYCH LUB INNE STRATY FINANSOWE), BĘDĄCE NASTĘPSTWEM UŻYWANIA ALBO

NIEMOŻNOŚCI UŻYWANIA NINIEJSZEGO OPROGRAMOWANIA FIRMY MICROSOFT BĄDŹ ŚWIADCZENIA USŁUG POMOCY TECHNICZNEJ ALBO NIEMOŻNOŚCI ŚWIADCZENIA TAKICH USŁUG, NAWET JEŚLI FIRMA MICROSOFT ZOSTAŁA POWIADOMIONA O MOŻLIWOŚCI WYSTĄPIENIA TAKICH SZKÓD. POWYŻSZE WYLICZENIE SZKÓD, ZA KTÓRE FIRMA MICROSOFT NIE ODPOWIADA, MA CHARAKTER PRZYKŁADOWY I NIE JEST WYCZERPUJĄCE. CAŁKOWITA ODPOWIEDZIALNOŚĆ FIRMY MICROSOFT NA PODSTAWIE NINIEJSZEJ UMOWY JEST OGRANICZONA DO WIĘKSZEJ Z NASTĘPUJĄCYCH KWOT: SUMY PIENIĘŻNEJ, KTÓRĄ LICENCJOBIORCA RZECZYWIŚCIE ZAPŁACIŁ ZA OPROGRAMOWANIE LUB RÓWNOWARTOŚCI KWOTY 5,00 DOLARÓW AMERYKAŃSKICH W LOKALNEJ WALUCIE. JEŚLI LICENCJOBIORCA PODPISAŁ Z FIRMĄ MICROSOFT UMOWĘ O ŚWIADCZENIU POMOCY TECHNICZNEJ, CAŁKOWITA ODPOWIEDZIALNOŚĆ FIRMY MICROSOFT W DZIEDZINIE ŚWIADCZENIA POMOCY TECHNICZNEJ WYNIKA Z POSTANOWIEŃ TEJŻE UMOWY. PONIEWAŻ USTAWODAWSTWA NIEKTÓRYCH PAŃSTW NIE DOPUSZCZAJĄ WYŁĄCZENIA LUB OGRANICZENIA ODPOWIEDZIALNOŚCI, POWYŻSZE OGRANICZENIE MOŻE NIE MIEĆ ZASTOSOWANIA DO LICENCJOBIORCY.

W przypadku, gdy OPROGRAMOWANIE zostało nabyte poza terytorium Stanów Zjednoczonych, prawem właściwym dla niniejszej Umowy Licencyjnej może być prawo obowiązujące w miejscu nabycia OPROGRAMOWANIA.

Szanowny Licencjobiorco, jeżeli masz jakieś pytania dotyczące niniejszej umowy lub jeśli z jakiegokolwiek powodu pragniesz skontaktować się z firmą Microsoft, skontaktuj się z lokalną filią firmy Microsoft lub napisz pod następujący adres: Microsoft Sales Information Center. One Microsoft Way, Redmond, Washington 98052-6399. USA

Caso tenha adquirido o seu Produto Microsoft em Portugal, a seguinte garantia limitada aplica-se ao Adquirente:

GARANTIA LIMITADA. A Microsoft garante que (a) a execução do PRODUTO DE SOFTWARE decorrerá substancialmente de acordo com os materiais impressos relacionados por um período de noventa (90) dias a contar da data do recibo; e que (b) a prestação do Suporte Técnico pela Microsoft decorrerá substancialmente de acordo com os materiais impressos aplicáveis fornecidos ao Adquirente pela Microsoft, e os técnicos de suporte da Microsoft envidarão todos os esforços razoáveis, do ponto de vista comercial, para resolver os problemas que possam ocorrer. Atendendo ao facto de alguns estados ou jurisdições não permitirem limitações à duração de uma garantia implícita, pode dar-se o caso de a limitação acima não se aplicar ao Adquirente. Dentro dos limites permitidos pela legislação aplicável, as garantias implícitas do PRODUTO DE SOFTWARE, se houver, estão limitadas a noventa (90) dias.

DIREITOS DO ADQUIRENTE. A responsabilidade integral da Microsoft e dos seus fornecedores, e o único recurso a que o Adquirente poderá recorrer, não poderá exceder, por opção da Microsoft, (a) a devolução da quantia paga pelo Adquirente, se for o caso, ou (b) a reparação ou substituição do PRODUTO DE SOFTWARE que não esteja de acordo com a Garantia Limitada da Microsoft e que seja devolvido à Microsoft acompanhado de uma cópia do recibo do Adquirente. Esta Garantia Limitada será nula caso a falha do PRODUTO DE SOFTWARE tenha resultado de um acidente ou de utilização abusiva ou indevida do mesmo. Qualquer PRODUTO DE SOFTWARE de substituição estará abrangido pelo restante período de garantia original ou por um período de trinta (30) dias, o que for mais prolongado. Fora dos Estados Unidos, o Adquirente só poderá dispor destes recursos ou do suporte técnico prestado pela Microsoft para o produto mediante a apresentação da prova de compra emitida por uma entidade internacional autorizada.

GARANTIAS NÃO INCLUÍDAS. DENTRO DOS LIMITES MÁXIMOS PERMITIDOS PELA LEGISLAÇÃO APLICÁVEL, NEM A MICROSOFT NEM OS SEUS FORNECEDORES OFERECEM QUALQUER GARANTIA OU CONDIÇÃO, QUER EXPRESSA QUER IMPLÍCITA, INCLUINDO MAS NÃO SE LIMITANDO ÀS GARANTIAS IMPLÍCITAS DE COMERCIALIZAÇÃO, DE ADEQUAÇÃO A UM FIM ESPECÍFICO E DE NÃO INFRACÇÃO RELATIVAMENTE AO PRODUTO DE SOFTWARE E À PRESTAÇÃO OU INCAPACIDADE DE PRESTAÇÃO DE SUPORTE TÉCNICO. ESTA GARANTIA LIMITADA CONCEDE DIREITOS JURÍDICOS ESPECÍFICOS AO ADQUIRENTE, PODENDO BENEFICIAR DE OUTROS DIREITOS, QUE VARIAM CONSOANTE O ESTADO/JURISDIÇÃO.

LIMITAÇÃO DA RESPONSABILIDADE. DENTRO DOS LIMITES MÁXIMOS PERMITIDOS PELA LEGISLAÇÃO APLICÁVEL, NEM A MICROSOFT NEM OS SEUS FORNECEDORES SE RESPONSABILIZAM POR QUALQUER PREJUÍZO ESPECIAL, ACIDENTAL OU INDIRECTO (INCLUINDO MAS NÃO SE LIMITANDO A PREJUÍZOS POR PERDA DE NEGÓCIOS OU DE LUCROS, INTERRUPÇÃO DE NEGÓCIOS, PERDA DE INFORMAÇÕES COMERCIAIS OU QUALQUER OUTRO TIPO DE PREJUÍZO MONETÁRIO) RESULTANTE DA UTILIZAÇÃO OU INCAPACIDADE DE UTILIZAÇÃO DO PRODUTO DE SOFTWARE, OU DA PRESTAÇÃO OU INCAPACIDADE DE PRESTAÇÃO DE SUPORTE TÉCNICO, AINDA QUE A MICROSOFT TENHA SIDO NOTIFICADA DA POSSIBILIDADE DE OCORRÊNCIA DE TAIS PREJUÍZOS. SEJA QUAL FOR O CASO, A RESPONSABILIDADE INTEGRAL DA MICROSOFT E O ÚNICO RECURSO A QUE O ADQUIRENTE PODERÁ RECORRER DE ACORDO COM ESTE EULA NÃO PODERÁ EXCEDER O MONTANTE QUE O ADQUIRENTE PAGOU EFECTIVAMENTE PELO PRODUTO DE SOFTWARE OU UMA QUANTIA EQUIVALENTE A CINCO DÓLARES (U.S.$5,00) NA MOEDA LOCAL, O QUE FOR MAIOR; TODAVIA, SE O ADQUIRENTE TIVER CELEBRADO UM CONTRATO DE PRESTAÇÃO DE SUPORTE TÉCNICO DA MICROSOFT, A RESPONSABILIDADE INTEGRAL DA MICROSOFT RELATIVAMENTE À PRESTAÇÃO DE SUPORTE TÉCNICO SERÁ REGULADA PELOS TERMOS DESSE CONTRATO. ATENDENDO AO FACTO DE A EXCLUSÃO OU LIMITAÇÃO DA RESPONSABILIDADE NÃO SER PERMITIDA EM ALGUNS ESTADOS OU JURISDIÇÕES, PODE DAR-SE O CASO DE A LIMITAÇÃO ACIMA NÃO SE APLICAR AO ADQUIRENTE.

Caso tenha adquirido este produto em Portugal, este EULA é regulado pela legislação portuguesa.

Caso este produto tenha sido adquirido fora de Portugal, poderá ser aplicada a legislação local.

Caso o Adquirente tenha quaisquer dúvidas relativamente a este EULA ou, por qualquer motivo, queira contactar a Microsoft, contacte a subsidiária da Microsoft no seu país ou escreva para: Microsoft Sales Information Center/One Microsoft Way/Redmond, WA 98052-6399, E.U.A.

Dacă ați cumpărat produsul dumneavoastră Microsoft în România, beneficiați de următoarele garanții limitate:

GARANȚII LIMITATE. Microsoft garantează că (a) PRODUSUL SOFTWARE va funcționa, în general, în conformitate cu materialele scrise ce îl însoțesc pentru o perioadă de 90 (nouăzeci) de zile de la data achiziției, și (b) orice servicii de Suport Tehnic acordate de Microsoft vor fi, în general, așa cum sunt descrise în materialele scrise corespunzătoare acordate dumneavoastră de Microsoft, iar inginerii ce asigură Suportul Tehnic Microsoft vor depune eforturi rezonabile din punct de vedere comercial pentru a rezolva eventualele probleme. Unele state și jurisdicții nu permit limitarea duratei unei garanții implicite, astfel încât este posibil ca limitarea de mai sus să nu vi se aplice. În limitele permise de legile aplicabile, garanțiile PRODUSULUI SOFTWARE, dacă există, sunt limitate la 90 (nouăzeci) de zile.

DREPTURILE CLIENTULUI. Întreaga răspundere a Microsoft și a furnizorilor săi, și totalitatea drepturilor dumneavoastră , se rezumă , în funcție de opțiunea Microsoft, fie la (a) rambursarea prețului plătit, dacă există, sau (b) repararea sau înlocuirea PRODUSULUI SOFTWARE care nu corespunde garanțiilor limitate Microsoft și care este returnat la Microsoft însoțit de dovada achiziției. Aceste garanții limitate sunt anulate dacă deteriorarea PRODUSULUI SOFTWARE este rezultatul unui accident, al abuzului sau folosirii necorespunzătoare. Orice PRODUS SOFTWARE livrat în schimbul celui defect va fi garantat pentru durata cea mai mare dintre perioada rămasă din garanția inițială sau o perioadă de 30 (treizeci) de zile. În afara Statelor Unite, nici una din aceste garanții, ca și serviciile de Suport Tehnic oferite de Microsoft nu sunt disponibile fără a se face dovada achiziției de la o sursă internațională autorizată.

NICI O ALTĂ GARANȚIE. ÎN LIMITELE MAXIME PERMISE DE LEGILE APLICABILE, MICROSOFT ȘI FURNIZORII SĂI NEAGĂ ORICE ALTE GARANȚII ȘI CONDIȚII, EXPRESE SAU IMPLICITE, INCLUZÂND, DAR FĂRĂ A SE LIMITA LA, GARANȚII COMERCIALE IMPLICITE, POSIBILITATEA REALIZĂRII UNUI ANUMIT SCOP, TITLU SAU NEÎNCĂLCAREA LEGILOR, REFERITOR LA PRODUSUL SOFTWARE, ȘI ACORDAREA SAU IMPOSIBILITATEA DE A ACORDA SUPORT TEHNIC. ACESTE GARANȚII LIMITATE VĂ OFERĂ DREPTURI LEGALE SPECIFICE. PUTEȚI AVEA ALTELE, CARE VARIAZĂ ÎN FUNCȚIE DE JURISDICȚIA FIECĂRUI STAT.

LIMITAREA RĂSPUNDERII. ÎN LIMITELE MAXIME PERMISE DE LEGILE APLICABILE, MICROSOFT SAU FURNIZORII SĂI NU VOR FI, ÎN NICI UN CAZ, RĂSPUNZĂTORI PENTRU NICI UN FEL DE DAUNE SPECIALE, ÎNTÂMPLĂTOARE, INDIRECTE SAU DEPENDENTE ÎN ORICE MOD (INCLUZÂND, FĂRĂ LIMITĂRI, DAUNE PENTRU PIERDERI DE PROFIT, ÎNTRERUPERE A ACTIVITĂȚII, PIERDERE DE INFORMAȚII, SAU ORICE ALTĂ PIERDERE FINANCIARĂ) DECURGÂND DIN FOLOSIREA SAU IMPOSIBILITATEA DE A FOLOSI PRODUSUL SOFTWARE SAU DIN ACORDAREA SAU IMPOSIBILITATEA DE A ACORDA SERVICII DE SUPORT TEHNIC, CHIAR DACĂ MICROSOFT A FOST AVERTIZAT DE POSIBILITATEA UNOR ASEMENEA DAUNE. ÎN ORICE CAZ, ÎNTREAGA RĂSPUNDERE A MICROSOFT ÎN CONFORMITATE CU PREVEDERILE ACESTUI ALB (ACORD DE LICENȚĂ BENEFICIAR) SE VA LIMITA LA VALOAREA CEA MAI MARE DINTRE SUMA PLĂTITĂ DE DUMNEAVOASTRĂ PENTRU PRODUSUL SOFTWARE SAU ECHIVALENTUL A U.S.$5.00 ÎN MONEDA LOCALĂ; ÎN CAZUL ÎN CARE, TOTUSI, AȚI SEMNAT UN CONTRACT DE SUPORT TEHNIC CU MICROSOFT, ÎNTREAGA RĂSPUNDERE A MICROSOFT PRIVIND SERVICIILE DE SUPORT TEHNIC VA FI GUVERNATĂ DE TERMENII ACELUI CONTRACT. DEOARECE UNELE STATE SI JURISDICȚII NU PERMIT EXCLUDEREA SAU LIMITAREA RĂSPUNDERII, ESTE POSIBIL CA LIMITAREA DE MAI SUS SĂ NU SE APLICE ÎN CAZUL DUMNEAVOASTRĂ.

Dacă ați cumpărat acest produs în România, acest ALB este guvernat de legile României.

Dacă acest produs a fost cumpărat în afara Statelor Unite și României, atunci este posibil să se aplice legile locale.

Dacă aveți întrebări privind acest ALB, sau dacă doriți să contactați Microsoft, indiferent de motiv, vă rugăm să contactați reprezentanța Microsoft din țara dumneavoastră, sau scrieți la adresa: Microsoft Sales Information Center/One Microsoft Way/Redmond, WA 98052-6399, U.S.A.

Ee ste Microsoftov izdelek dobili v Sloveniji, zanj veljajo naslednje omejitve garancije:

OMEJENA GARANCIJA. Microsoft jamči, (a) da bo programski izdelek deloval zanesljivo in v skladu s spremljajočo pisno dokumentacijo devetdeset (90) dni od datuma prejema in (b) da bodo vse podporne storitve s strani Microsofta izvršene, kot je to opisano v ustreznem tiskanem gradivu, ki ga priskrbi Microsoft, ter da se bodo Microsoftovi strokovnjaki za podporo potrudili v okviru možnosti, da bodo rešili vse nastale probleme. Nekatere države in sodne oblasti ne dovoljujejo omejitve trajanja jamstva, zato zgoraj omenjene omejitve zanje ne veljajo. Do obsega, dovoljenega z veljavnim zakonom, so vsa jamstva v zvezi s programskim izdelkom omejena na dobo devetdeset (90) dni.

PRAVICE DO POVRAČILA. Microsoftova celotna obveznost in celotna obveznost njegovih dobaviteljev ter vaša izključna pravica do povračila je, po Microsoftovi izbiri, ali (a) vrnitev kupnine, če je bila plačana, ali (b) popravilo ali zamenjava programskega izdelka, ki ne ustreza Microsoftovi omejeni garanciji in ki ga vrnete Microsoftu skupaj s kopijo računa. Ta omejena garancija se razveljavi, če do napake programskega izdelka pride zaradi nesreče, zlorabe ali napačne uporabe. Vsak zamenjani programski izdelek ima jamstvo do konca prvotnega garancijskega roka ali trideset (30) dni, kar je dlje. Izven ZDA niso na voljo niti pravice do povračila niti kakršna koli podpora izdelka, ki jo nudi Microsoft, brez potrdila o nakupu pri pooblaščenem mednarodnem prodajalcu.

IZVZETE GARANCIJE. DO NAJVEČJEGA OBSEGA, DOVOLJENEGA Z VELJAVNIM ZAKONOM, MICROSOFT IN NJEGOVI DOBAVITELJI ZAVRAČAJO VSA DRUGA JAMSTVA IN POGOJE, VKLJUČNO S PRODAJNIM JAMSTVOM (A NE OMEJENO NANJ), USTREZNOSTJO ZA DOLOČEN NAMEN, UPRAVIČENOSTJO IN JAMSTVOM ZA NEKRŠITEV V ZVEZI S PROGRAMSKO OPREMO TER NUDENJEM ALI NEZMOŽNOSTJO NUDENJA PODPORNIH STORITEV. TA OMEJENA GARANCIJA VAM DAJE DOLOČENE ZAKONSKE PRAVICE. LAHKO IMATE TUDI DODATNE PRAVICE, KI PA SO ODVISNE OD DRŽAVE (SODNE OBLASTI).

OMEJITEV ODGOVORNOSTI. DO NAJVEČJEGA OBSEGA, DOVOLJENEGA Z VELJAVNIM ZAKONOM, V NOBENEM PRIMERU MICROSOFT ALI NJEGOVI DOBAVITELJI NISO ODGOVORNI ZA KAKRŠNO KOLI POSEBNO, NENAMERNO, POSREDNO ALI POSLEDIČNO ŠKODO (VKLJUČNO (IN BREZ OMEJITEV) S ŠKODO ZARADI IZGUBE DOBIČKA, PREKINITVE POSLOVANJA, IZGUBE POSLOVNIH INFORMACIJ ALI DRUGE GMOTNE ŠKODE), KI IZVIRA IZ UPORABE ALI NEZMOŽNOSTI UPORABE PROGRAMSKEGA IZDELKA OZIROMA NUDENJA ALI NEZMOŽNOSTI NUDENJA PODPORNIH STORITEV, ČEPRAV JE BIL MICROSOFT OPOZORJEN NA MOŽNOST TAKE ŠKODE. V VSAKEM PRIMERU JE MICROSOFTOVA CELOTNA ODGOVORNOST GLEDE KATEREGA KOLI POGOJA TE LICENČNE POGODBE OMEJENA NA ZNESEK, KI STE GA DEJANSKO PLAČALI ZA PROGRAMSKI IZDELEK ALI PET AMERIŠKIH DOLARJEV (5,00 USD) V TOLARSKI PROTIVREDNOSTI, KAR JE VEČ. ČE STE SKLENILI POGODBO O MICROSOFTOVIH PODPORNIH STORITVAH, JE MICROSOFTOVA CELOTNA OBVEZNOST GLEDE PODPORNIH STORITEV VEZANA NA DOLOČILA TAKE POGODBE. KER NEKATERE DRŽAVE IN SODNE OBLASTI NE DOVOLJUJEJO IZLOČITVE ALI OMEJITVE ODGOVORNOSTI, ZANJE ZGORAJ NAVEDENE OMEJITVE NE VELJAJO.

Če ste izdelek dobili izven ZDA, veljajo zanj krajevni zakoni.

Če imate kakršno koli vprašanje v zvezi s to pogodbo ali če želite iz kakega drugega vzroka stopiti v stik z Microsoftom, poiščite Microsoftovo podružnico v svoji državi ali pišite na naslov:

Microsoft Sales Information Center, One Microsoft Way, Redmond, WA 98052-6399, USA.

Ak ste nadobudli produkt spoločnosti Microsoft v Slovenskej republike, vzťahuje sa na vás nasledujúca obmedzená záruka:

OBMEDZENÁ ZÁRUKA. Microsoft ručí za to, že (a) SOFTWÉROVÝ PRODUKT bude pracovať v súlade s priloženými písomnými materiálmi počas deväťdesiatich (90) dní od dátumu obdržania, a (b) akékoľvek služby technickej podpory, ktoré poskytuje spoločnosť Microsoft, budú v podstate také, ako je to opísané v príslušných písomných materiáloch, ktoré vám spoločnosť Microsoft poskytne, a technici, obstarávajúci služby technickej podpory spoločnosti Microsoft, vyvinú pri riešení akýchkoľvek problematických záležitostí komerčne optimálne úsilie. Nakoľko niektoré štáty a právne predpisy nedovoľujú obmedzenie dĺžky implicitnej záruky, horeuvedené obmedzenie sa na vás nemusí vzťahovať. V miere, ktorú povoľuje príslušný zákon, sú implicitné záruky na SOFTWÉROVÝ PRODUKT, pokiaľ existujú, obmedzené na deväťdesiat (90) dní.

OPRAVNÉ PROSTRIEDKY. Jedinou zodpovednosťou spoločnosti Microsoft a jej dodávateľov a vaším výlučným opravným prostriedkom bude na základe voľby spoločnosti Microsoft (a) vrátenie zaplatenej čiastky, alebo (b) oprava alebo výmena SOFTWÉROVÉHO PRODUKTU, ktorý nespĺňa podmienky obmedzenej záruky a ktorý bol vrátený spoločnosti Microsoft spolu s kópiou potvrdenia o zaplatení. Táto obmedzená záruka stráca platnosť, ak bola porucha SOFTWÉROVÉHO PRODUKTU spôsobená nehodou, zneužitím alebo nesprávnym používaním. Akýkoľvek vymenený SOFTWÉROVÝ PRODUKT bude mať záručnú lehotu rovnú zbytku pôvodnej záručnej lehoty alebo 30 dní podľa toho, ktorá z lehôt je dlhšia. Mimo územia USA je použitie opravných prostriedkov alebo služieb technickej podpory spoločnosti Microsoft podmienené preukázaním dokladu o nadobudnutí od autorizovaného medzinárodného predajcu.

ŽIADNE INÉ ZÁRUKY. V MAXIMÁLNEJ MIERE, KTORÚ POVOĽUJE PRÍSLUŠNÝ ZÁKON, ODMIETA SPOLOČNOSŤ MICROSOFT I JEJ DODÁVATELIA AKÉKOĽVEK ĎALŠIE ZÁRUKY A PODMIENKY, ČI UŽ VÝSLOVNÉ ALEBO IMPLICITNÉ, VRÁTANE, ALE NIE VÝHRADNE, IMPLICITNÝCH ZÁRUK TÝKAJÚCICH SA OBCHODOVATEĽNOSTI, VHODNOSTI NA TEN-KTORÝ ÚČEL, VLASTNÍCKYCH PRÁV A ZÁRUK NA DODRŽANIE PREDPISOV V SÚVISLOSTI SO SOFTWÉROVÝM PRODUKTOM A POSKYTNUTÍM ČI NEPOSKYTNUTÍM SLUŽIEB TECHNICKEJ PODPORY. TÁTO OBMEDZENÁ ZÁRUKA VÁM DÁVA ŠPECIFICKÉ ZÁKONNÉ PRÁVA. MÔŽETE MAŤ AJ ĎALŠIE PRÁVA V ZÁVISLOSTI NA ŠTÁTE A PRÁVNYCH PREDPISOCH.

OBMEDZENIE ZODPOVEDNOSTI. V MAXIMÁLNEJ MIERE, KTORÚ POVOĽUJE PRÍSLUŠNÝ ZÁKON, SPOLOČNOSŤ MICROSOFT, ANI JEJ DODÁVATELIA NEBUDÚ ZODPOVEDNÍ ZA NIJAKÉ ŠPECIÁLNE, NÁHODNÉ, NEPRIAME, ČI NÁSLEDNÉ ŠKODY AKÉHOKOĽVEK DRUHU (VRÁTANE, A BEZ OBMEDZENIA, ŠKÔD, VYPLÝVAJÚCICH ZO STRATY OBCHODNÉHO ZISKU, PRERUŠENIA PODNIKANIA, STRATY OBCHODNÝCH INFORMÁCIÍ, ALEBO AKEJKOĽVEK ĎALŠEJ PEŇAŽNEJ STRATY), KTORÉ VYPLYNÚ Z POUŽÍVANIA ČI Z NEMOŽNOSTI POUŽIŤ SOFTWÉROVÝ PRODUKT, ALEBO Z POSKYTNUTIA ČI NEPOSKYTNUTIA SLUŽIEB TECHNICKEJ PODPORY, A TO AJ VTEDY, KEĎ BOLA SPOLOČNOSŤ MICROSOFT NA MOŽNOSŤ TAKÝCHTO ŠKÔD UPOZORNENÁ. CELÁ ZODPOVEDNOSŤ SPOLOČNOSTI MICROSOFT PODĽA AKÉHOKOĽVEK USTANOVENIA TEJTO LICENČNEJ ZMLUVY BUDE OBMEDZENÁ NA SUMU, KTORÚ STE SKUTOČNE ZAPLATILI ZA SOTFWÉROVÝ PRODUKT, ALEBO NA SUMU 5 USD, PODĽA TOHO, KTORÁ Z NICH JE VÄČŠIA; AK STE VŠAK UZAVRELI SO SPOLOČNOSŤOU MICROSOFT ZMLUVU O SLUŽBÁCH TECHNICKEJ PODPORY, CELÁ ZODPOVEDNOSŤ SPOLOČNOSTI MICROSOFT, POKIAĽ IDE O SLUŽBY TECHNICKEJ PODPORY, SA BUDE RIADIŤ PODMIENKAMI TEJTO ZMLUVY. NAKOĽKO NIEKTORÉ ŠTÁTY A PRÁVNE PREDPISY NEDOVOĽUJÚ VYLÚČENIE ALEBO OBMEDZENIE ZODPOVEDNOSTI, HOREUVEDENÉ OBMEDZENIE SA NA VÁS NEMUSÍ VZŤAHOVAŤ.

Ak ste nadobudli tento produkt mimo Spojených štátov, potom sa môžu použiť miestne zákony.

Ak máte akékoľvek otázky, týkajúce sa tejto licenčnej zmluvy, alebo ak sa chcete z akéhokoľvek dôvodu obrátiť na spoločnosť Microsoft, obráťte sa na pobočku spoločnosti Microsoft vo vašej krajine, alebo napíšte na adresu: Microsoft Sales Information Center/One Microsoft Way/Redmond, WA 98052-6399.

Mikäli olette hankkinut Microsoft-tuotteenne Suomesta, sovelletaan Teihin seuraavaa rajoitettua takuuta:

RAJOITETTU TAKUU. Microsoft takaa, että (a) OHJELMISTOTUOTE toimii olennaisilta osiltaan oheistetun tuoteoppaan (-oppaiden) mukaisesti vastaanottopäivästä 90 päivän aikana ja (b) Microsoftin tukipalvelut ovat olennaisilta osiltaan sovellettavien oppaiden mukaisia. Lisäksi taataan, että Microsoftin tukihenkilöt pyrkivät ratkaisemaan ongelmat siinä määrin, kuin on kohtuullisin kustannuksin mahdollista. Joissakin valtioissa tai joillakin lainkäyttöalueilla ei hyväksytä rajoituksia oletetun takuun kestoaikaan, joten edellä esitetty rajoitus ei koske kaikkia asiakkaita. Sovellettavan lain sallimissa rajoissa kaikki OHJELMISTOTUOTTEEN oletetut takuut on kestoajan osalta rajoitettu yhdeksäksikymmeneksi (90) päiväksi.

ASIAKKAAN OIKEUDET. Microsoftin ja sen toimittajien koko vastuu ja asiakkaan kaikki oikeudet rajoittuvat, Microsoftin valinnan mukaan, joko (a) maksetun kauppahinnan palauttamiseen tai (b) sellaisen OHJELMISTOTUOTTEEN korjauttamiseen tai uusimiseen, joka ei vastaa Microsoftin rajoitettua takuuta ja joka palautetaan Microsoftille kuittijäljennöksen kanssa. Tämä rajoitettu takuu on mitätön, jos OHJELMISTOTUOTTEEN vika on aiheutunut onnettomuudesta, väärinkäytöksestä tai väärinasentamisesta. Jokainen korvattu OHJELMISTOTUOTE kuuluu takuun piiriin jäljelle jäävän alkuperäisen takuuajan tai 30 päivän ajan sen mukaan, kumpi ajanjakso on pitempi. Yhdysvaltain ulkopuolella Microsoftin tarjoamat tukipalvelut tai korvaukset ovat käytettävissä vain, jos asiakas todistaa ostaneensa tuotteen valtuutetulta kansainväliseltä jälleenmyyjältä.

EI MUITA TAKUITA. SIINÄ MÄÄRIN KUIN SOVELLETTAVA LAKI SEN SALLII, MICROSOFT JA SEN TOIMITTAJAT TORJUVAT PÄTEMÄTTÖMINÄ KAIKKI MUUT TAKUUT JA VASTUUT, MUKAAN LUKIEN OLETETUT VASTUUT SOVELTUVUUDESTA JOHONKIN ERITYISEEN TARKOITUKSEEN, SOPIVUUDESTA KAUPANKÄYNNIN KOHTEEKSI TAI OIKEUKSIEN LOUKKAAMATTOMUUDESTA, KÄSITTÄEN OHJELMISTON JA TUKIPALVELUJEN TARJOAMISEN TAI KYVYTTÖMYYDEN NIIDEN TARJOAMISEEN. TÄMÄ RAJOITETTU TAKUU ANTAA TEILLE NIMENOMAISET OIKEUDET. TÄMÄN LISÄKSI TEILLÄ SAATTAA OLLA MUITA OIKEUKSIA, JOTKA VAIHTELEVAT VALTION TAI LAINKÄYTTÖALUEEN MUKAAN.

RAJOITETTU VASTUU. SIINÄ MÄÄRIN KUIN SOVELLETTAVA LAKI SEN SALLII, MICROSOFT TAI SEN TOIMITTAJAT EIVÄT OLE MISSÄÄN TAPAUKSESSA VASTUUSSA YLLÄTTÄVISTÄ, SATUNNAISISTA TAI VÄLILLISISTÄ VAHINGOISTA (MUKAAN LUKIEN RAJOITUKSETTA VAHINGONKORVAUKSET LIIKEVOITON MENETTÄMISESTÄ, LIIKETOIMINNAN KESKEYTYMISESTÄ, LIIKETOIMINTAAN LIITTYVÄN TIEDON MENETTÄMISESTÄ TAI MUUSTA RAHALLISESTA VAHINGOSTA), JOTKA AIHEUTUVAT MICROSOFT-TUOTTEEN KÄYTÖSTÄ TAI KYVYTTÖMYYDESTÄ KÄYTTÄÄ SITÄ TAI TUKIPALVELUJEN TARJOAMISESTA TAI KYVYTTÖMYYDSTÄ NIIDEN TARJOAMISEEN, VAIKKA MICROSOFTILLE OLISI ILMOITETTU VAHINKOJEN MAHDOLLISUUDESTA. JOKA TAPAUKSESSA MICROSOFTIN VASTUU ON RAJOITETTU SIIHEN MÄÄRÄÄN, JOKA OHJELMISTOTUOTTEESTA ON MAKSETTU. JOS ASIAKAS MAKSOI OHJELMISTOTUOTTEESTA ALLE VIITTÄ YHDYSVALTAIN DOLLARIA VASTAAVAN SUMMAN, MICROSOFTIN VASTUU ON RAJOITETTU VIITTÄ YHDYSVALTAIN DOLLARIA VASTAAVAAN SUMMAAN. JOS ASIKAKAS ON SOLMINUT MICROSOFTIN KANSSA TUKIPALVELUJA KOSKEVAN SOPIMUKSEN, MICROSOFTIN VASTUUT ON SÄÄDETTY SOPIMUKSEN EHDOISSA. KOSKA JOTKIN VALTIOT TAI LAINKÄYTTÖALUEET EIVÄT SALLI KULUTTAJIEN OIKEUKSIEN RAJOITTAMISTA TAI VAHINGONKORVAUSVASTUUN POISSULKEMISTA TAI RAJOITTAMISTA, KUN KYSE ON TÖRKEÄSTÄ HUOLIMATTOMUUDESTA TAI TAHALLISUUDESTA, EDELLÄ MAINITTU RAJOITUS EI KOSKE KAIKKIA ASIAKKAITA.

Jos tuote on hankittu Suomesta, tähän käyttöoikeussopimukseen sovelletaan Suomen lakia.

Jos tuote on hankittu muualta kuinSuomesta, tähän käyttöoikeussopimukseen saatetaan soveltaa paikallista lakia.

Jos Teillä on tätä Käyttöoikeussopimusta koskevia kysymyksiä tai haluatte jostain muusta syystä ottaa yhteyttä Microsoftiin, kääntykää Microsoftin paikallisen tytäryhtiön puoleen tai kirjoittakaa osoitteeseen Microsoft Sales Information Center, One Microsoft Way, Redmond, WA 98052-6399.

Om Ni har förvärvat Er Microsoft-produkt i Sverige, gäller följande begränsade garanti för Er:

BEGRÄNSAD GARANTI. Microsoft garanterar (a) att PROGRAMVARUPRODUKTEN i allt väsentligt fungerar i enlighet med tillhörande skriftligt material för en period om nittio (90) dagar från dagen för mottagandet; och (b) att eventuella supporttjänster som tillhandahålls av Microsoft i allt väsentligt överensstämmer med vad som anges i tillämpligt skriftligt material från Microsoft och att Microsofts supporttekniker kommer att vidta skäliga åtgärder för att lösa eventuella problem. Eftersom begränsningar av giltighetstiden för underförstådda garantier inte är giltiga i vissa länder, är det möjligt att ovanstående ansvarsbegränsning inte är tillämplig i Ert fall. Eventuella underförstådda garantier avseende PROGRAMVARUPRODUKTEN är begränsade till nittio (90) dagar, om inte annat följer av tvingande lag.

PÅFÖLJDER. Microsofts och dess leverantörers ansvar på grund av garantin är, efter Microsofts val, begränsad till antingen (a) återbetalning av eventuell köpeskilling eller (b) reparation eller utbyte av den PROGRAMVARUPRODUKT som inte uppfyller Microsofts begränsade garanti och som returnerats till Microsoft tillsammans med en kopia på Ert kvitto. Garantin gäller ej om fel eller brist i PROGRAMVARUPRODUKTEN beror på olyckshändelse, eller oriktig användning eller hantering. Utbytt PROGRAMVARUPRODUKT omfattas av en garantitid motsvarande för den utbytta varan återstående garantiperiod, dock minst trettio (30) dagar. Dessa påföljder samt de supporttjänster som tillhandahålls av Microsoft är endast tillgängliga utanför USA genom uppvisande av Ert inköpsbevis från en auktoriserad leverantör.

INGA YTTERLIGARE GARANTIER. MED UNDANTAG AV VAD SOM FÖLJER AV TVINGANDE LAG, FRISKRIVER SIG MICROSOFT OCH DESS LEVERANTÖRER FRÅN ALLT YTTERLIGARE GARANTIANSVAR, SÅVÄL UTTRYCKLIGEN SOM UNDERFÖRSTÅTT, AVSEENDE PROGRAMVARUPRODUKTEN. DENNA FRISKRIVNING GÄLLER SÄRSKILT FÖR GARANTIER AVSEENDE PROGRAMVARUPRODUKTENS ALLMÄNNA LÄMPLIGHET ELLER LÄMPLIGHET FÖR ETT SÄRSKILT ÄNDAMÅL, SAMT GARANTIER AVSEENDE FRÅNVARO AV INTRÅNG I TREDJE MANS RÄTTIGHETER ELLER MICROSOFTS EVENTUELLA TILLHANDAHÅLLANDE AV SUPPORTTJÄNSTER. DENNA BEGRÄNSADE GARANTI MEDFÖR SÄRSKILDA RÄTTIGHETER FÖR ER. NI KAN HA ANDRA RÄTTIGHETER SOM VARIERAR FRÅN LAND TILL LAND.

ANSVARSBEGRÄNSNING. MED UNDANTAG AV VAD SOM FÖLJER AV TVINGANDE LAG, ANSVARAR INTE MICROSOFT ELLER DESS LEVERANTÖRER FÖR NÅGRA SOM HELST INDIREKTA SKADOR ELLER FÖLJDSKADOR (INKLUSIVE UTEBLIVEN VINST, DRIFTAVBROTT, FÖRLUST AV INFORMATION ELLER ANNAN EKONOMISK SKADA) TILL FÖLJD AV ANVÄNDNING AV ELLER SVÅRIGHET ATT ANVÄNDA PROGRAMVARUPRODUKTEN, SAMT TILLHANDAHÅLLANDE AV ELLER OFÖRMÅGA ATT TILLHANDAHÅLLA SUPPORTTJÄNSTER. DETTA GÄLLER ÄVEN OM MICROSOFT UPPMÄRKSAMMATS PÅ MÖJLIGHETEN TILL SÅDANA SKADOR. MED UNDANTAG AV VAD SOM FÖLJER AV TVINGANDE LAG, ÄR MICROSOFTS TOTALA ANSVAR ENLIGT DETTA LICENSAVTAL BEGRÄNSAT TILL DEN FÖR PROGRAMVARAN ERLAGDA KÖPESKILLINGEN ELLER ETT BELOPP MOTSVARANDE USD5.00 I SEK ELLER LOKAL VALUTA. DOCK GÄLLER ATT OM NI HAR INGÅTT ETT AVTAL MED MICROSOFT AVSEENDE SUPPORTTJÄNSTER REGLERAS MICROSOFTS TOTALA ANSVAR I ENLIGHET MED VILLKOREN I DET AVTALET. ANSVARSBEGRÄNSNINGAR ÄR INTE GILTIGA I VISSA LÄNDER VARFÖR OVANSTÅENDE BEGRÄNSNINGAR EVENTUELLT INTE ÄR TILLÄMPLIGA FÖR ER.

Om Ni förvärvade denna produkt i Sverige är svensk lag tillämplig på detta Licensavtal.

Om denna produkt förvärvades utanför Sverige kan lokal lag vara tillämplig.

Om Ni har några frågor angående detta Licensavtal, eller om Ni vill kontakta Microsoft av någon annan anledning, kan Ni kontakta Microsofts dotterbolag i Ert land eller skriva till: Microsoft Sales Information Center/One Microsoft Way/Redmond, WA 98052-6399/USA.

Если продукция корпорации Microsoft приобретена на территории бывшего СССР, то действует следующая ограниченная гарантия.

ОГРАНИЧЕННАЯ ГАРАНТИЯ. Корпорация Microsoft гарантирует, что а) программа будет работать в соответствии с сопутствующей документацией в течение 6 (шести) месяцев после приобретения, согласно дате на квитанции; б) любые услуги по техническому обслуживанию, предоставляемые корпорацией Microsoft, осуществляются так, как описано в письменных материалах переданных вам корпорацией Microsoft, и инженеры технического обслуживания корпорации Mcrosoft предпримут любые экономически оправданные усилия для устранения возникших технических неполадок. Если действующее законодательство не допускает ограничений действия подразумеваемой гарантии, то последнее ограничение к вам не относится. В той степени, в которой это разрешено действующим законодательством, подразумеваемые гарантии в отношении программы, если таковые имеют место, ограничены сроком действия в 90 (девяносто) дней.

ВОЗМЕЩЕНИЕ УБЫТКОВ. Совокупная ответственность корпорации Microsoft и ее поставщиков ограничивается по выбору представителей корпорации Microsoft: либо а) возвратом уплаченных денег, если продукт был приобретен, либо б) исправлением или заменой программы, не удовлетворяющей ограниченной гарантии, предоставляемой корпорацией Microsoft, по возвращении ее представителям корпорации Microsoft вместе с копией документа, удостоверяющего ее приобретение. Данная ограниченная гарантия недействительна, если неполадки в работе программы возникли в результате внешнего повреждения, неверного использования или использования не по назначению. На любую замену данной программы будет распространяться гарантия на оставшийся гарантийный срок, но не менее чем на 30 дней. За пределами территории США ни возмещение убытков, ни услуги по техническому обслуживанию корпорации Microsoft не осуществляются без копии документа, удостоверяющего приобретение продукта от авторизованного продавца.

ОТСУТСТВИЕ ПРОЧИХ ГАРАНТИЙ. В НАИБОЛЬШЕЙ СТЕПЕНИ, РАЗРЕШЕННОЙ ДЕЙСТВУЮЩИМ ЗАКОНОДАТЕЛЬСТВОМ, КОРПОРАЦИЯ MICROSOFT ОТКАЗЫВАЕТСЯ ОТ ВСЕХ ДРУГИХ ГАРАНТИЙ И УСЛОВИЙ, КАК ЯВНЫХ, ТАК И ПОДРАЗУМЕВАЕМЫХ, ВКЛЮЧАЯ (НО НЕ ОГРАНИЧИВАЯСЬ ТОЛЬКО ИМИ) ПРЕДПОЛАГАЕМЫЕ ГАРАНТИИ ТОВАРНОСТИ, ПРИГОДНОСТИ ДЛЯ ОПРЕДЕЛЕННОЙ ЦЕЛИ, ТОВАРНОСТИ И БЕЗВРЕДНОСТИ, А ТАКЖЕ ПРЕДОСТАВЛЕНИЕ ИЛИ НЕПРЕДОСТАВЛЕНИЕ УСЛУГ ПО ТЕХНИЧЕСКОМУ ОБСЛУЖИВАНИЮ. ЭТА ОГРАНИЧЕННАЯ ГАРАНТИЯ ПРЕДОСТАВЛЯЕТ ВАМ ОПРЕДЕЛЕННЫЕ ЮРИДИЧЕСКИЕ ПРАВА. ВЫ МОЖЕТЕ ТАКЖЕ ИМЕТЬ И ДРУГИЕ ПРАВА, СОГЛАСНО ДЕЙСТВУЮЩЕМУ НА ВАШЕЙ ТЕРРИТОРИИ ЗАКОНОДАТЕЛЬСТВУ.

ОГРАНИЧЕНИЕ СУММЫ ОТВЕТСТВЕННОСТИ. В НАИБОЛЬШЕЙ СТЕПЕНИ, ДОПУСКАЕМОЙ ДЕЙСТВУЮЩИМ ЗАКОНОДАТЕЛЬСТВОМ, КОРПОРАЦИЯ MICROSOFT И ЕЕ ПОСТАВЩИКИ ОТКАЗЫВАЮТСЯ НЕСТИ ОТВЕТСТВЕННОСТЬ ЗА КАКОЙ-ЛИБО УЩЕРБ (ВКЛЮЧАЯ ВСЕ БЕЗ ИСКЛЮЧЕНИЯ СЛУЧАИ ПОТЕРИ ПРИБЫЛИ,

ПРЕРЫВАНИЯ ДЕЛОВОЙ АКТИВНОСТИ, ПОТЕРИ ДЕЛОВОЙ ИНФОРМАЦИИ ИЛИ ЛЮБЫЕ ДРУГИЕ УБЫТКИ), СВЯЗАННЫЙ С ИСПОЛЬЗОВАНИЕМ ИЛИ НЕВОЗМОЖНОСТЬЮ ИСПОЛЬЗОВАНИЯ ПРОГРАММЫ, А ТАКЖЕ С ПРЕДОСТАВЛЕНИЕМ ИЛИ НЕВОЗМОЖНОСТЬЮ ПРЕДОСТАВЛЕНИЯ УСЛУГ ПО ТЕХНИЧЕСКОМУ ОБСЛУЖИВАНИЮ, ДАЖЕ ЕСЛИ ПРЕДСТАВИТЕЛЬ КОРПОРАЦИИ MICROSOFT БЫЛ ИЗВЕЩЕН ЗАРАНЕЕ О ВОЗМОЖНОСТИ ТАКИХ ПОТЕРЬ. В ЛЮБОМ СЛУЧАЕ ВСЯ ВОЗМОЖНАЯ СОВОКУПНАЯ ОТВЕТСТВЕННОСТЬ КОРПОРАЦИИ MICROSOFT ПРИ ВОЗМЕЩЕНИИ УЩЕРБА ПОЛЬЗОВАТЕЛЮ ПО ДАННОМУ СОГЛАШЕНИЮ НЕ МОЖЕТ ПРЕВЫСИТЬ СУММЫ, СООТВЕТСТВУЮЩЕЙ ПЯТИ ДОЛЛАРАМ США. ЕСЛИ ДЕЙСТВУЮЩЕЕ ЗАКОНОДАТЕЛЬСТВО НЕ ДОПУСКАЕТ ОТКАЗ ОТ ОТВЕТСТВЕННОСТИ ИЛИ ОГРАНИЧЕНИЕ ОТВЕТСТВЕННОСТИ, ТО ПОСЛЕДНЕЕ ОГРАНИЧЕНИЕ К ВАМ НЕ ОТНОСИТСЯ.

Если же программа была приобретена за пределами США, то действует местное законодательство.

При возникновении вопросов по данному соглашению или необходимости связаться с представителями корпорации Microsoft по любому другому поводу обращайтесь в представительство корпорации Microsoft, обслуживающее вашу страну, или пишите по адресу: Microsoft Sales Information Center/One Microsoft Way/Redmond, WA 98052-6399, USA.

Microsoft Ürününüzü Türkiye'de aldIysanIz sİzİn İçİn aşağIdakİ sInIrlI garantİ hükümlerİ geçerlİdİr:

SINIRLI GARANTİ. Microsoft şu sınırlı garantileri vermektedir: (a) YAZILIM ÜRÜNÜ, teslim alındıktan itibaren doksan (90) gün, ekteki yazılı belgelerde belirtildiği gibi çalışır, ve (b) Microsoft tarafından sağlanan tüm Destek Hizmetleri, ekteki basılı malzemede belirtildiği gibidir ve Microsoft destek mühendisleri çıkan tüm sorunları çözmeye çalışacaktır. Bazı eyalet/yargı mercileri, sözü edilen garantilerde süre sınırlamaya izin vermezler, dolayısıyla yukarıdaki sınırlama sizin için geçerli olmayabilir. Geçerli yasanın izin verdiği ölçüde, YAZILIM ÜRÜNÜ için garanti, doksan (90) gün ile sınırlıdır.

MÜŞTERİNİN TELAFİ HAKLARI. Microsoft'un ve sağlayıcılarının tüm sorumlulukları ve size tanınan münhasır telafi hakkı, Microsoft'un seçimine bağlı olmak koşuluyla, (a) ya ödediğiniz miktarın geri verilmesi, veya (b) bu Sınırlı Garanti şartlarına uymayan YAZILIM ÜRÜNÜ'nün, faturanın bir kopyası ile birlikte Microsoft'a geri gönderilip tamir ettirilmesi veya değiştirilmesidir. YAZILIM ÜRÜNÜ, kaza, suistimal veya yanlış kullanım nedeniyle gerektiği gibi çalışmaz duruma gelmişse, bu Sınırlı Garanti geçerliliğini yitirir. Eskisinin yerine verilmiş herhangi bir YAZILIM ÜRÜNÜ, özgün garanti süresinden geriye kalan süre için veya bu süre otuz (30) günden az ise otuz (30) gün için garanti altındadır. Microsoft tarafından sağlanan telafi hakları ve ürün destek hizmetleri, ürünün yetkili uluslararası kaynaktan satın alınmış olduğunun kanıtlanamaması durumunda, Amerika Birleşik Devletleri dışında uygulanmaz..

BAŞKA GARANTİ YOKTUR. MICROSOFT VE SAĞLAYICILARI, YASALAR İZİN VERDİĞİ ÖLÇÜDE, YAZILIM ÜRÜNÜNÜN TİCARİ KULLANIMI VE UYGUNLUĞU KONUSUNDAKİ ZIMNİ GARANTİLERİ VE KOŞULLARI, DESTEK HİZMETLERİ SAĞLAMA YA DA SAĞLAYAMAMA VE BUNLAR İLE DE SINIRLI OLMAMAK ÜZERE TÜM DİĞER AÇIK VEYA ZIMNİ GARANTİLERİ REDDETMEKTEDİR. BU SINIRLI GARANTİ SİZE BELİRLİ YASAL HAKLAR TANIR. DİĞER SAHİP OLABİLECEĞİNİZ HAKLAR ÜLKE/YARGI MERCİSİNE GÖRE DEĞİŞİR.

SORUMLULUĞUN SINIRLANMASI. MICROSOFT YA DA SAĞLAYICILARI, GEÇERLİ YASANIN İZİN VERDİĞİ ÖLÇÜDE, YAZILIM ÜRÜNÜ'NÜN KULLANILMASINDAN YA DA KULLANILAMAMASINDAN VE DESTEK HİZMETLERİ'NİN SAĞLANMASINDAN VEYA SAĞLANAMAMASINDAN KAYNAKLANAN HASARLARDAN (İŞ GETİRİLERİNİN KAYBINDAN DOĞAN ZARARLAR, İŞTEKİ DURAKSAMALAR, İŞ BİLGİLERİNİN KAYBI YA DA DİĞER PARASAL KAYIPLAR GİBİ), MICROSOFT BU HASARLARIN OLUŞABİLECEĞİ KONUSUNDA UYARILMIŞ OLSA BİLE, HİÇBİR ŞEKİLDE SORUMLU DEĞİLDİR. MICROSOFT'UN, SÖZLEŞMENİN HERHANGİ BİR HÜKMÜNDEN KAYNAKLANABİLECEK TÜM SORUMLULUĞU, YAZILIM ÜRÜNÜ'NE ÖDEDİĞİNİZ ÜCRET VEYA US$5.00 KARŞILIĞI YEREL PARA BİRİMİNDEN BÜYÜK OLAN İLE SINIRLIDIR; MICROSOFT DESTEK HİZMETLERİ SÖZLEŞMESİ YAPTIYSANIZ, DESTEK HİZMETLERİ İÇİN MICROSOFT'UN TÜM SORUMLULUĞUNU BU SÖZLEŞMENİN HÜKÜMLERİ BELİRLER. SORUMLULUK ALINMAMASINA YA DA SORUMLULUĞUN SINIRLANMASINA BAZI ÜLKELER VE HUKUKSAL DÜZENLEMELER İZİN VERMEDİĞİNDEN, YUKARIDAKİ SINIRLAMA SİZİN İÇİN GEÇERLİ OLMAYABİLİR.

Bu ürünü Washington Eyaleti dışında bir yerden aldıysanız, bulunduğunuz yerin yasaları geçerli olabilir.

Bu sözleşme hakkında sorularınız varsa ya da Microsoft ile herhangi bir nedenle ilişki kurmak isterseniz, lütfen ülkenizdeki Microsoft bürosunu arayın veya aşağıdaki adrese yazın:

Microsoft Sales Information Center/One Microsoft Way/Redmond, WA 98052-6399, USA.

If you acquired you Microsoft Product in any other country, the following limited warranty applies to you:

LIMITED WARRANTY. Microsoft warrants that (a) the SOFTWARE PRODUCT will perform substantially in accordance with the accompanying written materials for a period of ninety (90) days from the date of receipt, and (b) any Support Services provided by Microsoft shall be substantially as described in applicable written materials provided to you by Microsoft, and Microsoft support engineers will make commercially reasonable efforts to solve any problem issues. Some states and jurisdictions do not allow limitations on duration of an implied warranty, so the above limitation may not apply to you. To the extent allowed by applicable law, implied warranties on the SOFTWARE PRODUCT, if any, are limited to ninety (90) days.

CUSTOMER REMEDIES. Microsoft's and its suppliers' entire liability and your exclusive remedy shall be, at Microsoft's option, either (a) return of the price paid, if any, or (b) repair or replacement of the SOFTWARE PRODUCT that does not meet Microsoft's Limited Warranty and which is returned to Microsoft with a copy of your receipt. This Limited Warranty is void if failure of the SOFTWARE PRODUCT has resulted from accident, abuse, or misapplication. Any replacement SOFTWARE PRODUCT will be warranted for the remainder of the original warranty period or thirty (30) days, whichever is longer. Outside the United States, neither these remedies nor any product support services offered by Microsoft are available without proof of purchase from an authorized international source.

NO OTHER WARRANTIES. TO THE MAXIMUM EXTENT PERMITTED BY APPLICABLE LAW, MICROSOFT AND ITS SUPPLIERS DISCLAIM ALL OTHER WARRANTIES AND CONDITIONS, EITHER EXPRESS OR IMPLIED, INCLUDING, BUT NOT LIMITED TO, IMPLIED WARRANTIES OF MERCHANTABILITY, FITNESS FOR A PARTICULAR PURPOSE, TITLE, AND NON-INFRINGEMENT, WITH REGARD TO THE SOFTWARE PRODUCT, AND THE PROVISION OF OR FAILURE TO PROVIDE SUPPORT SERVICES. THIS LIMITED WARRANTY GIVES YOU SPECIFIC LEGAL RIGHTS. YOU MAY HAVE OTHERS, WHICH VARY FROM STATE/JURISDICTION TO STATE/JURISDICTION.

LIMITATION OF LIABILITY. TO THE MAXIMUM EXTENT PERMITTED BY APPLICABLE LAW, IN NO EVENT SHALL MICROSOFT OR ITS SUPPLIERS BE LIABLE FOR ANY SPECIAL, INCIDENTAL, INDIRECT, OR CONSEQUENTIAL DAMAGES WHATSOEVER (INCLUDING, WITHOUT LIMITATION, DAMAGES FOR LOSS OF BUSINESS PROFITS, BUSINESS INTERRUPTION, LOSS OF BUSINESS INFORMATION, OR ANY OTHER PECUNIARY LOSS) ARISING OUT OF THE USE OF OR INABILITY TO USE THE SOFTWARE PRODUCT OR THE PROVISION OF OR FAILURE TO PROVIDE SUPPORT SERVICES, EVEN IF MICROSOFT HAS BEEN ADVISED OF THE POSSIBILITY OF SUCH DAMAGES. IN ANY CASE, MICROSOFT'S ENTIRE LIABILITY UNDER ANY PROVISION OF THIS EULA SHALL BE LIMITED TO THE GREATER OF THE AMOUNT ACTUALLY PAID BY YOU FOR THE SOFTWARE PRODUCT OR AN AMOUNT EQUIVALENT TO U.S.$5.00 IN LOCAL CURRENCY; PROVIDED, HOWEVER, IF YOU HAVE ENTERED INTO A MICROSOFT SUPPORT SERVICES AGREEMENT, MICROSOFT'S ENTIRE LIABILITY REGARDING SUPPORT SERVICES SHALL BE GOVERNED BY THE TERMS OF THAT AGREEMENT. BECAUSE SOME STATES AND JURISDICTIONS DO NOT ALLOW THE EXCLUSION OR LIMITATION OF LIABILITY, THE ABOVE LIMITATION MAY NOT APPLY TO YOU.

U.S. GOVERNMENT RESTRICTED RIGHTS. The software product and documentation are provided with restricted rights. Use, duplication, or disclosure by the government is subject to restrictions as set forth in subparagraph (c)(1)(ii) of the rights in technical data and computer software clause at dfars 252.227-7013 or subparagraphs (c)(1) and (2) of the commercial computer software—restricted rights at 48 cfr 52.227-19, as applicable. Manufacturer is Microsoft corporation/one Microsoft way/Redmond, WA 98052-6399.

This EULA is governed by the laws of the State of Washington.

Should you have any questions concerning this EULA, or if you desire to contact Microsoft for any reason, please contact the Microsoft subsidiary serving your country, or write: Microsoft Sales Information Center/One Microsoft Way/Redmond, WA 98052-6399.

For information about Microsoft Press® products, visit our Web site at

mspress.microsoft.com

Microsoft®